SPROUT LANDS

ALSO BY WILLIAM BRYANT LOGAN

Air: The Restless Shaper of the World

Dirt: The Ecstatic Skin of the Earth

Oak: The Frame of Civilization

SPROUT LANDS

Tending the Endless Gift of Trees

William Bryant Logan

W. W. NORTON & COMPANY
INDEPENDENT PUBLISHERS SINCE 1923
NEW YORK   LONDON

For information about permission to reproduce selections from this book, write to
Permissions, W. W. Norton & Company, Inc., 500 Fifth Avenue, New York, NY 10110

For information about special discounts for bulk purchases, please contact
W. W. Norton Special Sales at specialsales@wwnorton.com or 800-233-4830

Manufacturing by LSC Communications, Harrisonburg
Book design by Daniel Lagin
Production manager: Beth Steidle

Library of Congress Cataloging-in-Publication Data

Names: Logan, William Bryant, author.
Title: Sprout lands : tending the endless gift of trees / William Bryant Logan.
Description: First edition. | New York : W.W. Norton & Company, [2019] | Includes
    bibliographical references and index.
Identifiers: LCCN 2018055376 | ISBN 9780393609417 (hardcover)
Subjects: LCSH: Trees. | Human-plant relationships.
Classification: LCC QK475 .L635 2019 | DDC 582.16—dc23
LC record available at https://lccn.loc.gov/2018055376

W. W. Norton & Company, Inc., 500 Fifth Avenue, New York, N.Y. 10110
www.wwnorton.com

W. W. Norton & Company Ltd., 15 Carlisle Street, London W1D 3BS

1 2 3 4 5 6 7 8 9 0

To my mother and her father.
And to Ray Donahue.

How beautiful the sprout-land seen from the cliff! No more cheerful and inspiring sight than a young wood springing up thus over a large tract, when you look down on it, the light green of the maples shaded off into the darker oaks; and here and there a maple blushes bright red. . . . Surely this earth is fit to be inhabited, and many enterprises may be undertaken with hope where so many young plants are pushing up. In the spring, I burned over a hundred acres till the earth was sere and black, and by midsummer this space was clad in a fresher and more luxuriant green than the surrounding even. Shall man then despair? Is he not a sprout-land too after never so many searings and witherings?

—Henry David Thoreau, *Journal*, II, 488–89

[The] lack of interest in the humble everyday mainsprings of one's own existence is mandarinism. We know mandarin attitudes have been a sure sign of decay in past civilizations; it probably is a sign in our own culture.

—Edgar Anderson, *Plants, Man and Life*

CONTENTS

ACKNOWLEDGMENTS

This book is almost completely owed to what others showed and taught me. It began when Dennis McGlade, Scott Dismukes, Allison Harvey, and their colleagues from the Olin Studio hired us to train the trees in front of the Metropolitan Museum of Art in New York City. I had to study pollards. In California, Scott McCormick of the San Francisco Parks Department, Phil Cody and Jim Horner of the University of California at Berkeley, and Alex Fernandez of Filoli all shared their expertise and their puzzlement with me.

In the United Kingdom, a drive on the Somerset Levels with Neville Fay and a visit to Burnham Beeches, where Helen Read gave a group of us a guided tour of the amazing commons of ancient beech pollards, set me off on the path to look at the ancient traditions of pollard and coppice. Reading and attending Fay's Transformational Nature seminars was also important. The fine arborist Reg Harris was tremendously generous with his time and effort, among many other things setting up visits to Bradfield Wood, where we met the wonderful Pete Fordham, and to Staverton, where Gary Battell showed us the finest group of oak pollards that I have ever seen. Bill Cathcart gave us an amazing tour of the trees at Windsor Great Park and introduced me to Clive Leake, whose hedge-laying class I was privileged to observe. Tony Kirkham showed me formal and retrenchment pruning at Kew Gardens, and Matthias Anton led me around his wonderful Deepdale Nursery, showing me their aerial hedge materials and pollards, while Lisa Edinborough helped me understand the fine mature aerial hedges and other formal pruning at Hidcote Manor. Ted Green, who was introduced to me as "a force of nature," was generous, forthright, and memorable in his thoughts and comments on the pruning of pollards and coppice. Jill Butler was equally generous and asked some of the most pertinent questions I have ever heard about wood pastures.

Through Helen Read, I met others. Her colleague Vikki Bengtsson generously led me on a lightning tour of Swedish pollards and informed me that I was becoming a "pollard geek." Read told me to contact Ingvild Austad in western Norway, who was among the first to study pollarded landscapes there. Professor Austad spent day after day showing me sites all over the Sognefjord and patiently explaining to me her work and that of her colleagues, including Leif Hauge. Austad kept me supplied with study materials and introduced me to others, including Ingeborg Mellgren-Mathiesen, who shared with me her research on the farm garden of Nikolai Astrup. She also introduced me to the young farmer Kare Solhaug, who is trying a new method to make pollarding function in a mechanized world.

Read introduced me as well to those who knew about pollards and coppicing in Spain, foremost among whom was José Miguel Elosegui, an extraordinary student of everything about the town of Leitza and maker of one of the finest local-area maps I have ever seen. He introduced me to many remarkable people who still practiced the traditional skills of the town, included the shepherd Patxi Barriola and the axe cutter Gabriel

Sarralegi. The arborist Samuél Álvarez walked my legs off, showing me whole woodlands of pollard oaks and beeches in Álava and Navarra. Oscar Schwendtner walked with me through other pollard woods and showed me the huge commons atop the Sierra de Urbasa.

In Japan, two professors from Morioka University, Harashina Koji and Azuma Atsuki, organized a two-day excursion to show me efforts at carrying the virtues of *satoyama* woodlands into modern plantation forests. Among the people they introduced me to was Chiba Nagomi, who runs Tohno Econet to teach forestry to ordinary citizens and who as it turned out was also an accomplished *kagura* dancer. Koyama Sayako graciously organized and led a trip on the Noto Peninsula to meet traditional and coppice foresters there. A number of students of traditional Japanese coppice forestry and woodland management accompanied us, including Iida Yoshihiko of the United Nations Institute for Advanced Study of Sustainability and the young forester Ifumi Yuho. Ohno Choichiro showed us all his coppice oak woodlands, some recently cut and some with ten or more years of growth, as well as his charcoal-making operation.

Kuramoto Noburo of Meiji University organized a trip near Tokyo to look at coppice woodland restoration projects. The work in Tama New Town of the Sakuragaoka Park Volunteers was being led by Kishimoto Koichi, who walked me through their woodland and shared with me the work of the volunteers there. Tsushima Ryoichi, Andoh Naoko, and Andoh Toshihiko explained and led a visit to many of the forest and paddy restorations of the Totoro no Furusato Foundation.

I was not able to visit Africa, but Professor A. Endre Nyerges graciously spoke with me by telephone about his work on the coppice forests of the Guinea savanna and guided me to the work of other researchers.

In California, the fine writer and anthropologist Kat Anderson helped me to understand her work on the California Indians. She introduced me to the extraordinary basket maker Lois Conner Bohna, who showed me her exquisite work and demonstrated how to make it, while talking all the while of the culture from which the baskets came. Anderson also led me to curator Natasha Johnson of the Phoebe A. Hearst Museum of Anthropology at the University of California, Berkeley, who patiently cured my ignorance about the role of baskets in the cultures of the California Indians.

Melanie Locay at the New York Public Library gave me a place in the Wertheim Study Room that was important to my research, and Esther Marie Jackson of the New York Botanical Garden Library helped me find difficult-to-access studies in journals.

The first drafts of the book were dense and difficult. I owe a great deal to David Sassoon, Joseph Charap, and Wayne Cahilly, who read and commented on early sections, to Joseph's reading of an entire later draft, and to my wife, Nora, who read the whole thing in more than one draft. I owe deep thanks to Susan Kessler, who coached me to at least recover my basic Japanese. Her teaching was both informative and enjoyable, and helped me enormously.

None of this would have been possible, nor would we have been pruning pollards, were it not for the remarkable men and women of Urban Arborists, whose hard work, craft, and persistence are the foundation of the company.

Finally, I am once again in debt to my editor Alane Mason, whose comments were as always copious, accurate, and very important to the book. She is the kind of editor who is not supposed to exist anymore, but thank goodness she does.

SPROUT LANDS

A TREE TO SAVE NEW YORK

We take care of trees in New York City. We had never seen a tree we didn't like, with the possible exception of this one. It had been right in the middle of one of the loveliest common gardens in Manhattan. It had amounted to a trunk as big in girth as a water main and as long as a New York City bus standing on its windshield. Like a pipe, the shaft was almost entirely hollow, with a thin veneer of sound wood enclosing the vacant cylinder. Atop this stem, and here and there along its sides, sprouted anemic twigs and branchlets, trickles of life leaking out of the hulk. A year or two prior to our becoming its caretakers, someone had removed most of the branches in the tree's crown, for reasons unknown, though likely because the sound wood in the trunk was gossamer thin, and the crown teetered on it like a flowerpot set atop a cylinder of cardboard, ready to collapse on passersby. Perhaps, too, many of the branches had died. There was a cable tethering the top of the tube to another, sounder tree nearby.

What was this cadaverous willow doing there? we asked. A willow is the very definition of vigor. If one of them falls over, it invariably sprouts.

A storm-broken branch makes a new tree where it landed, or more likely a new grove. A line of willows on the Somerset Levels, a very flat bottomland of rivers, wetlands, and peat bogs in the southwest of England, has had its branches cut back again and again for millennia—a practice called pollarding—each season yielding new straight and pliable stems. There are still companies that weave these into beautiful salmon-colored wattle fences, the warp and weft so tight that it resembles fine cambric shirting seen under a microscope. In Massachusetts and New Hampshire, the Indians burned off willows and turned the returning young sprouts into fish traps that now and again an enterprising explorer—usually under twelve years old—will turn up with wonder in a backwater, exposed by drought. Thoreau met a pair of Irish boys catching fish with what they called a Dully Chunk, a four-foot length of new-sprouted willow stem with a horsehair noose at the end. They would slip it gently over a resting fingerling pike, and jerk the creature unceremoniously out of the water, the flexing of the willow wand sealing the trap. Willows are world-champion sprouters, but the tree we faced was scarcely sprouting at all. It obviously had serious root decay. Might we get permission to remove it?

Heaven forbid! It turned out the tree was famous. E. B. White had written about it in an essay entitled "Here Is New York" in *Holiday* magazine in 1949. In the article, he had distilled into a form that still brings tears to my eyes the reasons that those of us who love that city do so. New York is not a monolith, he claimed, but a tight and squirming breeding ball of tiny neighborhoods, each with its own independent suppliers: its dry cleaner, its bodega, its haberdasher, its shoe repair shop, its newsstand, its fruit stand, and in his day still its ice and coal shed. The city welcomed people from everywhere on a footing of at least tolerance and at most embrace. Each person came with a dream in their hearts, a scheme in their heads, or a manuscript in their suitcase. A place where 8 million hopes interwove. White wrote, "A poem compresses much in a small space, and adds music, thus heightening its meaning." New York City was to him a great poem, where the celebrated rubbed up against the strung-out, the greatest art against the meanest theft, the merchant prince against the gypsy king.

At the end of the piece, he had raised the then novel specter of atomic destruction. "A single flight of planes," he wrote, "no bigger than a wedge of geese can quickly end this island fantasy, burn the towers, crumble the bridges, turn the underground passages into lethal chambers, cremate the millions."

What did he have to set against this horror?

You have guessed it: the cadaverous, threadbare willow. He described it as "long suffering and much climbed, held together by strands of wire, but beloved of those who know it." If that tree were to go, he wrote, the whole city would go. As long as it could be saved, then New York would remain.

Uh-oh.

So.

We did our duty to nurse it. We pruned it as though it were a bonsai, twice annually, keeping every living stem as perfectly exposed to the sun as we could. We cleared back the branches of nearby trees to give the willow the advantage. We kept back competitors in the root zone. We encouraged its absorbing roots with humic and fulvic acids. And we added three more cables—one of wire and two of more flexible polypropylene—to keep it in place. For about five years, we preserved it safe and more or less alive.

Then, during an early spring inspection of the garden, I noticed that a cable had failed. It hadn't broken in the middle. The wood had cracked at the attachment point, broken away like a piece of pottery. We had long since stopped putting our weight on the tree. We got to the top—the climber depending on a rope attached to the branches of a nearby maple—in order to inspect the hollow stem. There was almost no wood left. It was indeed thinner than crockery and not much stronger. Cracks were forming where two other cables were attached. We reluctantly asked permission to remove it.

The owners at length agreed that there was no choice. We took the tree down one fine spring day. You could have framed round paintings with each cross section of the trunk wood. There were two dead roots at the base that had already begun to buckle. Surprisingly perhaps, Grand Central Station, the Chrysler Building, and the Empire State Building did not shudder or collapse as we hauled the last of it away. A *New York Times* reporter got wind of what had happened and wrote a story portraying us as the unfortunates who had had to do the dastardly deed. On the contrary, we actually felt that we had in the course of nursing the tree come to love it, and like hospice practitioners we had lovingly laid it to rest.

Little did we know that mortality was foreign to it.

Most of the tree had gone into the chipper to make mulch. We had a few unchipped branches. I took three slender young poles from the tree and stuck them in the dirt in the back corner of our yard in Red Hook, Brooklyn. Each was about the size of a broom handle.

Just in case. Or as a memorial.

Then I went away and forgot all about them.

That fall, we were taking inventory of the trees in the yard.

Honey locusts:	6
Willow oaks:	2
Kentucky coffee trees:	4
Serviceberries:	3

What was that knot of slim yellow leaves back in the corner? Not another willow oak, although it looked like one. This tree wasn't balled in burlap or container grown. It was coming out of the dirt that ordinarily we'd take to use on planting sites.

My god, it was the willow!

I bushwhacked my way back to its corner. All three of the broomsticks had sprouted and were growing vigorously. So much for its being a dying tree! I was reminded of the wonderful crazies in Germany and England who had recently designed and planted scale models of cathedrals, made of willow wands. They sprout. You can visit them in Taunton, Somerset, in Great Britain and in Auerstedt, Germany. We thought it a pretty good witticism to have made a building that grows, but in our willow we had a genuine vegetable resurrection.

All that the willow had needed was a fresh set of roots, and the tree's removal, surprisingly enough, had provided them. The cambium, that thin layer of regenerative cells that lies not far beneath the bark of every woody creature, say botanists, with their latinate palaver, is *totipotent*. Had they been Stan Lee or one of his Marvel minions, they would have been frank and just called the cambium All Powerful. Same difference. The cambium can make from scratch any part of the tree it needs, roots included. When our fresh-cut broomsticks had entered the dirt, the all-powerful cambium had remarked, "Hmm! Looks like we need roots here." And out they came.

With hope in our hearts, we left the new grove alone. Within a year, the three stems had grown into a large clumped, multistem tree. Five years later, it was by far the tallest thing in the yard. Our landlord called to complain that the leaves were blocking up the gutters. We cleaned the gutters and cut back the tops. Undaunted, they returned the same year to where they had been, and tacked on another foot and a half for good measure. Now we must pollard the tops annually. When I look out the office window, there it waves, about thirty-five feet tall and growing, the broomsticks now as thick as lampposts.

So willy-nilly, the famous willow is still protecting New York City. It is just that for the present it has moved to Brooklyn.

When we are upset with some new bureaucratic silliness in the city or when we see Manhattan turning into the Isle of the Rich, it occurs to us that we could use the willow to our advantage. If New York City's safety and well-being depend upon it—according to the revered E. B. White—perhaps we could address the city father, thus, in a gruff voice:

"Mr. Mayor, we *have* your tree."

After all, without it, the city might, as White opined, just go.

We are, however, a part of that neighborhood breeding ball that still is wriggling and alive on the outskirts of the golden circle. We still more or less believe in things like White's willow. We might use a sprout from it to catch a fish, but extortion is not in its repertoire.

We have had a better idea. Every year now, we pollard the White willow in our yard, creating about a hundred straight sticks a quarter inch in diameter and two to four feet long. They are the very image of uncounted new hopes. Instead of just weaving rough fences out of them, we plant them.

Where?

Everywhere.

We are planting out every stick somewhere in New York. How many will take and grow? We have no idea, but I bet at least 5 percent. That means maybe five or six new willows per year.

Keep your eyes open. Maybe you will see one. Or more. They grow somewhere waiting for you.

If we can save enough sprouts as the mother grows, maybe we can build a small cathedral, too.

FORGOTTEN WORDS

E. B. White was not the first to admire a strange and apparently ever-lasting tree. In England, at the National Arboretum in Westonbirt, among all the mature and lovely woodland specimens, is an ancient monument. When I saw it, it consisted of several dozen low tree stumps. They were set out along the edges of a rough ring of ground about as big around as the light a street lamp casts. Within the ring, the center was empty of all but sparse grass. To one side, bound with a cord, was an amazing sheaf of several hundred poles, each about twenty feet high and four to eight inches in diameter. It looked like a gigantic sheaf of har-vested wheat. All were slender trunks that during the previous winter had been cut from the ring, leaving the stumps.

The witches had told Macbeth that he would be defeated only when Birnam Wood should come to Dunsinane. The murderer-king in his cas-tle had laughed, but the soldiers had cut trees and advanced behind them. These tall stems indeed would have done the trick. Each soldier could have carried one, the whole approaching like a wave of lime trees—limes

are what the British call lindens—small for the species but big enough
and many enough to hide a lot of men.

This unlikely monument was older than Big Ben. It was older than
Westminster Abbey, older than London Bridge, older than the Roman
baths at Bath. It was a tree that had been cut and allowed to sprout again
for about two thousand years. When it had been a seedling, Jesus had
been teaching in Galilee. Then, it might have grown into a tree with a
trunk about a foot in diameter. Likely, there had been many more limes
around it. The people who lived there had cut each tree to the base, confident that it would sprout new stems.

Every decade or so, they repeated the process, harvesting the tall
slender trunks that had grown back. The cut poles might simply be used
for firewood, or converted into charcoal to fuel pottery, iron, or glass
works. They might be used for wattle and daub, the infill that made the
walls for houses. They could be used for posts or turned for chair legs.
The inner bark—the tough and stringy phloem layer—might be peeled
and woven into a durable, serviceable rope. New trunks on the periphery
of the old ones grew back again, and so decade by decade, the original
trunk expanded to a fairy ring of dozens and eventually of hundreds of
rising stems. The cycle had gone on for centuries, as dark ages came and
went, royal wars were fought, the parliament rose, and the modern age
came on. Until the beginning of the twentieth century, the wood was still
harvested for use.

It is as important a monument as many that are much taller and that
look much finer. It is not a dead thing: a house or a castle or a church. It is
a living cathedral dedicated to the power of sprouting. As often as you cut
it, all by itself it grows its pillars again. It remembers the long age when
such self-renewing wood was the foundation of cultures around the
world—from Japan to Norway to Bulgaria to Afghanistan to Morocco to
Sierra Leone to California—and when it led to the birth and the long long

life of the healthiest woodlands that human beings have ever known. It is a monument to the world founded on coppice and pollard.

I say the words with love and reverence: coppice and pollard. My listeners, whether they be students, clients, friends, or strangers, say, "What are you talking about?" From ten millennia to about two hundred years ago, every person in every forested part of the world would have known exactly what I meant. Indeed, they themselves would have been alive and thriving because of coppice and pollard. We should know these words again, for by means of them, people built their world out of wood for ten thousand years. The persistence, power, intelligence, patience, and generosity of the trees guided them. Home, culture, poetry, and the spirit were shaped by the cutting of trees. Long before the word "sustainable" had ever been coined, human beings learned a way of living with their woodlands that benefited and sustained them both.

The idea is a simple one: when you break, burn, or cut low the trunks of almost any leafy tree or shrub, it will sprout again. New branches will emerge from behind the bases, either from buds that were dormant, waiting for their cue to grow, or from twiglets newly formed by the all-powerful cambium.

A tree can't move. It has to live where it first came up. For 400 million years, in order to stay alive, trees and shrubs learned to respond actively to damage. A wind took down a branch. An aurochs chewed a young tree right to the ground. A vascular disease killed everything above the root system. A bigger tree fell on a smaller one. A flood tipped a whole tree over. A decay fungus like the artist's conk, *Ganoderma applanatum*, caused most of the plant to die back to the base. Each and all of these disasters did not necessarily end the tree's life, because it had learned how to sprout again. Eighty percent of the trees in a leafy forest are not virgins from seed, but experienced sprouts.

At least a hundred centuries ago, people had observed what living wood could do. They needed to make fires, to weave fences, to build houses, to make bridges. Found wood was good, but what if they could multiply it? When a section of a woodland burned, they saw, many of the plants sprouted again right from the ground. The new branchlets, arching up from an existing root system, grew fast and straight. The woodsmen learned how to burn or to cut a part of a woodland intentionally and to harvest the trunks and branches that grew back. Once cut, the shrubs and the trees responded by sprouting again. If people were not greedy and timed the cuts to allow the woods time to recover, they could repeat the operation again and again.

The old Indo-European word for tree, *varna,* also means "to cut." This language was spoken in the seventh millennium BC, and already embodied the idea that trees are to cut. In Europe, the cutting came to be called coppice—from Old French meaning to chop, that is, to cut with a blow. The very sharp and precise Neolithic stone axes could cleanly part a stem from its root. The earlier, Mesolithic axe had been easy to make, simply by chipping a flint, but it was more a bludgeon than a cutting tool, and it did not last long. The Neolithic axe was laboriously worked from a large flint to a size like our present axe head, sharpened carefully by pressure flaking and polished for a day or two on sandstone so that it would hold its edge.

The Neolithic went wild with *varna,* with coppice and sprouts. The piers on which stood the lakeside dwellings of the Swiss and German Alps, the fen bridge supports at the Somerset Levels Sweet Track, the fences and gates of every pasture, the stems for the baskets, all were made with wood that had been coppiced. How do we know that? Because each used hundreds of poles, all of about the same dimension. All must have been cut and regrown for a similar period of time, then selected and cut again. Had they not been coppiced, the people would never have been able to find so many stakes of like length and breadth.

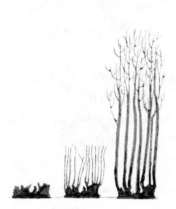

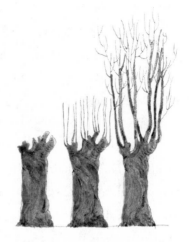

COPPICE STOOL   POLLARD TREE

At left, a coppice stool, cut near the base. At right, a pollard tree, cut at about six-foot height on the trunk. In each drawing, from left to right, are new-cut, one-year-old, and five-year-old stems.

In many parts of the globe, however, cutting to the base was not a good idea. People depended upon their animals—cattle, sheep, goats, pigs—to concentrate the goodness in ephemeral grasses and leaves into a form that humans could eat. If you turned your animals loose in a new-cut coppice woodland, their mumbling mouths would munch the new sprouts as they arose. Once cut, your coppice would never come again, because every time it sprouted, the slender green new stems would go down the gullets of the stock.

One solution was to keep the animals out until the new trunks were strong enough to resist them. Ditches and banks, sometimes topped with hedging, were one solution. So were fences made of woven wood. A third idea did not require fencing. They called it pollarding. The word comes from "poll," meaning to cut, crop, or shear, as in "polled Hereford," a heifer whose horns have been cut off. The Hebrew prophet Ezekiel wanted the priests of God to be pollards: "Neither shall they shave their heads, nor suffer their locks to grow long; they shall only poll their heads." That is, priests had to have haircuts. Because the hair is on the head, the word came to be used to describe an individual person, a pate, a head. The "poll tax" was a tax by the head, or the individual, and going to the polls is going to register the opinions of your individual head.

Pollarding a tree meant creating a number of "heads," each of which would get periodic haircuts. To start a pollard, instead of cutting back to the ground, you pruned the trunk or the branches at a spot where the tree was at least six to eight feet tall, high enough that no cow or sheep or goat could stretch its jaws to reach it. You might cut right to the trunk, or cut back all the branches that were six feet or higher off the ground. If you first cut back to the trunk, it answered with a rosette of rising branches. Those branches became the scaffold on which to cut and cut again. Then, just as with coppice, you let the new sprouts grow for anything from one to thirty years, depending upon the size of the wood you want to harvest and the willingness of the tree to respond. As you continued to cut each branch at the same place, new sprouts emerged only from those blunt ends.

There were wonderful, graphic names for these strange, prolific, bulbous tips. The French called them *têtes de chat*, the Spanish *cabezas de gato*. Each meant "cat's heads." In English, they were heads or knuckles. The end of each branch got fat and thick. (On some species, it could get so large and heavy that it eventually threatened to break its branch.) The ends thickened because the tree responded intelligently to the cutting. It ceased to make new sprouts up and down the length of each stem, as would happen on an ordinary branch. Instead, it directed its buds to form and sprout only at the ends of each branch. There, hundreds of buds gathered, together with great quantities of starch to feed their release and their rapid growth. If you have seen a piece of furniture or a bowl made from burl, you have been able to look at the polished evidence of the thousands of swirling dormant buds that wait beneath the bark for their moments in the sun. A pollard head or knuckle is in essence a kind of burl, created by the mutual action of trees and people.

From the Mesolithic onward, at the latest, coppice and pollard not only supported human beings but changed their minds, opened their hearts, and instructed their hands. Food, fire, cooking, building, boundaries, bridges, and even ships all depended upon the twin practices. The more the people cut, the more they learned; the more they learned, the more they could imagine. As we shall see, the idea of springtime turned upon coppice; the eight-hundred-year tradition of classical Japanese poetry did too. The street, summer vacation, and homecoming all were invented in the cultures of coppice and pollard, but the most important thing that the trees taught people was to live in the presence of their days. You had to cut, all right, but you also had to know when to stop, and you had to learn how to wait before you cut again. If you failed in your response, it wasn't that the authorities fined you or the editorials criticized you, but that you were cold and hungry in the coming year. Great Nature herself would punish you. For ten thousand years, trees were our companions and our teachers. They brought us this far, and perhaps they will carry us on. The only trouble is that we have forgotten almost everything they taught us.

REMEMBERING

For me, remembering started with a job. Just another job. Thanks to the wonderful landscape designers at Olin Studio, we got the opportunity to train ninety-two new trees in front of the Metropolitan Museum of Art on Fifth Avenue in New York City. Fifty-two of them were lindens. We were to create aerial hedges—that is, tall hedges held up above the ground on the trunks of trees—in two sets of two rows. When we were done, they would look much like a boxwood or a yew hedge, but about forty feet tall. My company had done this work before, and we loved it.

The other forty trees were to be pollards of London plane trees. They were planted in four small, regularly spaced rectilinear groves that the designers called bosques. The idea was to make a place with a beautiful pattern of branching in winter and a small-scale place to sit in the shade come summer. Ornamental pollarding was meant to carry into the city the beauty that was produced in the country almost as a by-product of producing wood for people's use. We had done some experimental pollarding in our work, but this style of pruning was so out of fashion that we had not done very much of it.

Allison Harvey, one of the designers, and I stood in front of a grove of ten young London plane trees, one of the four new bosques that had recently been planted in front of the museum. It was the end of March. A late cold storm had lined each branch with a white highlighter of wet snow. The trees surely did not look normal. Indeed, they looked more like a child's first drawing of a tree. Each trunk was prominent, but each branch was either a single fat line or a rough V in shape. The ends were stubbed: each had been cut off short, and most of the slender branchlets at the tips had been removed. On some, we'd left a single stub about the size of a cigar or cigarette butt. On others, where two little branchlets had emerged, we'd cut them back to a double stub that looked like the two biggest knuckles on your fist. Etched in snow, each tree as a whole looked more like a bottle brush of a size suitable to clean tanker trucks. I half expected the sun to come up like an orange slice of pizza in a corner of the page, with a smiling face and a halo of spikes, and my stick-figure mother to put her five stiff fingers across my flat-line back.

I smiled. Allison smiled back. In my heart, I was thinking, "I have killed them all. The museum has spent millions of dollars on this place, and I have killed them all." Everything I had ever learned about trees told me that that was not true. For 400 million years, woody plants have learned to deal with the inevitable damage and destruction of fungi, beetles, storms, plant eaters, and pruners, by sprouting back when they were wounded. Still, these trees were only recently transplanted and so did not have a normal root system. They had lived happily in southern New Jersey until we ripped them up and brought them to Manhattan. I was convinced that they would be the exception that proved the rule.

I recited to myself the mantra that I tell my students every winter as my pruning class begins: "When a tree is wounded, there are only three things it can do: 1. It can adapt remaining branches to replace what was lost; 2. It can release dormant or suppressed buds to create new branches to replace what was lost; or 3. It can create brand-new buds and twigs out of the cambium layer inside the stem." This was meant to comfort and encourage me, but I suddenly realized that I had left out an additional possibility: "4. It can die."

I was not new to these forty trees. For two years, we had been training them in the nursery. First, we had cut off the tops, so they would remain at the height we'd chosen. Then, we had begun to select from the thirty or forty lateral branches on each tree, removing a few at a time. We wanted each to have eight to twelve branches when it was finally trained. We had created an elaborate trellis system, using slender wire and bamboo poles lashed to the trunks to tie down the top branches so they would grow more outward than upward. Where a branch had many smaller branches, we had removed most of those, or left only a couple.

We knew what we were aiming at: urban pollards. These highly trained trees are still common in France and in Southern Europe. Instead of a tall-growing tree with arrays of branches that themselves ramify into smaller and smaller branchlets and then twigs, these would have a low, fixed height and instead of sprouting all along each lateral branch, they would sprout only (and prolifically) from the stubbed ends. In winter, the selected branches and their starbursts of sprouts cast a wonderful shadow on the ground, like a living rose window. In summer, they make a lovely place to sit and picnic or to listen to a band concert, well protected from the sun, but not smothered in the deep shade of forest giants. That was the program.

But how to achieve this end in the heart of Manhattan? I thought I knew just where to go to learn. As a boy on the Peninsula, about fifteen miles south of San Francisco, I had been obsessed with the Steinhart Aquarium in Golden Gate Park. At the time, as you entered the building, you stood immediately before half a city block of swampland, sunken into the ground and surrounded with a brass railing, but otherwise uncaged. It was full of alligators, some as big as drag racers, some as small as bagpipes, piled one atop the other in irregular heaps. We boys waited for one to move, or even better, to slide into the water and promenade. Around the open tank, in glass terrariums on the wall was an array of highly colored snakes and lizards from around the world. To me, it was paradise.

Every weekend, my brother and I wheedled our parents to take us there. When we succeeded, there was almost always a bargain: if we take you to the gators, you have to go with us to the De Young Museum. The latter was full of horrible Chinese ceramics. We had no choice but to agree if we wanted our reptile fix. But we had to do something to escape the awful shiny pots.

Pollards were the answer. The Music Concourse separates the two museums. It was built as a sunken garden—lowered out of the afternoon wind and paved with crushed stone and gravel—to make room for as many as twenty thousand people to listen to the concerts that emanated from the Spreckels Temple of Music, a Venus-on-the-half-shell-style Beaux Arts bandshell at one end. Built in 1900, the concourse has had pollarded trees from the very beginning. Now, there are almost three hundred of them, about two thirds of them mature, gridded through the vast space. Among the older trees, the majority are wych elms, with London planes a close second, plus all kinds of other experiments, even a field maple and a black walnut. The older trees are no taller today than they were sixty years ago, when I was five years old, although they are much larger in girth.

Back then, replete from our watching of alligators and caimans, we had had to walk the prisoner's mile across the concourse toward the dreaded De Young. Inevitably, we had started out under the first pollards: "Hey, you guys, we'll just play here! Okay?" Parental disapproval. "Look, we won't leave the trees. It'll be fine." When they had reflected upon how whining kids would spoil their museum visit and how the space was a bowl naturally bounded by the trees and the steep banks at the edge, they usually at last relented. So I had got to know the trees quite well. You couldn't climb them, because the first branch was eight feet in the air, a stratospheric height to a kid. And you couldn't play hide-and-seek, because the lower trunks were completely without branches, unless you learned to stand very straight and still.

I had never before seen trees like them. I asked my dad, "Are they real?" He averred that they were, but he had little more to say about them. He was a doctor and so, I thought, knew everything. His silence on these creatures had seemed deafening.

But the people who still cared for these very trees . . . *they* would know. Five decades after I had first met the concourse pollards, I thought I would at last find out all about them, particularly about how to make and to care for them.

Through the nearby Strybing Arboretum, I found out that the city Parks department was in charge of the trees. They put me in touch with Scott McCormick, who agreed to show me his work on the concourse. There were also many pollarded trees on the campus of the University of California at Berkeley, he told me. Perhaps the gardeners there would be able to help? I thanked him for the thought and contacted the men in charge at Berkeley, Phil Cody and Jim Horner. Finally, I remembered an estate garden called Filoli, about 20 miles south of the city on the Peninsula near Woodside. My mother had helped to open it to the public during the 1970s. I knew that it had London plane pollards. I arranged to meet its horticulturist, Alex Fernandez, there.

My relief at finding advisers was not long-lived. McCormick was a fine young man. "This was the job everybody hated," he told me. "It takes so long, and you have to be careful where you cut." He loved it and willingly took it on. "It is very very interesting to me," he went on, "and I have a few guys now who agree. Trouble is we don't know what we are doing."

Many of the trees first planted in Golden Gate Park a hundred years ago were gone, and in more difficult places, some had been replaced three or four times. The pruners were not sure whether to cut back new trees a lot or a little, whether to leave the stumps of one or two sprouts when they pruned back the younger pollard heads or not. When a head got so heavy that it threatened to break the branch, they didn't know whether if they removed it the branch would form a new one. They were not sure whether to use more planes, more elms, or even something completely different. "We try everything," he said, "and we try to keep a record of what works." There was no old hand to advise them.

Never mind. At UC Berkeley, they would be able to help. I got to the campus two hours before my meeting with Cody and Horner, so I could have a look around. The place was awash in pollarded London planes. Hallelujah! Up hill and down, through the whole campus, if it was not a grove of eucalyptus, it was a line or a bosque of pollards. One group of thirty stood in a rectangle, with tops that had been trained flat. Others were finished trees with large pollard heads and branches upraised in acclamation. Still more were brand-new trees, their first stubby branch cuts just executed. I thought there was something wrong with these last, but I could not quite tell what. It looked as though someone had tried to imitate the shape of the mature pollards exactly in the form of the young ones, on the theory that the latter would grow up simply by adding girth and length, as though they were very large balloon animals and Great Nature's were the lungs that would inflate them.

The prize of the whole campus was four rows of plane pollards that stretched north in parallel rows from the campus monument, the obeliskine campanile. The trees had been transplanted from the grounds of the

Panama Pacific International Exhibition after that fair closed in late 1915. Since the trees were already established when planted at the fair, they were well over a century old when I saw them. This in itself surprised me, because I did not think that trees so deeply pruned would live so long. Since these had survived for so many years, I reasoned, if I could learn how they were started, I would know how to proceed.

Because they had been pollarded, the rows did not tower. As I walked among them on a sunny winter day, waiting to meet Horner and Cody, I had the impression of walking underwater. The crown branches arched up and out like a many-headed candelabra. The end of each was dark and heavy, like a flattened burl, knotty, knobbly, scaly, rough. Each of them looked as though it should be at the bottom of the tree, not at the top, unless of course they were floating underwater, like the inflated bulbs of bull kelp that bob just beneath the surface of Monterey Bay.

Atop each of these pimply scabs waved the most unexpected things imaginable: long thin twigs of rising wood—each two or three feet long— supple, blond, delicate. If you have ever seen clams or mussels feeding— with delicate pink nets of translucent tissue that float like a skirt around the half-opened shell—you have seen the contrast: out of something gross and solid rose something bright, almost filamentous.

Each of the fifty-six trees had between twelve and twenty branches, each branch topped with a fistful of the same long slender sprouts. Each tree was only about twenty-five feet tall, a third the size that you would expect in a centenarian London plane tree. Each year (or sometimes every other year) the new sprouts were pruned back to the burls. During the growing season, they created a regular rounded canopy of leaves. In the winter they cast their concentric shadows on the ground.

In the year 1915, the Panama Pacific Exhibition had announced not only San Francisco's recovery from the 1906 earthquake, but also its arrival as a city on the world stage. Immodestly, its makers had dubbed the event "the greatest, most beautiful and most important in history." The neighborhood later called the Marina was its setting. A lot of the land was fill dirt, which in many subsequent earthquakes has liquefied, causing foundations to crack and houses to tilt. The phantasmagoric structures of the fair—the Tower of Jewels, the Fountain of Energy, the Court of Abundance—went up in 1915, and with a few exceptions were removed at the conclusion of the fair. (Most were made of plaster mixed with burlap, not a lasting material.) The fair featured the first steam locomotive on the Southern Pacific line, searchlights to illuminate the towers, a submarine, and a transcontinental telephone call that let New Yorkers listen to the crashing Pacific surf. Among all these modern miracles had stood these very fifty-six pollarded planes, modest memorials to a time when people still spoke the language of trees.

Here came Horner and Cody. I was excited to ask them how they did it all. "I don't know," said one. "None of us do. The last guy who had an idea retired some time ago, and no one thought to ask him while he was still alive." So they tried stuff. Sometimes they cut back all the sprouts every year in January or February. A few of the branches did not respond well. Instead they tried cutting back the sprouts every second year. But that made larger wounds that take longer to close, and sometimes whole heads went into decline. As for new pollards, they said they were just trying things out. Many of the young pollards looked like a push-me-pull-you; their branching rhythm was jerky, more zigzag than balletic. It appeared that Berkeley too had lost both the art and the science of making these trees.

Alex Fernandez at Filoli was my last chance. I drove down the Peninsula an hour to a valley just south of the Crystal Springs Reservoir to meet him.

The garden had once been the seat of a robber baron who had been among those who bought the land that San Francisco's water supply reservoir would occupy. He had then sold the property to the city. He had kept the southernmost portion of the land, just past the water, to be his estate, Filoli. Later, the place had belonged to the Matson Line heiress, and finally opened as a public garden.

The entry gate was flanked by a dozen fine pollards. Inside, I could see that Fernandez had been hard at work renovating an overgrown garden. A double line of huge Irish yews—so prominent that pilots used them as landmarks when on final approach to SFO—had more than doubled in size since they had first been planted, in the 1920s. Recently, the gardeners had had to tie them together with wire to keep them from splaying out. "Whenever there was a storm, the wires would snap," Fernandez said. "The yews would fly apart like an old lady's girdle." He took them back from twenty-two feet high to only twelve, and from eight feet wide to only three. "At first, it looked like hell," he recalled. "But the next year, it was fine." He'd also taken down an aerial beech hedge by four or five feet, renovated a long holly hedge, restored a famous double allée of espaliered fruit trees, and rounded over everything from magnolias to hawthorns. Here was a man who liked to prune. Surely, he could help me.

We walked up to the head of the yew allée. There stood half a dozen young pollards. They were scarecrows. Each stark trunk had six or seven stiff awkward broomstick branches with a knot of long sprouts at the end. Fernandez assured me that his predecessor had made these trees. "I think he let the branches grow out too long before he cut them," he commented. "They are very stiff."

"What should he have done?" I asked.

"I haven't the slightest idea," he answered.

Nobody but nobody could tell me how to make this strange kind of tree. I had allies, all right, but we were partners in perplexity. We were doing our best in a vacuum of knowledge.

Given the predilections of postwar arborists, however, I guess I should not have been so surprised. Like most of my peers in tree care, I had been a student of Alex Shigo, the brilliant USDA scientist who had changed the way the whole world prunes. He had done for trees what the anatomists of fifteenth- and sixteenth-century Bologna and Padua had done for the human body: instead of taking the word of authorities for what was happening inside, he dissected the body to find out what was really happening. It was shockingly different from what had been assumed. The branch collar—a part of tree anatomy not even recognized before—took center stage, and guided our pruning. A shouldered ring of tissue where the branch is attached to its parent branch or trunk, the collar had evolved over millions of years to defend the tree from damage. If we made our pruning cuts to the collar, all would go well.

But deep in the Shigo teaching lay a prejudice. He worked for the Forest Service. His job was to produce clean timber: long knotless trunks that could best be cut into dimensional boards. A Shigo-style tree looks ur-natural, almost sculptural, the tree that nature would have made were there no accidents—that is to say, were there no world. Of the three things a wounded tree can do, he favored overwhelmingly the first—letting the tree adapt its remaining branches to replace what had been lost. We were to make our cuts to collars or at least back to branchlets capable of carrying on. Under few circumstances did we want to let the tree produce sprouts, either by releasing dormant buds or by making fresh buds.

Sprouts look a lot less neat when they first arise. In fact, they are a mess, a real bad hair day. They also eventually make knots in the wood that spoil the boards—think of knotty pine versus clear pine—or at least reduce their value. And I have heard arborists repeat this phrase again and again: "Epicormic sprouts are poorly attached, and most of them will die anyway" (epicormic means dormant). Shigo himself clearly understood how important sprouts were, he understood the place of sprouts in pruning, and he honored good pollards. Many of his followers had not.

And in his practice, the master never taught how to prune pollards. In some crevassed fold of my brain, I too was betting against the sprouts that I was trying to produce with my stub cuts on the London planes. What good were they anyway? I could not depend upon them, and even if they came, they were scrawny, unruly, inferior little things.

I had to look deeper in time, and elsewhere in space. Europe, everyone told me, is where they pollarded best. Off I went, at first to the library. I am good in a research room. To me, it is a distillery of the human heart, mind, and hand, where I can begin to find the truth of any matter.

What I found shocked me. At once, it encouraged and devastated me. The practice of pruning to intentionally cause sprouts was as old as the last Ice Age, and it had been practiced not only in Europe but around the world. Unfortunately, however, the modern age had decided that it was a bad thing and had mainly put a stop to it.

Shigo was only a small part of the matter, and indeed there was nothing at all wrong with his way of pruning. It made lovely, tall, upstanding, clean trees. Unintentionally, however, his focus on "natural" pruning had helped cut us off from 10,000 years of intimate exchange between people and trees. Not only are sprouts "important" in pruning, I found, they are the reason that there are any trees or shrubs at all, and they are the reason that there are any people at all. For all but the last two centuries of human history, the whole point of pruning was to produce sprouts—to stimulate the second and third of the possible wound responses that I teach in pruning class—for when those sprouts grew up they gave people firewood, charcoal, building wood, ship timber, fence posts, slender willow whips (called withies) to tie knots with, hedges, fodder, fiber, rope, and baskets. They gave us a way to stay warm, to eat, to live, a way to travel. Without them, human beings would not have made it past the Neolithic.

Also, I discovered, the way trees sprouted when cut gave people an intimation of immortality. When Isaiah envisioned the coming kingdom, he sang that no child would die or old person not live out their days; rather, each would have the life of a tree. Job too saw it plainly: in chapter 14, as he demanded that God tell him why He had broken him, he complained that death simply puts an end to men. He wished he might have been a plant: "For a tree there is hope, if it be cut down, that it will sprout again and that its tender shoots will not cease. Even though its root grow old in the earth, and its stump die in the dust, yet at the first whiff of water, it may flourish again and put forth branches like a young plant." Unlike a man, a tree could revive although it seemed to have died.

By means of coppice, I discovered—and as we shall see—West Africans had created a timed system of agriculture that gave lumber, grain, and vegetables and renewed the forest. By means of pollards and coppice, the Iberians had got wood, charcoal, vines, cork, ink, sweeteners, and fat pork. By means of coppice, the people of Japan had got an integral system of living that brought them rice, wood, pottery, poetry, and fire. By means of coppice and pollard, the peoples of Sweden and Norway since the Bronze Age had grown fodder for their sheep, goats, and cattle and wood for their stoves. By means of pollards, the Basques had got charcoal to make iron, wood to build and heat their houses, and they had crafted trees to make ship's timber. By means of fire coppice, the Indians of North and South America had cleared land for growing and got back poles to make houses, fashioned traps and weirs, and stimulated the production of fruit and nuts. By means of coppice, the women of California tribes had got slender stems to make the baskets to hold food and supplies, to carry burdens, to sift, and to cook a meal. By means of pollards on the Somerset Levels in England, the Neolithic and Bronze Age peoples had got poles to build the armature for foot bridges and withies to weave fences and the frames for walls. By means of pollard and coppice, Europeans had got the small wood to burn with limestone, kilning the quick lime from which they made fertilizer, disinfectant, and paint. By bending Douglas firs, the people of Mesa Verde had got upright poles to become the lintels of the cliff dwellings. By means of fire coppice, the people of the Amazon basin had created a shifting agriculture that enriched the rain-forest soils with slow-to-decay charcoal.

What? I wondered. Hadn't they denuded their landscapes, destroyed their forests, reduced biological diversity, and caused massive erosion?

No. Because they left the live roots in the ground, they prevented erosion. The landscape was not denuded because the trees sprouted back. Whole suites of creatures joined the rhythm of regrowth, colonizing the coppice and pollard woods. The resulting lands were more diverse, not less. The poetic language of classical Japan enshrines certain key creatures in its word-hoard; six of the autumn creatures so used are threatened by the real estate developments that destroy their coppice woods. In England, beetles, lichens, and other creatures that once inhabited the wildwood now survive only in ancient pollard woodlands.

But don't the trees soon disappear? I wondered.

No. Coppiced and pollarded trees, it turns out, lived longer than their uncut cousins.

These woods of coppice and pollard around so many villages and settlements were no peaceable kingdoms. Heretics were burned. Rival sects warred. The well-off lived off the rest of the world. Droughts, floods, and plagues winnowed populations. A savvy politico could mine the system for its riches, whether the boss was a hereditary lord, a warlord, a landlord, or a municipal council. But people lived in nature in a way that now we seldom do. Harmony is not the right word to describe it. A better phrase is creative engagement. They lived that way because they knew they had to, in order to live at all, and it was a good way to live, for both the people and the plants. In essence, they learned to talk to trees.

In coppice and pollard, both people and trees were reciprocally active. One acted, and the other responded. When the parties listened and answered, the results created new possibilities for both. One party harvested for its needs, the other lived longer and continued indefinitely upon the land. The relationship cost a tremendous effort on the part of both. To cut a hundred trees, even with a sharp steel blade, was a hard day's work. For their part, the trees had their leaves stripped from them in whole or in part every few years. Leaves are not decorative. They are the one and only way in which trees can get food. It takes a great deal of energy to replace them all at once, but unless the tree did so, it died.

The relationship could be abused. If you did not let the trees alone for long enough, and cut them again more quickly to get more wood faster or to open new ground for planting, the plants might indeed die rather than regenerate. In the times when the alternative sources of livelihood were few or none, however, the failure of a tree had put a quick brake on excess. When growing populations overwhelmed the land in the nineteenth century, it was the destruction of pollard systems in places like Norway that brought so many immigrants to the United States.

Only when coal began to be mined in quantity and when at last saws became cheaper than axes—that is, in the late eighteenth and early nineteenth centuries—did this millennial relationship to living wood begin to dwindle. Suddenly, the woods surrounding villages that had been repeatedly cut and repeatedly sprouted since time immemorial (a phrase used throughout the Middle Ages to justify common rights to a coppice or pollard woodland) no longer gave a feeling of security, but a fear that they had fallen behind the times.

John Evelyn, the father of modern forestry, had written in 1664 that pollarding made "so many scrags and dwarfes of many trees, which else would be good timber." He called those who did the pollarding "unskillful wood-men and mischievous bordurers," who left trees "a mass of knots, boils, cankers and deformed branches, to their utter destruction." Many writers and modern foresters took up the chorus. More than a century later, the English essayist William Cobbett summarized the complaint: He called pollards "trees that have been beheaded . . . than which nothing in nature can be more ugly."

In England, the enclosures despoiled commoners of their common lands, parts of which had been in coppice or pollard. The rich began to make parks. Majestic, untouched trees were prized along the long vistas of these naturalistic forest and meadow confections. In his "Epistle to Bathurst," Alexander Pope uttered his justly famous maxim "Consult the genius of the place in all." He was counseling lords to remake their landscape into an ideal nature, shifting trees, building hills, installing vales, and sculpting views to imitate an imaginary, untouched landscape. (Real woodlands were of course much messier than the designed ones.) They invented the ha-ha, a hidden sunken fence, to keep potentially unsightly sheep and cattle at a picturesque distance in the unspoiled vistas.

The often lopped trees of the commons around villages were thought hideous disfigurements, signs of the backwardness of the stupid hidebound country bumpkin. The best idea was to burn them or to cut them down and sell them. "Pollards, which by reason of their decay or stintedness will not, in the course of eighteen or twenty years, throw out tops equal in value to their present bodies," wrote the up-to-the-minute agriculturist William Marshall in 1785, "should . . . be taken down;—for the principal and interest of the money will be worth more at the end of that time, than the body and top of the pollard; besides the desirable riddance of such unsightly encumbrances." John Locke himself, in his *Second Treatise on Government*, had praised the person who enclosed and cleared an acre of land, making it pure farmland, rather than allowing it to continue "lying waste in common."

Lord Bathurst's seat at Cirencester Park is still in a tolerable state of repair, and the beautiful vistas framed by uncut woods are certainly a delight to see. The landscape seemed to represent a rapprochement between man and wild nature, but in fact it built an impassible, invisible wall, a ha-ha of the mind and heart. In the older woodlands, man and trees were co-actors in nature, of equal dignity and power. They had to respect and respond to each other. In the new picturesque landscape, man became the spectator of an idea of nature that he himself had made in the image of a primordium that had never existed. If you traveled back to the end of the last Ice Age, for example, it is very likely that the wildwood browsed by large herbivores like mammoths, mastodons, and aurochs much more closely resembled pollard woods than it did our notion of a pristine forest.

Allison and I stood before the snow-whitened outlines of the scalped London plane trees in front of the Metropolitan Museum. She and her colleagues had designed the pollard bosques, based upon European precedents. I honored their work and their trust in us to produce it. Still, I could not keep from thinking I'd done wrong. I felt a confused press at my back, as though Fifth Avenue at six a.m. had suddenly filled with honking impatient cars and buses faced with a detour that ran them right up our backs and over the trees. Evelyn is the father of forestry, Pope one of my favorite poets and garden thinkers, Cobbett a fine defender of the common lands, and Shigo my teacher. They and hundreds more looked over our shoulders and groaned.

What could I do? It was a job. It had been late winter, time to cut the trees. *Varna.* I had reread my notes, looked at my favorite pollard pinups, remembered that they were living beings, and then we had taken a deep breath and pruned them. Modesty had been rule number one. We had left enough branches so that if one failed, we'd have a backup. We had selected some single branches and some that forked, trying to create the beginning of what might grow into a mature pattern. We had been careful to make sure each got plenty of light. I had reminded myself and my crew that this was not a one-shot event but the beginning of a training process that would take a decade. The pollards could not all at once look like finished trees. We had to begin a conversation.

The more I had learned, the more I felt keenly the lack of a teacher. I have often wished to have beside me a fen dweller from the English Neolithic or a medieval Japanese farmer. He would certainly have been able to tell me how best to prune these trees. But for now, under an untimely March snow, I was more than half afraid that they were dead, dead, dead.

Allison looked hard at the trees, smiled again, and said with a lilt in her voice, "Well, that's done! Now what?"

I looked at her and back at the white stick figures of the trees.

I said, "Silent prayer."

THE SPROUT LANDS

A few weeks later, I was studiously avoiding the plaza in front of the museum. I feared the worst. I wanted to delay the hour of doom. I was checking some trees we'd planted on upper Fifth Avenue, when I got a call from a client down in the 60s on Fifth. She is always worried about her fine katsura trees. Trundling down the road, I suddenly realized that I was abreast of the pollard plaza at the museum, and there, on two trees nearest me, I could see tiny light green shadows at the edges of the knuckled stems.

I slammed on the brakes and pulled to the curb. Could it be true? There is no parking in front of the museum. I was not parking, I reasoned. I was "loading and unloading." I was taking a tremendous load off my mind. I tried to walk nonchalantly toward the fuzzy-ended planes, though to a stranger it may have appeared like an eyes-closed rush.

There they were: Yes, they were leaves. Yes, there was more than one of them. Yes, there were numbers of leaves emerging! Yes, they were emerging on each and every—or almost each and every—stem. "Say Amen!, somebody!" I breathed. I felt like my old friend and boss, then the dean of the Cathedral of St. John the Divine, who, whenever he found a parking place in Midtown Manhattan, threw up his hands and exclaimed in jest, "There *is* a God!"

I was excited to touch them. I felt something like what Thoreau must have felt when he first saw the acres of sprouts coming up from an oak wood that he had recently burned. Like the native peoples before him, his people had still cultivated some of the woodland by fire coppice: by burning and letting grow again. "How beautiful the sprout-land (burnt plain) seen from the cliff!" he wrote. "No more cheering and inspiring sight than a young wood springing up thus over a large tract, when you look down on it, the light green of the maples shaded off into the darker oaks; and here and there a maple blushes quite red."

I had not scorched the London planes, but I had certainly whacked them. I shared the feeling of inner renewal that Thoreau drew from the sprout's persistence. "Shall man then despair?" he continued. "Is he not a sprout-land too, after never so many searings and witherings?" No doubt about it. As I hurried back to the car before it flowered with traffic summonses, there was a sproutish spring in my step.

I began to trust in the power of sprouting, and the more I learned, the more I came to believe that trees are more perceptive, more intelligent, more generous, and more persistent than we are. We could learn from what they knew and what they did. Thoreau saw them as clearly as anyone ever has. "If you examine a wood-lot after numerous fires and cuttings," he wrote, "you will be surprised to find how extremely vivacious are the roots of oaks, chestnuts, hickories, birches, cherries, etc. The little trees which look like seedlings of the year will be found commonly to spring from an older root or horizontal shoot or stump." Commonly, indeed. In a review of the literature on sprouting among leafy trees, Arnold Arboretum botanist Peter del Tredici estimated that 80 percent of trees in a broadleaf forest are not seedlings but sprouts from a preexisting stem.

Woodlands *are* sprout lands. Scrabbling in the dirt, Thoreau looked at young trees. One four-year-old red oak about a foot high rose from an acorn an inch beneath the pine-needle duff. It had already died back once and sprouted again. A black oak of about the same age was only six inches tall and much branched, having been chewed down by rabbits at least once. The stem was just a quarter inch in diameter, but the root beneath it in the soil was three times fatter. The tree was storing up the will and the food to grow or to sprout again. Another taller white oak stem, maybe seven years old, had also shot up again after a rabbit had eaten it down. "These little oaks in their earliest years," he observed, "are forming great fusiform vigorous roots on which they can draw when they are suddenly left to seek their fortunes in a sprout-land."

Some trees can grow again from the base indefinitely. Most conifers can do so only when they are seedlings, but ever after if their branches hit the ground, the tips can root again. Leafy trees can sprout from the base for at least fifteen or twenty years, many of them for half a century or more, and some for as long as they live. Sprouters that make clonal groves—like quaking aspens or the Tasmanian Lomatia—can in theory keep sprouting forever (see page 291).

There are trees that possess a lignotuber, a specialized organ at the base that maintains viable dormant buds for the entire lifetime of the tree. Lindens all have lignotubers. They sprout promiscuously, causing arborists headaches, because we must explain to our client that the tree is not dying, just vivacious. When you find a multistem basswood in the forests in the Northeast, it is very likely the result of many stems that sprouted from the lignotuber when the previous tree died. It is a kind of natural coppicing. The flare at the base of each tree is a colony of buds, ready to recruit new stems. The word "recruit" itself comes from the French meaning "to grow again," referring to the ability of trees to sprout after cutting. It was an ironic way to speak of armies as being indefinitely refillable.

To branch and branch again was no innovation, not something trees learned to do because of an Ice Age or some other recent perturbation. It was rather a way of life that they had gradually perfected over 400 million years. Back in the early Silurian, before plants came on land, the seaweeds had learned to fork as they grew. Each stem had sprouted two daughter stems. Each daughter had done the same. And so on and so forth, ad infinitum. In this way, a single plant had been able to spread across the surface of the water, exposing as much of its green surface to the sun as possible and so making by photosynthesis the most food that it might.

These branches had been leafless. All the tissue of each stem had been green—suffused with chlorophyll—and all of it had made food out of sunlight, water, and carbon dioxide. (Still today there are some trees—sassafras, box elder, and sweet bay magnolia are three—whose youngest stems are green and photosynthetic.) The surface of the water had been the roof of their world. Growing up had not been an option, since the roof had contained them, but spreading out across it had been a big help. It had been as though the vegetable world were growing in some enormous conservatory under glass. The stems had multiplied, feeling at the upper edge of their world, like hands exploring a glass ceiling—only these hands had made food and so had given rise to more hands.

Now and again, an alga had broken from its holdfast, and washed up on shore. It had dried out, but likely not before it had been attacked by terrestrial fungi, among the earliest land creatures, whose branching hyphae had woven in and out among the plant cells and digested the remains. In this way had come early dirt, a new creation forged from broken rock, clay, and the mineralized remains of the dead. Again and again, many thousands of times, however, a fungus had been slow on the uptake. It had fed on nitrogen from the alga's cells while still attached to and feeding on the detritus in the dirt. The water and minerals it had absorbed from the soil had leaked into the tissues of the plant. The plant could stay alive, because the parasite now gave it what the sea had given it before. The fungus had got its food, not only for a moment, but for as long as the plant could stay alive. The two had acquired a common interest. Roots had been born.

This proto-plant might have simply sprawled across the land. Indeed some did. They looked rather like guts, oozing in bulbous lobes over the shallows and the rocks. The plant's fungal roots gave it the water it needed to survive. Each organism had a core of hardened tissue, the aptly named sclerenchyma, that both channeled water to the green photosynthesizing cells and gave a bendy backbone to the stem.

One year, a plant stood up. Its descendants—that is, every tree and shrub—eat by acclamation. They raise their hands to the sky. For many years, many decades, even centuries, and in principle eternally, a woody plant can hold up and out its continually self-renewing leafy branches. Goethe derived the whole plant from the leaf. As he saw it, the root, the stem, the twig, the flower, and the fruit all arose as modifications of the leaf. From the spleenwort to the redwood, it was all one idea, elaborated, adapted, ramified, repeated. Once the roof of the conservatory was removed, only the height of the atmosphere and the load limits of standing wood could contain the upward growth.

It was a wonderful way to understand growth and form, because it worked not from arcane cellular and subcellular minutiae, but from observations of whole living plants. Recent morphologists—scientists who look at form for clues to the life history of creatures—think it was the stem, not the leaf, that came first, but they honor Goethe's method. The German poet and scientist had called his great work *The Metamorphosis of Plants*. In the telome theory, botanist Walter Zimmerman and his colleagues distinguished four metamorphoses that they believe gave rise to trees and shrubs, and eventually to all living plants. The four are overtopping, flattening, webbing, and reduction.

According to the telome theory, woody plants were originally dichotomous, each branch dividing into two equal daughters. Soon, one branch overtopped another creating a leader with lateral branches. Then, groups of laterals flattened into a plane. Webbing grew among the flattened twigs, giving rise to the first leaves.

The story as they tell it is about learning to branch, to leaf, to flower, and to fruit. Once there was a sprout. It stood up on the land. It was glad because now it could expose all of its aboveground surface, not just the top side, to the light. It strained upward toward the sun. It did just as its waterborne cousins had always done. One branch forked into two equal daughters, only now there was no roof over their heads. Each shot up into the sky. One got a little more light than the other, so it grew a little faster and a little taller. It overtopped its sister, so the little sister moved its growth out sideways, where it too could get enough light. Here was the distinction between a lateral branch and an upward-leading branch. Then it rested.

When growth began again, the two daughters each forked, each making two granddaughters. Again, on each, one overtopped the other. One granddaughter on the tallest stem continued to grow upward. Again, the slightly weaker sibling branched off to make her way. On the weaker of the original daughters, one granddaughter might get uppity and turn upward to compete with the rising leader, or both it and its sister might just fork wider, seeking their way to the sun in spreading extension, not vertical erection. Still, one grew more than the other, so the branch extended outward at its angle. Season by season, the new growth continued in this way, the leader zigzagging into the sky, and the lateral branches zigzagging outward and upward, a compound gesture of acclamation, increasing as the plant grew taller. You can still see today this zigzag habit in the twigs of some trees like the sycamore, hackberry, linden, and beech.

This way of growing harvested more sunlight and made more food. The plant was emboldened. What if instead of zigzagging, it just grew straight up? With each new season, one daughter would begin life as the upright leader, and two or three more would start out as lateral branches. Look at the top of a spruce or a young white pine. It shoots up straight as an arrow with its laterals fanning out at angles beneath it. As it branched and rebranched, the plant could be more sure that each of its new daughters would find her slice of sun. The bud developed as a branch in embryo, protected by hardened leaflets. Year by year, a new season would release the new buds at the tips of the youngest branches, continuing the pattern of growth.

Life could be even surer with another metamorphosis. Some successive ranges of branches, subbranches, branchlets and twigs might grow in a single plane. To be sure, not all of the branches of the tree should do this or it would sacrifice 340 degrees of the circle. But if close-fit groups of lateral branches or their branchlets flattened into a single plane, many more sprays could orient themselves to reach the light. Walter Zimmerman called this planation—that is, the flattening of sprays of daughters and their progeny.

A strange thing happened to some of these flattened sprays. When the twigs were near one another, they began to sprout flags or standards of fine thin green tissue. These flags met. They webbed the space between the leader twiglet and its laterals. All of this tissue could use the light to make food. It was the first leaf.

In this story, the leaf is outcome, not origin, as Goethe had claimed, but one can understand Goethe's love of the leaf form, for through it the power of plants to grow multiplied by orders of magnitude. Through it, the system that powers the uptake of water came to be. The leaf allows plants today to take more than 56 billion metric tons of carbon from the air each year, creating the organic compounds upon which all the rest of life subsists.

When the sprouts were simply forking, the tips did for reproduction, with both male and female organs meeting there. As some stems overtopped others, webbed, and fused, they folded modestly over on the sexual parts and fused into the carpel, closed seed vessels, the spores of ferns, and the stamens of the flowers. They protected and enclosed the reproductive parts by reduction of some growing tips to form vessels for the seeds.

The whole tree is thus woven by the growth and the metamorphosis of its sprouts. A tree is in a forest, but there is also a forest in each tree. Every new branch arises on its parent's stem in exactly the same way that its first parent arose from the dirt. If you look closely at the trunk of an old tree, you can sometimes see how its largest branches attach to the trunk with fingers of tissue that closely resemble the roots of the parent stem. The great French botanist Francis Hallé called the young branch an epiparasite, because when it is young, it depends upon the existing branches for its food, as did those branches before them. Only as one makes enough of its own leaves does it feed itself and then finally begin to export surplus food to the rest of the tree.

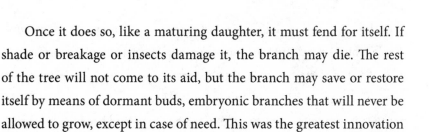

Once it does so, like a maturing daughter, it must fend for itself. If shade or breakage or insects damage it, the branch may die. The rest of the tree will not come to its aid, but the branch may save or restore itself by means of dormant buds, embryonic branches that will never be allowed to grow, except in case of need. This was the greatest innovation in the life of shrubs and trees: They learned to keep spare parts, extras, *recruits*, not only at the base but on the trunk and branches. Each of these could be called upon in the event of damage or disease to come forth and begin to branch again.

Conifers dominated the early world of trees. Their idea was to start life as green pyramids. They occupied more ground space at the bottom than the top. The base of the tree made elbow room for the crown, so that the slender tops would be more likely to get sun, even were the forest packed with fellow trees. Spare buds were needed not near the base of branches, but at the tips, where they could hit the ground, root, and start a new member of the tribe. Leafy trees, on the other hand, began life fighting for space and light in a world dominated by conifers. They had to be sneaky, and they had to be quick. They kept recruits all up and down each branch, so a new stem could immediately shoot up toward any ray of light.

Tree people have many different names for these extra buds. For some they are dormant, for others suppressed, for still others reserve buds. The names reflect more the variety of human feelings about nature than any difference in the buds themselves. The friendly Rousseauian sees them sleeping, the tough-minded Hobbesian sees them violently quashed, the calculating Adam Smithian sees them as handy spares. They are all of these at once. Trees are much closer to the facts of their nature than are we to the facts of ours. On those branches are many such buds, ready to sprout if needed.

The evolution of tree structure is astonishing, but the really brilliant thing were those spare buds, whether you call them dormant, suppressed, or reserve. Only through them can the plant replace lost leaves, make food, and stay alive. If an ice storm, a big wind, an infestation or disease, or a pruner like me takes down a branch, and if the tree could not then have made a new branch to replace what had been lost, it would have had to go hungry. Each of those buds contains a copy of the tree's plan, ready to release it should the need arise.

Learning this, I felt more secure about my new-sprouted baby plane trees at the Metropolitan Museum. As the season went on, each of the new twigs from the stubbed ends grew to three feet or more in length, making wonderful wild heads like a hundred fright wigs, and their big sycamore leaves beautifully shaded the tables and chairs beneath them. I felt they were at once indispensable to the tree, beautiful to see, and a delight to sit beneath. I was willing to bask in the glow of our new companionship, though I thought it likely that late in the following winter, when we would have to cut them again, my terror would return.

FAVORITE THINGS

Learn your chops, learn your charts. Then throw them both away.

—Instruction to a young saxophone player

To study how trees grow is to admire not only their persistence but their imagination. Live wood just won't quit. Every time you knock it down, it comes back again, but when a plant sprouts back, it is not a random shot, like some finger simply raised to make a point. Rather, the growing tip of any stem—what botanists call the meristem—answers with an inborn, complex pattern, like a musical tune. Something had knocked the top off a London plane tree in Brooklyn. It had already been forty feet tall. It hadn't just sprouted a new arrow-upright stem. The sprouts at the broken edge had ramified into a set of eight complete little plane trees, each one closely resembling what its parent had looked like twenty years before, a bouquet atop the trunk.

In a grove of ancient junipers beside a village in the Spanish province of Castile, one trunk had cracked and bent until it ran horizontal, parallel to the ground. All along the trunk had sprung a linear grove of new young junipers, each with the same ancestral shape.

A little branch had broken off a willow and fallen into a stream. Where it had fetched up at an eddying edge farther downstream, it had rooted, sprouted, and up had come a new tree, whose structure had been just like its parent's.

Charlie Parker is supposed to have given the above advice to a young saxophone player. First, you had to learn your instrument. Next, you had to learn to play the tunes. Finally, you were free to improvise, to play jazz. John Coltrane's "My Favorite Things" is a terrific example of what he meant. It begins with a perfectly clean statement of the tune, beautiful in itself for the richness of its tone, notes that are almost solid, so you could build a house of out of them. Within three minutes, the tune has modulated into completely unexpected shapes, sizes, rising and falling glissades, stops and starts, pianissimos to fortes, but it never loses the thread of that original tune. Every tree is a jazz player, in just this way, although where a long Coltrane piece might last a quarter of an hour, a tree's performance may go on for half a millennium or more.

The tropical botanists Francis Hallé and Roelof Oldeman were the first to articulate the idea that every plant first grows to fill a form—that is, to play its tune. It does not matter whether it is a weed by the wall or a giant sequoia, whether it is a tropical *Terminalia* or a subarctic birch. They, along with P. B. Tomlinson, in their 1978 book *Tropical Trees and Forests*, wrote that every species of the higher plants can grow in only one of twenty-three different patterns. (They have since added one more.) In fact, they noticed, a few modulate from one pattern to another, and a few more seem to grow in a hybrid pattern, but all conform to the same morphology that their ancestors had.

The tree's "chops" are inborn, a part of its inheritance. It knows how to grow in the way its parents did. The seed contains the knowledge. To

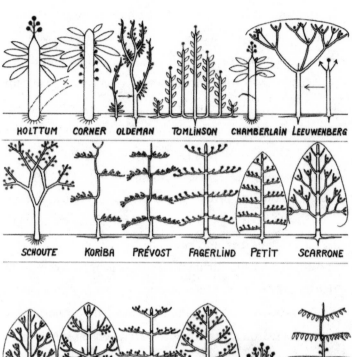

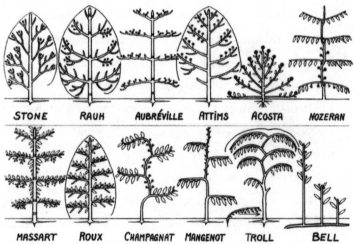

Twenty-four architectural models of trees.

learn its "charts," the plant grows to elaborate this knowledge into its basic shape. This first statement of its tune may take a few weeks for the weed or twenty years for the oak or may last a lifetime for a fir, but in physiological time, it is just the same. All seek to fill out the pattern of stem, lateral, flower, and fruit that was handed down to it by its forebears.

What are its notes, its scales, its sharps, its flats, and its time signatures? According to the three botanists, every plant plays upon six choices:

The First—To branch or not to branch. Palms, for example, never branch, though some clustering palms make the second choice, below.

The Second—If you branch, do you do so only at the bottom, or all along a stem? Bamboo, for example, is simply a colony of stems, each repeating from the base, and the small grove is in fact a single plant. Quaking aspen seems the same, but each of its new sprouts itself branches all up and down the stem. Shrubs, likewise, in general prefer the mode of living that sprouts again and again from the base.

The Third—Do your trunk and branches grow without a rest, or is there a dormant season? Most trees in the temperate zone choose the latter gambit. Trees with a definite dormant season—like spruce and fir— tend to have a very clean and open habit of growth.

The Fourth—Do all of your branches want to grow upward, all outward, or do some want to grow upward and others outward? Pagoda dogwood prefers to grow mainly outward. Staghorn sumac wants to grow mainly upward. On upward-growing, or orthotropic, stems, the leaves and twigs tend to be organized symmetrically around the stem, in spirals of opposite pairs. On outward-growing, or plagiotropic, branches, the leaves and twigs appear in flattened planes along the edges of the branch, like a phalanx of wings.

The Fifth—Do you flower at the branch tips, or on smaller lateral branches? Again, sumac flowers at the terminals, so each year's new growth must start from dormant laterals below the tips. It makes what look like buck's horns, hence the common name "staghorn sumac." (In one species, the sprouts even have the velvet of young horns.) If you flower on laterals—like most temperate zone trees, such as maples and ash—you can continue to grow more or less straight upward while your branches go straight outward, and if any difficulties occur, one growing tip can substitute for another.

The Sixth—Do your branches change back and forth between growing outward and growing upward? This is a flexible arrangement that lets a plant fill the space above and around it. Frequent changes of upward-growing top branches allow it to exploit more sun to one side or the other. Hemlock is one example. It is wonderful to see how, for all of its ability to reach eighty and more feet in height, it has a nodding top that easily trades off its leading upright branch. On average, the leader changes seven times in ten years. The top of a hemlock is a juggler.

Out of these six choices each plant plays its tune, the phrase that has characterized its kind for millions of years. No matter where its seed sprouts, each will try to play its melody. Many of the twenty-three-plus possible tunes are played only in the tropics, where abundant water and little cold let plant imaginations run wild. In the temperate zone, where winter is *winter* and where inundation may be followed by drought, fewer and more flexible tunes are the rule. The three botanists named all of the models in honor of other botanists who had studied the trees that exemplify that form. Rauh's model is the most common among temperate trees. Here, the trunk and branches are functionally equivalent, so if necessary one can become the other. It flowers on lateral branches, not tips, so it does not need to bifurcate to go on growing. It rests in winter and leafs again in spring. Troll's model is the next most common. Here again, the flowers are lateral, and the plants take a rest in dormancy. The plants are never merely a single trunk or assembly of trunks. Their branches waffle: when they begin life, they want to grow out, not up, but at the end of the season their tips turn upward. Here is a tune with a phrase that stretches out all year, only to run up the scale at the end, but again, as in Rauh, the effect is to let the plant expand both out and up. A third common model in the temperate zone is Massart's, although it is a relic of an older world. Spruces, firs, and many of the conifers play this tune. Their trunks are upright, but their branches only want to grow outward. Because they rest in winter, they tend to have a very neat and consistent growth habit, both upward and outward. They grow both up and out in what look like whorls.

When conifers ruled the world, in the warm and equable time before the ice, they had little need of improvisation. Massart's conical model is well adapted to capturing light, and it holds its neighbor at arm's length. Even on mountaintops at tree line, the balsam fir simply loses its tops to the wind, but its long-reaching plagiotropic branches spread out in a carpet over the ground.

Leafy trees never had it that good. They began to spread through the evolving continents as the weather started turning nastier, around 150 million years ago. Not only that, but the damn conifers had already taken over almost every place worth living. The flowering plants, dominant today, were then marginal, sneaky, eking out a living along streamsides, on rock ledges, any place where light could get in and where a conifer couldn't make it. From the beginning, they specialized in not specializing. Not only did they not grow in such a regular shape, they also took whatever shape they had made and reiterated it throughout their lives. Perversely, the leafy trees often started with competing branches, letting them fight it out on their way to sky, so that if one perished, another might make its way higher and wider.

Most of us, even those of us who take care of trees, have a vague notion that there are different ways of growing. Yes, an oak or an ash or a maple look qualitatively different from a catalpa or an ailanthus or a horse chestnut, from a honey locust, a beech, or an elm. But just how, we can seldom say anymore, though our ancestors almost certainly could have told us quite certainly what the difference was. They lived constantly among the trees, and their lives depended upon how those trees grew.

Still, a few species stand out. Staghorn sumac races along the edge of difficult disturbed sites much as the first leafy plants must have done during the early and middle Cretaceous period. It loves the loaf-shaped substrate upon which superhighways perch. Spreading clonally—that is, by means of an aggressive underground root system—it occupies more and more of the exposed soil of the raised berms. Often, it is in a race with quaking aspen, another clonal spreader. There is a spot near Oneonta, New York, on Interstate 88 where the two spread so quickly, you can almost see them charging into each other like linemen trying to open a hole for the back. Who gets there first tends to get to stay there, and the slopes are a great place to catch the light they need to grow.

The pair are like Laurel and Hardy. Each aspen is straight, skinny, and gray. They stand close together like a room full of partygoers. Each sumac is beyond paunchy. It is downright fat and squat. A flower blooms always at the end of a new stem, so that end will never grow again. Two lateral buds beneath the flower sprout instead, and they grow out in wide open arcs like two hands raised to signal a touchdown. Next year, those two branches flower, so the same thing happens all over again. The plants less climb into the sky than they reach out to capture as much aerial real estate as they can. Two by two by two by two, each trunk ramifies into an impossibly complicated candelabra.

Most of the models make ways to mix the tall and the broad. Many of the trees in the temperate forest—the oak, the ash, the maple, the pine— grow straight up with lateral branches that also arch upward. All have spiral or opposite twigs, leaves, and flowers. The form is marvelously supple. If the top stem fails, the next lateral down turns upward to take over the leader position. Any branch can take the place of any other. If you are looking for opportunity in the dense forest, this is a fine model to follow.

Trees of equal or even greater size—the elms, the beech, the honey locust—instead grow only spreading branches. They get taller only because one new sideways branch sprouts atop the previous one, and so on sometimes to heights of more than one hundred feet. They get a little additional upward boost because in the dormant season of their first year, the new floppy branch may slightly straighten up. A quarter of all temperate forest trees grow this way. It is even more flexible than the upright model, since the sideways branches can stretch in any direction to find light, staying short if light is scarce or stretching out forty feet to reach a hole in the forest canopy. So a tree of this kind can go upward or outward as conditions change. These are the trees that make great vase-shaped canopies, so that a double row of elms or even of honey locusts above a roadway shuts out the sky above.

Still others play a tune that sends up each year a trio or more of fresh stems, all fighting one another for the light. Ailanthus trees do this, as do catalpas and horse chestnuts. Of the three or more fresh upright stems, one dominates and the others bend off sideways. As these are often lovely flowering trees, at the right time of year the tree looks like a fireworks display, with explosions of leaf and flowers at each elevation, measuring back to when the tree was small. They seem to thrive on complication.

If every tree seeks to express its model, why then does the world of plants not resemble immense phalanxes of similar shapes? Why is a forest not an array like the bottles of different brands of seltzer on the supermarket shelf?

Because of the many accidents.

Because of the uncertain world.

Because of heat and cold, storm and wind, pests and diseases.

Because of neighbors, those that are rooted, and others that are two, four, six, and eight legged.

Because of opportune openings to the sun.

Because of the subsequent improvisation.

Reiteration is the wonderful name that Oldeman gave the tree's ability to respond to the world around it by in whole or in part replaying its melody, but in very different contexts at ever different scales. It is jazz: take the tune, stretch it, cut it into pieces, put them back together, transpose it up or down, flatten it out, or shoot it at the sky. Each tree gets its chops, gets its charts, and then throws them away. It knows the chart by heart, and so can repeat it with a thousand variations for hundreds of years, as it grows to its full stature, lives among its peers, and grows back down to the ground. Positive and negative morphogenesis, they dubbed the cycle: growing up and growing down.

As soon as the tune is played, the initial reiteration is the first major branch. As a leafy tree grows, it will generate what arborists call scaffold branches. These are the few—maybe five to eight—very large stems upon which the tree will hang most of its crown—that is, most of its smaller branches and their millions of leaves. As horticulturalist Liberty Hyde Bailey saw as far back as 1908, "A tree is essentially a collection or a colony of individual parts. . . . Branches are not so much organs as competing individuals." The skill of the tree as an organism is like Coltrane in his vamping: it brings the variations back to the persisting theme.

Atop these scaffold branches—big, thick, and arching—come a series of smaller reiterated steps at the scale of trees, as though they were dogwoods or cherries, filling up what will be the middle story of the mature tree. Next are reiterations at the scale of a shrub, bushing out the leafy twigs to all sides where life-giving sun is to be found. Finally, when the tree is about to achieve its full size, the repetitions are practically the size of herbaceous plants. Each new sprout complex extends only a foot or two from the parent branch. All the new branchlets will remain forever small in diameter. The tropical botanists call this last layer the Monkeys' Lawn.

The first third of the tree's life is positive morphogenesis. "Building up" is what it means. The phase may last one hundred years. Then, for another century or two, the tree may maintain its full stature, no longer able to grow much taller or wider, but still replacing every lost piece of the Monkeys' Lawn or the shrub layer with fresh improvisations. Finally, it enters on the third stage of its life, negative morphogenesis, or "growing down." An old saying about oak trees put it succinctly: "Three hundred years growing, three hundred years living, three hundred years dying."

Growing down is not just decay. It is as active and improvisational as was the building up. Roots are damaged or die. Branches are lost to storms. Hollows open up on the trunk and are colonized by fungi like the wonderful and aptly named Dryad's Saddle. The tree's solid circulation system resolves itself back into discrete pathways, some living and some dead. It becomes obvious that scaffold branches were once separate trees, as they become so again, some maintaining their root systems and others losing them. Now the tips of the higher branches begin to die back. Instead of growing new reiteration branchlets on their undersides, as they did in their youth, they now sprout perfect little trees of their species on the tops of the branches, between the trunk and the dead tips. It is a complete restatement of the thematic tune, happening dozens of times among the still living branches.

Now that we know trees can spend a third of their lives in this process, arborists are no longer so eager to remove a tree once symptoms of age set in. By studying and keeping up with the plant's own process of growing down, the pruner can keep the tree safe and lovely for many years longer than was once thought possible. People have determinate life spans. Trees do not. Although the trunk and branches are old and decaying, the creature is still producing the brand-new babies of the reiterated stems. An ancient tree is thus a mixture of newborns and Methuselah. By helping it to retrench, we can keep it for longer.

Little by little, a tree loses its crown, first small branches, then larger ones. Roots decay. The circulation system that carries water aloft to the leaves starts to break down. When no leaves emerge on a branch, it can no longer feed itself. It dies and falls to the ground, but the tree does not give up. When a giant that was once ninety feet tall has shrunk to a height of twenty feet, little images of itself may sprout from the lower trunk or even from the root flare, wherever a living connection between root and branch survives. I once saw an ash on the Somerset Levels that had left just a single sprout on the trunk and one from just above the roots. All the rest of the trunk was dead and its base stood in a posture that looked like a dancer's plié. It is not impossible that one or the other of those last sprouts—if only they can generate their own stable root systems—may grow once again to ninety feet tall. Phoenix regeneration is the name for this process. Potentially, every tree is immortal.

The fine British arborist Neville Fay outlined the seven ways that this regeneration can happen: One of the reiterations at the base of the trunk can make its own root system and its own new trunk, as the ash I saw on the Levels was doing. An old scaffold branch can do the same. Or the tree may completely resprout from the basal root system, rising again from the ground up. Or the tree's lowest branches may strike the ground, root where they hit, and generate a new tree. Or a small diameter trunk can form right inside the decaying ancient one and there make a fresh start. Or new roots may start in the hollow at the base of the tree, and touching ground, they may generate a new trunk and crown. Finally, the tree may fall right over, its lateral branches turning into new trees.

I had a client on the eastern shore of Maryland. Their house was bowered in a forest garden. They owned hundred-foot oaks, huge pecans, beautiful Chinese chestnuts, mature southern magnolias, a unique double allée of gigantic deodar cedars, but the very best of their trees was a fallen Osage orange. By most accounts, it is not a high-value species. Michael Dirr, whose *Manual of Woody Landscape Plants* is the standard refer-

Incipient phoenix regeneration of an ash on the Somerset Levels.

ence for park and garden trees, commented, "Not worth recommending for the residential landscape." It drops fruit like corrugated puke green cannonballs, and the wood is so hard that to hand-saw through a dead trunk can wear out two grown men. Indeed, my clients showed the tree to me sheepishly. We rounded a corner of their house, admiring a huge pin oak in the distance, and there in the foreground was the fallen tree.

I stopped, and I believe my mouth must have fallen open.

"What do you think of it?" asked the wife, wrinkling her brow. I could see she was mentally gritting her teeth against what I was about to say.

"Amazing!" I replied.

Their brows both unfurrowed. A smile broadened on her face, but she wanted to make sure.

"You like it?" she asked.

"It is extraordinary," I answered. "The best of all your trees."

"Oh, what a relief," she breathed. "We were told we should remove it."

I expressed shocked disbelief. I think I may have thrown up my hands and pretended to tear my hair.

There on the ground before us was a trunk about forty feet long and about three feet in girth. It had fallen over so many years ago that ferns, mosses, and small herbaceous plants had colonized the root plate that stood at one end taller than a tall man. Because it was an Osage orange, however—renowned for its resistance to decay—the entire length of the trunk was otherwise intact. At the opposite end was the wonder.

Once they had been branches on the trunk, but when the tree had fallen, the former branches had changed their minds. The original crown of the tree had died away. All the other branches had died, but these two had risen straight into the air, as though they were and had the perfect right to be new young Osage orange trees. Decades later, each of them was forty feet tall. One was evidently still depending upon the remaining roots in the ground on the bottom of the root plate. The other had also begun to put down its own root system, snaking over the dead trunk and into the ground.

It is as though a person rested her arm on the dirt, spread out her palm, and two perfect new arms emerged from her life line, complete with all the muscles and tendons and circulation, the hands, palms, fingers, and fingernails. Or perhaps more accurate, as though a person lay down at night and had two new people overnight sprout from his torso, complete from toenails to cowlicks. I think John Coltrane would have loved phoenix regeneration. It is like those moments in "My Favorite Things" where the whole piece seems about to jump off the top end of the soprano sax register, but suddenly the tune takes up again.

We think we know a tree when we can name its genus and species, perhaps place it in a family, and recount the tale of invisible processes like photosynthesis and the production of pigments. What if this were really a strange, abstract, and less useful way of knowing trees than to know them by the forms in which they grow, live, and die? Up until the Neolithic and probably even into the Middle Ages, human beings were better at the latter than the former way. In those times too, they had a very active relationship to trees, depending on them for energy, warmth, structure. (Nowadays, we think we have graduated to oil, but that is only a way of robbing the energy of ancient trees.) In those days, we knew trees the way we know friends: what they like and don't like, how they are likely to respond to a thing we do with them, what we should under no circumstances try with them. Each exchanged with the other. There is no call to think people had to be altruists to do this. Rather, they knew what was good for them better than we do.

BRANCHING

Say it, no ideas but in things—
nothing but the blank faces of the houses
and cylindrical trees
bent, forked by preconception and accident—
split, furrowed, creased, mottled, stained—
secret—into the body of the light!

—William Carlos Williams, *Paterson*, Book 1

Just as Walt Whitman in his poem "This Compost" foresaw Selman Waksman's cure for tuberculosis, so William Carlos Williams in the first book of *Paterson* (1946) foresaw what Francis Hallé, Roelof Oldeman, and P. B. Tomlinson would make plain in *Tropical Trees and Forests* three decades later (see page 42). By model and reiteration—by patterns of branching—every woody plant rises into the body of the light.

It is not only plants. The whole world is pregnant with branching.

In every place.

At every size.

If every branch is alive, then nothing in the whole world is dead.

Under the electron microscope, the sheets of montmorillonite clay are seen to stretch, bend, divide, extend. To join again and to divide again. When you pick the bark off an infected oak, the black whips of the rhizo-morphs of the fungus armillaria run in parallel lines, only to branch in every direction. The mycelia of the fungus are running through the oak's cells in the same way. When they come to a wall, they digest and breach it, then divide entering the next cell, and so on until the plant stops them. The branches of the mycorrhizal fungi, without which few trees could live, ramify within the cells of the roots and into the surrounding dirt, helping the plant absorb water and phosphorus. All the rivers of the earth are questing downhill, meeting resistance, worming their way through, breaking into new streams and flowing onward. In the flats come the meanders, where the stream braids, its separate channels meeting, then dividing again. Henry David Thoreau was delighted with the intestinal branching that the water made as it flowed down new railroad banks, freezing and thawing on the way.

As water percolates into the dirt, it creates an interlocking system of channels through which it flows to the water table. This makes soil struc-ture. There is no more penetrating and persistent force in the world than the one that shows itself in branching. Even underground, the dirt is a net-work of stems made by percolating water, which finds the pathways among the aggregates of mineral and organic matter. "Water is the strongest thing on Earth," wrote the Taoists, "because it is not afraid to go to the lowest place." It breaks rock, carries down iron into the depths, changes crystals of silica and aluminum into the arabesques of clays, distributes organic matter, frees and spreads the elements that plants need to grow.

The roots of all plants inhabit this network, mirroring the branch work through which the water flows. As the roots take up the water from these passageways, they pass it upward to the crown of the plant.

The branches above ground are an answer to the ones beneath it. Pollards, with their repeatedly trimmed and resprouting branches, I have observed, often occasion finer fibrous branching in the roots. What is above responds to what is below.

What a wonderful word is anastomosis. You can hear it happening as you say the word: *ah-nass-tow-mow-sis*. It is the way in which branches that have separated, rejoin, then repart. Ahnass . . . we part; towmow . . . rejoin, sis . . . we part again. The rivers of airways in the lungs through which the blood flows to harvest oxygen anastomose. The meandering slows the blood enough to fill it with oxygen. In your guts the same principle slows the passage of digested food so that its goodness can be harvested for the body's use. Veins and arteries anastomose. Every leaf of every plant is a network of anastomosed veins that distribute water to the chloroplasts, as well as distribute the products of photosynthesis. Slime molds anastomose. So do highways.

A network of vessels, the xylem, ascends each tree. Its long, winding, interconnected cells stretch from roots through trunk and branch to the slimmest newest twig, bringing water and nutrients from the dirt to the leaves. It constantly anastomoses as the tree grows. The interlacing vessels not only slow the flow, they also make a wildwood of forking paths, so that if one channel is blocked, another can find the way. This happens inside every tree, and is the reason that they can live five hundred years, in spite of every effort of pathogenic, pestiferous, or storm-falling things to destroy them. How many such vessels are there in a mature tree? A ring porous tree like a red oak has fewer and larger vessels than does a diffuse porous tree like a sugar maple, which has more and smaller vessels. The former might on average have around 213 million vessels, the latter about 1.3 billion. In *each* tree. And every year, the new wood makes more of them.

The birth and persistence of the xylem shows that branching is one of the generative ideas by which the world goes on. Without the idea, how could it ever come to pass that millions of cells each year are formed, seek neighbor cells of the same kind, join each to each in a vast anastomotic network that ascends the tree from base to crown. Then, to add acclamation to calamity, the whole daisy chain of interconnected cells must die and empty out its contents, leaving just the cell walls. Only then can it begin to do what it was born for: to carry the water and nutrients all the way from the roots into the veins of the leaves. There, either the water evaporates, empowering more water to keep rising from the ground, or it enters the green cells where it is half the material of photosynthesis. If one path is blocked—by a fungus or a chain saw, it doesn't matter— another way up remains.

All these wanderings ask a question, and wood is the answer. What

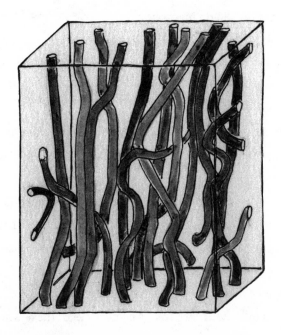

A sample of the xylem vessels in a square centimeter of wood. Wherever they meet, they connect, making a labyrinth of channels.

has fallen from the sky and percolated into the dirt, rises up against gravity through the river paths in every stem. A tree's array of sprouts, twigs, and branches, continually produced anew, is both the means and the memorial of this central idea in things, through which the world around us is created and maintained.

SPAGHETTI FOREST

Trees are closer to God than we are and, in the anagogical sense, smarter. They have no mass of gray matter to interpose between their being and their doing. When they see a need, they fill it. In this way, they are closer to the divine, of whom it is said that His thinking and doing are one and the same. I learned this from a spaghetti wood. Even where no tree at all should have grown, it found a way.

After the genteel pruning of the Metropolitan Museum planes, it seemed a nightmare job. I was supposed to evaluate weed trees eking out a living in the shade of the hideous viaduct that carries Amtrak trains over Randall's Island on their way out of New York's Penn Station bound for Boston. Where this woodland sits is no place for a forest. Twenty feet east, they rehabilitate New York City feces. Fences topped in helices of razor wire surround the place. (Who could possibly want in, I wonder, or is it to keep the poop tenders from getting out?)

Each of the trestles is 100 feet high, made of puce-tinted concrete. A curve of four tracks runs over the top of them. They stand on unadorned bases, each a cruciform of nooky corners, with indents about 175 feet square. The viaduct was completed during World War I, an arc of monumental Romanesque arches that stretched improbably tall like the arcade of a twelfth-century church tortured on the rack by the Holy Inquisition. The guy who designed them had been educated in Paris at the École des Beaux Arts. This viaduct is the totalitarian nightmare of that tasteful classical design. It anticipates Mussolini's fascist additions to Rome.

But why so high? Was it to spare the railway passengers the odor of the largest sewage treatment plant in New York? It couldn't have been. In 1917, there was no treatment facility here, only a scattering of the other things that an urban culture wants to hide. In those days, it was hospitals for people with infectious diseases and for the criminally insane. The fact is that the aptly named Hell Gate Bridge, to which it connects, had to be built tall enough for ships to pass beneath. The Gumbyesque arches were sequelae to the bridge.

What could grow there?

Anything the wind blew in or a bird pooped out.

Now, the New York City Department of Parks and Recreation wanted to make a walking and biking path in the shadow of the viaduct. This was a great idea when the wind was out of the north or west, blowing the infused fetor of the stink plant away, but when the wind was from the east or south, the path would be bathed in sticky stench. I first visited the site on an unlucky day, just as the wind shifted. The smell rolled along my nasal passages until it reached the lip of flesh that descends into the back of my mouth. From there it dripped, leaving a taste of metal and fish scraps. My nostrils were filled with a stinging vapor of shit marinated in chlorine.

How had I gotten into this job?

No matter. I had, and now I had to get done with it.

My job was to identify, locate, measure, and assess each tree. Okay. Here were three big cottonwoods in a row along a chain-link fence. Their parent's tumbling mass of cotton had lodged against the fence, and out of its thousands of seeds, three had become young trees. On the side of the trestle facing the sewage plant—where in fact the sun was much better—two or three Norway maple seeds had blown into the cruciform angle and sprouted. The three trees leaned out toward the light, reaching beyond the edge of the high tracks. (Because the roof was a railroad line, rain could come through, but little light did.) Behind the Norway maples on the long edge of the trestle cross, deep under the tracks, two catalpa mustachios had taken root. They must have been surprised to find themselves not only in the shade cast by the trestle, but also behind the notoriously dark shade of fast-growing Norway maples. They had answered the challenge by growing out at an angle as steep as a jibboom, reaching south along the length of the trestle and then bending around beyond the maple leaves, toward the east light. In the next bay, an ailanthus seed had lodged against the trestle base. Accident or mowing had taken it down again, and five sprouts had arisen from the former root crown, turning the ailanthus into a multistem shrub. In another situation, one of the stems would likely have outraced the others, making a sort of queen and her court. Here, beneath the trestle, where it was a virtue to stay low enough to get the morning and evening light, the ailanthus shrub was happy to squat and spread. It was a teeming democracy of sprouts.

As I saw one after another of these heroic lurchings and burstings, I not only stopped despising the job, I began to enjoy it as much as any other tree inventory I had ever done. A couple of trestles to the south, I felt I was present at the birth of a world, one that showed the limitless creativity of sprouts. I came upon a black locust with its spiny stipules at each node. Like the catalpa and ailanthus, it had arisen in an inauspicious place, midway under the tracks. Little rain, little sun. "What to do?" mused the tree, and it instantly answered. It had begun to imitate the ailanthus shrub, putting out sprouts from the root crown at its base, making itself into a low multistem instead of a tall tree. Then too, it had sent out long superficial roots in all directions, not just as water carriers, I saw, but as an advance guard. Along the length of two of the roots, where better sun beckoned, the roots sent up reiterations, new young trees springing right out of the roots. There were nine of them on two roots, stretching farther and farther into the light. This was a very intelligent tree, or was it ten?

Black locust is so good at this game that most state forest agencies fulminate against it. "Black locust is difficult to control, due to its rapid growth and clonal spread," lamented the Missouri Department of Conservation. "Mowing and burning largely have proven only temporarily effective due to the tree's ability to spread vegetatively." Any one of the Indians of this continent could have told them that, without need for elaborate studies, since they had been burning woods to get the trees to sprout for about ten thousand years. The black locust is unusually talented in this regard, since it sprouts both from the swelling collar at the base of the plant and prolifically from the roots, not to mention from the trunk and branches. In fact, a stand of the plant in any wood is likely to travel by root suckers, so that a black locust grove has the oldest trees at its center, younger and younger ones on the periphery. Today, this behavior is regarded as a nuisance, though in the past it was highly valued, since the wood of the black locust is hard to beat for fence posts and doorsills and teepee frames. It does not decay in contact with the ground.

The prize of this spaghetti forest was on the west side of Trestle 79. Not many trees grew on this side of any of the pillars. The best light was from the east side. The west was higher and drier, and shaded by the Triborough Bridge. Like it or not, however, here is where a lot palm came up. (Lot palm is one of the fanciful if insulting names by which ailanthus is known. Ghetto palm and stink tree are others.) It was stuck in the darkest interior corner of the northwest cruciform base. It didn't have a chance. But ailanthus is resourceful. It can send up sprouts from the roots, the root crown, and the bole and the branches of the tree. In nature, more than 90 percent of all ailanthus trees have grown not from a seed but from some kind of sprout.

It died back once or maybe twice. Sprouts came from the root crown. It sent two roots pile-driving north, and others that looped around the inside corner, like arms joined to return a volleyball. More sprouts came from the lariat loop of root. Now the tree had six reiterated stems. One was trapped back in the deepest shade and would never amount to much. Two were heading north in a steep climb that left them with light both from west and east. Three more had used their advance position to reach out for as much western light as they could gather. And I will bet that those two northbound roots—they looked like the twin tailpipes of some skeletal hot rod—are now well out of the trestle's shade and heading wherever they find water and air. It was a big, self-gathered bouquet of a tree, held out to whoever was willing to see it. It was as though the bones of a prehistoric creature had decided to change kingdoms and build themselves into an improbable plant, a spaghetti tree, looping and draping and floating, turning what was once a simple repetitive shape into a unique and plastic growing pile. The seed had sprouted. A trunk had formed. It had died back to the ground. Two more sprouts had come from its edges. A root had reached south. It had hit the edge of the trestle and bent west. There, two sprouts had come up. Another root had headed due west. The two had met. There, another sprout emerged. . . .

I had stopped hating the job and almost stopped smelling it. Who could have imagined that such a thing would happen? Houdini could not have better escaped from a fatal prison. What had done this feat? Just a couple of dumb weed trees. No brain. No nerves. No blood. No instincts. No plans. Just a couple of dumb trees. Right?

Not only the lowly invasive black locust and lot palm can perform this feat. Almost any tree around the world can do it one way or another. Cut down a four-hundred-year-old coast redwood, and eight or nine redwoods will spring back. Knock the tree over, and its trunk will sprout a linear grove of youngsters (see page 232). Out on the isolated Galápagos, when a thirty-foot-tall endemic giant cactus keels over, a dozen new cacti spring from the nodes where its paddle stems were joined. Roots of a Canadian white spruce forest join forces beneath the ground, keeping a mere stump alive while the stump's roots help feed the rest of the grove. Deep in the shade of the hemlocks sprout apparently seedling beech trees. In fact, they are sprouts from the roots of a mother tree two hundred yards away. The mother supports the young, waiting perhaps for a hemlock to fail or blow down, so the young can race for the sun.

When a wound occurs anywhere on a stem, there are at least twenty ways that sprouts can go. About half make new roots, half new stems. Roots can form high in the crown to harvest water that gathers in the axils of leaves or in stem unions; roots can grow and hang down until they reach the ground, a kind of vine in reverse; or roots can sprout where decay is occurring, taking nutrition from the tree's own compost. Roots can also grow from callus tissue on a trunk wound, reaching down inside a hollow stem until they reach the ground. Roots can grow from a new coppice shoot, from low on the trunk into the soil, making stilts, from other dying roots, from suckers, or from rhizomes. New stems can sprout from dormant buds or direct from the cambium high in the crown, or they can sprout from callus tissue on branches or on the trunk, or from up and down the length of a wounded branch. New stems can rise from the collar as coppice, from old or adventitious roots, a new shoot on young coppice, or as sprouts from rhizomes or tillers or as layered sprouts from the tips of the branches when they dip to touch dirt. Some say the entire body of a tree is a source of repetitions of itself.

Trees are among the most creative creatures on Earth. What we do with words in language—making infinite combinations out of finite structures and finite parts—trees do with their branches out of their flesh. Their creativity is intrinsic, ours is extrinsic.

ON THE LEVELS

Half the first season was gone, and I still had nobody to advise me on pruning my pollards. They looked pretty good. People were sitting by the hundreds in the trees' aborning shade, but how would I get them to grow in beauty like my favorite pollard pinups? A friend of mine suggested Neville Fay. He specialized in such things. I sent him an email. Yes, he responded, he would be happy to ride around with me near his home in Bristol, England, looking at old pollards. We would visit the Somerset Levels, the nearby coastal bottomland, a place only borrowed from the water. In early February of 2014, it looked like the water was about to foreclose. More than 17,000 acres of the Levels had been flooded. A whole village had been abandoned, and another cut off from the rest of the country by the rising. Not anything like as bad as the flood in 1607—possibly a tsunami—which had killed two thousand people and inundated the whole lowland, where the average height above sea level is only eleven feet. But bad enough.

We went for a drive. The ribbon of tarmac was ebony black and polished, since the water had receded only the day before. We were inserted in thick fog like specimens kept from breaking in a bed of cotton wool. For a time, we were the only specimens in the place. There were ditches full of black water, beaten-down brown grass, and a green scruff of wild garlic on the road and channel verges.

That was when the apparitions started. One by one and then in lines, they began to appear resting on the cushion of fog. The first was an ash tree, set just behind the beginning of a gray winter hedge that punched a hole in the fog into which it quickly disappeared again. The ash had a trunk like a torso that rose only about 10 feet into the air, but was about eight times as broad as a man's waist. From there about a dozen branches snaked off in every direction like Medusa's hair, only sparser and each strand thicker. Every stem was maybe 8 to 12 inches in diameter, and each stretched anywhere from 12 to 25 feet from the bole—that is, from the spot where the tree had first been pollarded, the top of the torso. Some stems arose alone, while others intertwined. A little farther along the hedge another ash appeared, this one with a shock of many branches, some rising from the bole and others from lower on the trunk, making a symmetrical fan of branches. Another punch through the fog and a third ash stood beside a gunmetal-gray steel farm gate, its torso the same height and girth as the others but its branches lopped crew cut–style. From these three alone, it was immediately clear that J. R. R. Tolkien had not invented the Ents, his tree people in *The Lord of the Rings*. He had seen them.

The hedge kept on, but the ashes disappeared. The fog settled lower, if that was possible, until it seemed to skim along the road like blown smoke. Then on the opposite side, a ditch of dark reflective water appeared, turning to parallel the track. Beside the ditch on the road side began to appear willow trees with boles only about five feet tall and dozens of gnarly branches rising at a steep angle from each, as though the willows were meant to be broomsticks for the much bigger ash trees. Then the fog closed in again. Next, half a dozen willows appeared, each cut

The head of a recently pollarded willow on the Somerset Levels.

with a trunk about the same height as the last, but this time the branches were younger, suppler, fresher, and more numerous, like a collection of buggy whips. One bole had a broad column of decay that spilled little blocks of pale wood onto the ground. The fog closed up on these specimens. The next appeared suddenly. They were blank boles, monster heads that arched over the water, with bright circles the color of wheat all over their heads, where the branches had been cut, perhaps only a few hours or a day ago. Arborists call these blond rings "cookies" and admire them when they are well made: at the branch collars and without rips or scorings into the remaining stem. Someone was still pollarding these willows, a hundred centuries after the first willows had been cut on this ground.

That someone was not far to seek. On the opposite bank appeared a farmstead with the gray ashlar block of a barn half covered in ivy and finished on the end with modern red-gold hollow bricks. A fence enclosed

Young pollard sprouts on willows near the main house and barn.

the farmyard: it was made entirely of slender woven willow withies. Thicker willow sticks bent into upright spindles were the warp on which the slender withies twined. There are companies still in business on the Levels that make and sell fences, hurdles, baskets, and brooms of pollarded and coppiced willow.

Along the far bank of the ditch grew a long line of willows. Each had a straight clean trunk five or six feet tall, and each was topped with a like array of straight slender stems, arching up and out like the strands of an old-fashioned shaving brush. They reflected perfectly in the still water before them. Rectilinear regularity and wild exuberance here met and embraced. They were as beautiful as any ornamental pollards I had ever seen. Fay assured me that they were made for use, not strictly beauty, but we could clearly see the impulse in the maker's hand. Near their house, they wanted the useful to be beautiful too.

Here was help for my perplexities. It was clear from all these willows of different sizes and styles that the pruners had trusted the trees and had listened to them. They cut with vigor, then responded according to what the trees gave back. Where they wanted thicker poles, they might thin the tops, and they might also remove some one year, some the next, choosing each size according to their use for it. When they wanted thinner poles, they might let all the sprouts remain, removing only unhealthy ones, and so let the stems get longer while still slim and unbranching. In many of the pollards I had seen in California, the pruners had seemed to want to create the finished shape from the first cut. In fact, I saw on the Levels, you could rather cut deeply, using timing and selection to get the stems you wanted. The result was a joint creation, the work of companions.

I found that I was learning much more than I had bargained on. I had wanted a book of instructions, but I began to glimpse a history that stretched back almost farther than I could imagine. This foggy flooded outpost of the sea opened for me a deep past where pollarded and coppiced trees were not an ornamental choice but a living need. These useful pollarded willows were by no means the first of their kind. Forty, fifty, sixty, seventy, ninety centuries back, it began, not only here, but around the world, wherever there were sprouting trees. In the Somerset Levels, however, a weaving of raised bogs, blanket bogs, reed swamps, marshes, and winding rivulets had given way today to 250 square miles of peat in which the perishable work of so many centuries had been preserved. This was a very good thing for me, because I now wanted to discover how these trees had been cut in the ancient past.

Where a dry land archaeologist finds only the postholes into which stakes had once been placed or at best traces of poles or boards in dried mud, the bog explorer finds the things themselves, cast in wet peat. Archaeologists called the ancient world the Stone Age, but that is because the rocks were all that had survived, rather than because they had been the primary products of those cultures. The Levels showed that that time might better have been called the Wood Age. In fact, archaeological work in Somerset had begun when people mining peat for fuel came upon inconvenient posts, planks, stakes, floors, fences, hurdles, roof thatch, clothing of flax and lime, lime rope, ladles, axe handles, cat and human figurines, toy wooden axes, coat racks. . . .

In 1975, men from the Eclipse Peat Works had been digging merrily along with a big loader. (Not many years before, the firm had created a small railway with moveable tracks that they shifted around the Levels, on-loading and off-loading the peat turves, which they then piled in storage in stacks larger than Westminster Hall.) They had come upon what seemed like a fallen fence of woven wood. "Better call the archaeologists," they had reasoned, referring to the Somerset Levels Project, which had been going on for a couple of years then. The peat guys knew the drill, but they didn't know what they had stumbled onto this time, though it sure looked like a farmstead fence.

The archaeologists recognized it right away, although they had never seen such a fine one. It certainly looked like a long fence made of panels, each about ten feet long and four feet wide, but it had never been stood on end or pounded into the ground. Within weeks, they had made another similar find nearby. These finds were not fences but trackways, ancient bridges. Both had stretched across the fen between Meare Island and the upland Polden Hills. They had brought neighbors and their sheep across the wet levels to each other's settlements.

Both had been made entirely of coppiced wood, harvested in the uplands, fabricated by skilled stem weavers, and brought to the bog. Some of the panels had simply been laid on the marsh surface, but most had been secured with stakes driven on either side of each panel. They had been woven with such care and skill that not only human or sledge traffic, but even the slender hooves of the sheep could pass without sinking. With care, two could pass abreast. Experiments showed that without these trackways a human foot would have squelched five or six inches deep with every step.

Since then, hundreds of tracks or parts of them have been discovered in the peat all over lowland Europe, more than thirty in the Levels alone. Some were made of whole slender trunks, some of hurdles—woven poles—and some of planks, but most were made from coppiced trees. During the Neolithic, and into the Bronze and Iron Ages, these handmade walkways were as common as sidewalks in a city.

A traditional Scottish game shows how life goes if you live on a trackless fen. It is called the bog race. Leave it to the Scots to create a sport that resembles torture and in which it is not a question of in what order you finish, but of whether you finish at all. In fact, a Bronze Age person has been found facedown in a bog, tacked under a hurdle, so perhaps the original bog race had been a form of capital punishment.

I participated in such a race set up at 10,000 feet, near a stream meander on Golden Trout Creek in the Sierra Nevada of California by my teacher, a Scot named Peter Reid. It was a simple course: somehow or other, the race committee managed to place a standing stake far out in a bog. The poor contestants had to make their way by foot and flounder from the bog edge, out to the stake and back again. As I found to my cost, not many do.

You sank only half a foot when you started, so you reasoned, Okay, this is going to be a slog but doable. Soon, you were up to your shins, then your knees. Quicksand nightmares ensued. Obviously, the best course was to make yourself flat and wide, but it was a task to lie down at all, when you had to laboriously extract both legs from depths where they seemed to have been set in concrete casts. You flopped forward, then back. Finally, you managed to stretch out over the surface, sinking only a few inches and smelling the anaerobic undersides of the disturbed bog. The race then became a swim across the scratchy surface, doing a flailing imitation of the breaststroke, remembering what it was like as a baby or a reptile to slither. Suddenly, you ran into a deep patch and you were really swimming, only to heave up against the semisolid surface once more. By halfway to the stake I was worn out. Only two people finished the race that day. The winners.

It took planning and skill to make a trackway, though the very first trackways may indeed not have been made by man at all, but by beavers. There is evidence that in the Mesolithic, people not only crossed marshes on beaver dams but sometimes made away with the beaver-cut wood for their own use. A 9,000-year-old man-made lakeside platform found in Yorkshire contains both wood cut and split by human beings and poles stolen from the beavers. The earliest trackway may simply have been piles of brushwood or lines of logs. To make woven hurdles took imagination and craft.

On the Somerset Levels at Walton Heath, the intact hurdles were remarkably similar. Each pole had come from trees—mainly hazel—coppiced and assembled at the same time. There had been a workshop on the Levels. Perhaps there had been a weaving season: the men wove hurdles, the women flax and wool. In the Neolithic, weaving was not a menial task, but a prestigious art. The most skillful and reliable practiced it. It was the way to humanize what Great Nature gave.

One intact hurdle of the Walton Track was about ten feet long by four feet wide. It consisted of six transverse warp rods, each of hazel around an inch in diameter. Woven over and under all of them was a weft of 64 long slim hazel rods, each about half to three quarters of an inch thick. The work was perfect: 32 rods over, 32 rods under each of the warp transverses and fitted so tight that the mud could not squelch through them. Were it a coat, you could have slipped it on and worn it. The hurdle had been stabilized by split willow withies, soaked in water and knotted or spliced to keep warp and weft together. On several of the hurdles, the knot could still be seen: a square knot, left over right, right over left, tied 44 centuries ago. John Coles, the archaeologist who led the Levels Project, estimated that a maker and his assistant could fashion about ten panels per day. The Walton Heath Track required about forty panels, because some were stacked on top of others to get across the deeper spots. It took about four days to make the hurdles, then a few days more to lay them.

At about the same time and using hazel and birch from exactly the same source, a different team made the panels for an eighty-meter track across the nearby Ashcott Heath. These panels were not quite as tightly woven as those nearby, but the maker had had a brilliant idea for the ties. Instead of using easily broken withies, he selected stems that had whippy slender ends. He bent and tied these stems back and over the other rods to stabilize the structure.

All the wood for both tracks was cut at one time, and woven green, while it was still pliable. There are more than 14,000 rods in these two tracks alone, a small fraction of the dozens of tracks that once crisscrossed the Levels. Where did they get the wood? Every bit of it had been coppiced. The understories of the open oak woodlands of the Polden Hills were carpeted with multistem hazel. Cutting each of these back to its base on rotations of from four to ten years, the craftsmen got several dozen stems to grow straight off each of the cut stools. The new stems typically grow straight and true, without lateral branching for at least the first six years. And even after ten years, the diameter of the wood at its upper end was only a little less than at the lower end. It was a natural factory of poles.

The Neolithic axe harvested this crop. So as not to damage the perennial stool—the stump to which all the roots were attached—the woodsman harvested the rods by pulling them back from the stool, peeling them back to expose the ingrown heel of bark (see illustration, page 76). He would then cut outward with his axe, severing the rod without scoring the stool. This left a long slender tongue of wood. He could then lay the sliced end against a hunk of down wood and crosscut the base, removing the tongue. The archaeologists studying the tracks diagnose coppice not only from the long straight poles without lateral branches but also because of the scalloped butts where the stem was joined to the stool and sometimes by the butt end itself, which contained both the current generation pole and a bit of wood left from the previous cutting. All of the rods showed a very wide first ring of growth, characteristic of the necessarily vigorous sprout that arises from the new-cut stool.

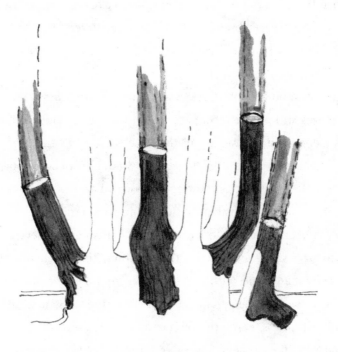

NEOLITHIC STOOL

The base of coppiced hazel rods from trackways on the Somerset Levels, showing the likely shape of the stool from which they were cut.

There were uses for the coppice besides. The system also made food and pottery. They would sometimes top the stems in summer, harvesting the leafy branches for livestock feed. And the same coppice stems that might be needed one year to make or mend a trackway might go the next year to make charcoal for the pottery kiln.

To our ancestors, fens and bogs were better than Scarsdale, San Rafael, or Brooklyn Heights as a place to live. They had all the materials for making, all the food to eat, and easy access to medicine, but without the tracks they were no easier to use than a suburb with no road to reach it, or a fine apartment in Brooklyn Heights from which you had to swim to work each day. In many ways, it was more difficult, because the water rose and fell on the Levels, not only with the storms but also with the not infrequent changes in climate pattern. When your road is a track laid on the surface, a rise in water can (and sometimes did) float it away.

Coppicing was not new to these fen dwellers of the 45th century BP. More than a millennium earlier, in the 59th century, at the dawn of the Neolithic in England, they had built the great Sweet Track, a bridge to link Meare Island to the glacial sandbar called Shapwick Burtle and then on to the Polden Hills. This track was not a few hundred feet but more than a mile long. In my book *Oak: The Frame of Civilization*, I have considered how oak planks split with wooden wedges out of whole logs made the surface of the Sweet Track, but the underlying coppice was what made it work. The Star Carr platform, which was discovered on a lake bank in Yorkshire, shows that almost 10,000 years ago Mesolithic people could split out clapboard, but it was apparently not until the Neolithic that they could reliably cut thousands of stems so they would sprout again.

To build the track, the makers of the Sweet Track coppiced hazel, ash, and oak on a ten- to twelve-year rotation. This gave them bigger poles to work with. First they stretched out long coppiced poles end to end to mark the track across the reed marsh. For the deepest section, they laid double poles, one atop the other. They then took stout poles by the dozen, cut them to size, and sharpened each of them at one end. They drove the sharp-ended poles in pairs into the marsh bottom, making an X that crisscrossed right on top of the long pole line. Every three feet or so along the length of the track, they made the same X. When they laid the notched oak planks onto the X-laid supports, the whole structure was supported three ways: the underlying poles kept it from sinking and the Xs from drifting apart; the Xs stabilized the boards along the trackway lines; and the boards prevented the Xs from warping or lying down. Just to make double sure, the makers cut holes in some of the oaks planks and drove slender pointed coppice stems through the planks to reinforce the connection to the marsh bottom.

Many of the new balletic bridges—in New York, Boston, Barcelona, and elsewhere—use much stronger materials and support much heavier weights, but they are based upon exactly the same X principle that was long ago enunciated in the Sweet Track. A crisscrossed structure atop a stabilizing base made it possible to run a long passageway over water.

We have not gone too far beyond our ancestors in intelligence, but we have forgotten one thing that they deeply knew: the instinct of thanksgiving. All along the edges of the Sweet Track and along other tracks, archaeologists have found sacrifices thrown into the marsh. One type consisted of pots full of hazelnuts. A toy wooden axe was also found beside the Sweet Track, but more impressive, a lovely green jadeite axe head—not a toy at all but a fine real axe imported all the way from what are now the French Alps. This axe head had never been hafted and never been used. It was offered in thanksgiving.

THE INVENTION
OF THE STREET

Flooding was one way to open up the land. Beavers showed how to do it. A beaver dam made a shallow pond. It drowned and killed trees in the flat basin that it flooded. This change brought in more sunlight, more sun-loving and fruit-bearing edge species, more fruit and nut trees, more game. A better and a quicker way—and one that could be used in uplands as well as on the flats—was fire coppice. By 8000 BC, European people had learned to burn off patches of forest intentionally. In their place came up blackberries, roses, currants, gooseberries, and hazel. People ate all of it, as did deer, aurochs, and other game animals, who were attracted to the open site. As the hazel grew in, it could also be harvested, even with the blunt Mesolithic axe, for poles and for firewood. By timing the burns, people could create a mosaic of woodland in different stages of regrowth, and so create the greatest possibilities for harvest of food, of medicine, of fuel, and of building materials. As the axe improved, a group could cut instead of burn.

The ice sheets of the Pleistocene never reached present-day Hungary, Bulgaria, or most of the rest of southern and eastern Europe. Broadleaf trees like oak, hornbeam, beech, and hazel took refuge in these southern mountains for the duration of the Ice Age. These were among the earliest places in Europe that people learned from the trees how to cut and renew them. In the Mattra and Bruk Mountains of northeastern Hungary, tribes began to manage the woods as long as 10,000 years ago. The forests were rich in hornbeam, which left to itself creates a very dense shade. That light-demanding species like hazel persisted for several thousand years there suggests that the forests were frequently cut. The hornbeam itself was cut to make winter feed for flocks and herds, and it made a good, hot-burning firewood. Hazel (see page 92) had use after use: feed for the animals, nuts for the people, fences, binding, hedging. Oak could be cut on a longer rotation for posts and other building needs, while its smaller branches were lopped for fodder.

In Bulgaria and Greece, more than 8000 years ago, trees were intensively pollarded and coppiced, for winter feed, for firewood, for house posts and beams, and for wattle and daub—a mixture of plaster and brushwood to make walls between the post and beams. Oak was much used, and in some uplands the easily worked dogwood was a principal constituent of wattle and daub. Archaeologists use pollen counts from ancient soil strata to determine what lived in a woodland then. In some areas, the very high counts for shrubs like rose, elderberry, blackberry, and raspberry, along with small trees like dogwood, suggest that the inhabitants had invented hedges—dense linear forests of light-demanding tree and shrubs species—that not only supplied provender but helped contain the stock.

As Mesolithic woodlanders all over Europe learned to live and work with their trees, the peoples grew in numbers, in affluence, and in skills. You had more living relatives, friends from the coppice work group, and people who would trade with you. One family was good at making rope from linden's inner bark, a few friends were great track weavers, another family was known for its textiles, a fourth specialized in willow, making little fences, and remedies for headache. How were they all to live together?

They did not aim for permanence or monumentality. They aimed for a way to reach, to meet, to talk, to trade and to sing with one another. And so they invented the street. The available wood from their coppiced forests made it possible to build, to repair, to rebuild, to move to a new village, almost at will. In the alpine foothills of what is now France, Switzerland, and Germany, along the edges of lakes and bogs, small settlements arose one after another. Archaeologists have now studied more than a thousand Neolithic settlements there, and that is only a fraction of what must have existed during the time, 65 to 50 centuries ago, when village building was at its height.

Oak was the principal species for building. A first settlement might use an uncut woodland. Thereafter, the posts and beams would be harvested on a ten- to twenty-year coppice cycle. The wood was never of great dimension. One of the posts from which to hang the roof and the walls might be only three to six inches in diameter. It might be of oak, of ash, or of the non-coppiced silver fir. The smaller wood for girts, wall plates and to make the infill for the walls themselves came from a whole group of coppiced leafy trees: from willow, maple, cherry, alder, poplar, birch or apple.

The resulting houses did not last long, nor were they meant to. They were an opportunity for discussion, for know-how, for working together. When a house turned two years old, it usually needed major renovations. Seldom was any dwelling occupied for more than fifteen or twenty years total. Each usually consisted of one or two lines of posts, with a pitched thatched roof. There were one or two rooms, at least one with a hearth or oven, and a covered front porch. Planks or wattle and daub filled in the walls. The floors were of packed clay, often inlaid with bark and moss. As Daniela Hoffman and her colleagues put it in their wonderful article "The Life and Times of the House," a structure was not so much built as "performed." Maintenance and renovation were continual. This was not for lack of skill. It was a conscious choice. Europeans had an abundance of material, and the building and rebuilding allowed them to work with their neighbors and to move and resettle as their needs, friendships, and alliances changed.

The oldest houses in a place were impromptu. First, one or two families would build contiguous houses on a site. If the site were good, a few more might join during the following year. Next, a building boom would add one or two dozen more houses over a space of half a decade. A catastrophe like a fire might make everyone start again. More often, the buildings would be gradually abandoned within twenty years, until not a single family remained. The inhabitants might found a new place together, or disperse to join with others in a new habitation. A new generation would likely make a new place to live. It has been claimed that this frequent moving was a result of resource depletion—chiefly of the coppice not being able to keep up with the building and repairs. That may indeed have been a part of the rhythm. Moving meant the area nearest the village could have untouched decades to recover, but it is more likely that the main reason was social: they wanted a change of scene or needed a change of friends.

The oldest settlements were arranged every which way, often with a trackway leading to or through them. There were widely spaced buildings, more or less facing one another. Later, there began to be more definite rows of houses, with a common track between them. You could easily call across the street if you needed to borrow a little butter. In the final centuries of the lakeside settlements, the houses were often tightly packed, one beside another. There was a main street, and there were side streets. Here you could not only call a friend to borrow some butter, but also hear the couple next door's argument, whether you wanted to or not.

Coppice made it possible to come into a relationship not only with a friend or relative but with neighborhoods. As the street evolved, the covered front porch became an important social meeting point. Houses were arranged with their porches facing the street. When you wanted to talk, you sat out on the porch, just as you might today in an older neighborhood in Davenport, Iowa, or Cocodrie, Louisiana, or San Jose, California. People with common interests or crafts tended to be neighbors. The coppersmiths lived next door to one another, as did the cloth makers. People who worked common pastures or cut a common coppice might live close by one another on the same street. If you needed something, you knew which neighborhood was likely to have it.

The residents all might share the tasks of maintaining the street and the trackways, of renovating a few of the ovens, of rethatching a root, raising a sunken floor, or repairing the wattle and daub. There was time for meeting, for singing, for gossip, for argument, for forming, dissolving, and re-forming a group of friends. Their monument was not a temple or a ziggurat, but the street, enabling a life among neighbors.

THE SPRING

New-cut coppice springs. After you cut to the ground, the wood jumps back into the sky, not quite as quickly but as surely as a spring trap. A coppice wood cut down in winter comes up in the season of flowers like so many tense erections. Each shoot reaches at least six feet tall in its first year's growth, some twelve feet or more. Springtime, the name by which every English speaker calls the May, means exactly that: the time when the coppice springs.

Shakespeare loved to pun on the season's word. In *Love's Labour's Lost*, the players sing a song called simply "Spring." In it, the flowers of meadow and of freshly coppiced woods appear, as does the cuckoo, a once widespread European migrant bird with a mixed reputation. Its cuckoo song means spring is here, but the bird lays its eggs in the nests of others, particularly in those of common coppice dwellers like reed warbler, garden warbler, pipit, robin, and dunnock. The host birds don't know it until a foreign chick grows up in their nest. A cuckold is the bird (or the man) who raises another's young. The cuckoo's song is "a word of fear to married ear," as it suggests the ungovernable power of all the season's erections.

The fact that thousands upon thousands of trees could be cut in a coppice wood and reliably return again and again was music to my ears. I, with my mere forty London planes to pollard, might relax a little bit. I was even happier when I saw such a coppice with my own eyes. Pete Fordham has cared for Bradfield Wood in England's Sussex since the 1980s. The site is a mix of heavy alkaline clays with lenses of acid sands. It likes to grow ash, hazel, sallow, oak, field maple, and especially alder. Where almost every other coppice in the United Kingdom had been lost by the time of World War II, this rural wood survived because it was the source of handles for a rake factory. That business had struggled on until 1964, so the wood had gone only two decades uncut when Fordham and his colleagues took it up again. Every species on it, they coppiced.

How quickly the locals had forgotten! When Fordham cut the first trees in the woods to the ground, some of the neighbors inquired, "Oh good! What are you going to plant there now?" It might even be that some of their parents had worked in the rake factory, but all that they had known had been forgotten. "We aren't planting anything," he had answered. "The trees will grow again all by themselves."

Indeed, until 1964, the trees at Bradfield Wood had been cut on a regular cycle of twelve to fifteen years since the twelfth century. Not only did Fordham not need to sow anything, but when he began to cut, a vast seed bank of ancient woodland plants saw the light of day again. Hundreds of species rushed into the newly opened spaces. You do not clear-cut an entire coppice wood, Fordham explained to me. Rather, you work in stages, a section at a time. In that way, the youngest newest sprouts stand cheek by jowl with veterans of fifteen years' growth. A wide-open meadow with new-growing stems adjoins one where the trees are beginning to limit the light that reaches the ground, which in turn adjoins another where the canopies have covered the entire space, making an even shade.

A coppice wood is a not a single thing, but a synthetic ecosystem in which human participation is the key. Far more species of plants, insects, birds, and other creatures inhabit such a mixed landscape than would live in an untouched woodland. And the fact that it is cut in a rhythmic cycle keeps a living seed bank in the dirt and reassures a tremendous variety of animal life that it can safely live there as long as it pleases. A coppice is a continuing performance, a long-running show. So important did Queen Elizabeth and her councilors regard its survival that they gave Fordham an MBE (Member of the British Empire), the next best thing to being made a lord.

A coppice woodland is divided into sections by a system of ditches and banks: The earth dug out to a depth of three feet or more around the edge of each part is thrown up to make a tall bank on the inside. Each piece was called by many different names: *coupe, sale, cant, fell, burrow,* or *hagg.* Within a given wood, each piece also had its own proper name, by which everyone in the neighborhood knew it: Strawberry Bank, Cottage Fell, Hannah's Close, Foxhunter's Fell, Lynderswood, Hearse Wood, Alsa Wood, Alice Tails, Tindhawe, Chertheage, Lodge Coppice, Beggarshall Coppice, Spittlemore Coppice, Old Women's Weaver, Six Wantz Ways. The system of barriers was in part to limit the intrusion of the stock—cattle, pigs, or sheep—into the young resprouting coppice. Sometimes, it was topped with a hedge. Mainly, it marked what to cut and what to leave in any given year.

To keep a coppice woodland is an art. Each of its woodsmen had a double aim: to renew the woods by harvesting wood. He had to manage not just the trees, but also flowers, berries, shrubs, birds, dormice, butterflies, deer, and visitors. The cutting came first. Different trees liked different ways. For hazel or alder, he cut as close to the dirt as he could get. For older stools of ash or willow, maple, birch, linden, sycamore, or elm, a forester like Fordham typically cut at an angle six inches or more above the ground. Some of the trunks so cut were as thick as telephone poles, others the breadth of a human arm, others slender and whippy like beanpoles, according to the species of the tree, to the sun regime in which it had grown, and to the purpose for which it was kept. The skill of the woodsman was to know the trees in the haggs and how each was likely to respond to a different kind of cut. The dirt, the species, the sun, the water might all play a role. He had to respond to the whole landscape.

A fell was between half an acre and five acres in size. When first cut, it looked stone dead, littered with stumps. The shade-loving, four-leaved woodland plant called herb Paris had burned tips. A few sedges bravely tried to poke up their heads. Especially if he looked next door at a maturing hagg, a young forester might well have thought he'd overdone it and killed them all. He rejoiced just as much when the first poles sprung as I did when my pollards first leafed. But where my landscape was carefully controlled, his was a flower bomb.

In the first three years following the cut, the sunlit dirt bloomed. At Queen's Wood in London, the gardeners counted 39 plant species in a hagg when they coppiced it in 2009. Three years later, the same acre had added 156 more. Most of them had waited dormant for the years since the last cut. Some jumped into the cant from nearby gardens.

Most of the plants had done the same decade by decade for more than a thousand years. As they lived with people, the plants told them their names. Moschatel, so called for its pungent odor, was also called five-faced bishop and townhall clock for its five-sided flower. Good Friday plant was another of its names, since it bloomed in Holy Week. The pignut was known as St. Anthony's nut. Its thick buried corm—a storage organ like those in daffodils or gladiolus—was delicious to swine. Anthony was the patron saint of pigs. People also ate the corm. They compared it with chestnut and swore it inflamed desire. Saint-John's-wort had little yellow flowers that were burned in the Midsummer's Bonfire on St. John's Eve. These flowers cured depression, prevented infection, and were treated as symbols of the sun. The wild daffodil or Lenten lily—a parent of so many thousands of daffodil cultivars and along with early purple orchid the first sign of spring on the ground—grew thickly when exposed to light and often persisted even into the final pole stage of the coppice cant. (In the 1930s, "daffodil special" sightseeing trains left London, bound for fields where they flourished.) The delicate wood speedwell, its light blue petals shot through with dark blue rays, was a universal tonic for everything from indigestion to gout. The Romans brought it back from their European conquests and spread it around the world. "Speedwell" is a lovely word. It means good fortune.

Herb Paris, which sprung prolifically in the new cut coppice as well as in the closed wood, had four equal leaves, disposed in two pairs. It was long thought that these represented the true lover's knot, where two half hitches are tied one into the other, making a very strong knot. Lovers made the knot with tree limbs and if the knot grew true in the coming year, their love would last. (As rock climbers, we know this as a knot that will securely join two ropes, even if they are frozen solid.) Be that as it may, the deep black button of fruit was deadly poison.

When my wife and I were courting, she taught me that the bright yellow buttercup, held beneath the chin, would tell if the chin's person loves butter. The yellow would show on the chin. (I suspect this was one of those games that brought men and women near to touching, in a gentle and exploratory way.) Called crowflowers in much of Britain, the buttercups also meant maidens, but they could suggest unfaithfulness.

John Clare, the great poet of the English countryside, loved the coppice for its early flowers. When all the ground was yet bare or even laced with snow at the blear end of winter, in the young cut copses, already flowers were stirring:

Beneath your ashen roots primroses grow
from dead grass tufts and matted moss once more
Sweet beds of vi'lets dare again be seen
In their deep purple pride and sweet display'd
The crow flowers, creeping from the naked green,
Add early beautys to thy sheltering shade

In the fourth year after the cut, the young poles of the resprouting coppice began to shadow the ground. Life changed in their shade. The bramble and raspberry that had sprouted with the sun-loving flowers, first in little spiny fingers, then in feathery sharp branchlets, suddenly covered every bit of open ground. By year's end, the meadowy landscape had become a thicket. All the other flowers had retreated to the edges or dropped down their seed to wait for a change of days. No new species were added at this stage. Not a square inch of ground could be seen. Two more years passed, the poles growing taller and spreading wider, the spiny shrubs rambling over everything beneath them.

By about the seventh year after the cut, the spreading tops of the coppice trees first closed the canopy. They quickly shaded out both raspberry and bramble. The two disappeared even more quickly than they had come. Under this canopy, the ground opened again and the shade dwellers emerged. Some of these, like herb Paris and daffodils, were the same as had grown at first, but now they were joined by bluebells, dog mercury, wood anemones, ivy, and an occasional insistent bramble. There are few things as lovely in all the world as nests of smooth, striped, or blocky gray, brown, and gray-brown tree stems shooting out of a carpet of bluebells like fireworks in a deep blue sky.

At Bradfield Wood there were only about seventy plant species in the closed coppice wood, a third of those that had grown in sun. Under the regime of the closed canopy, these plants would grow on until the coppice was felled again, somewhere between the fifteenth and twenty-fifth year.

Each coppice cant is a woodland history in miniature, repeated again and again as the cycle of cutting comes round. If there are fifteen cants in a given woods, though, it is only one scene in the performance. The art was to mix all of the stages in a way that could help the whole to thrive. The annual rhythm of cutting might move in a round, from one cant to the next in space. This brought better light to the young panels, but it also helped the animals that preferred a given stage to stay with it. Also, the scrubby tops of the new-cut coppice made effective fencing to keep animals out of the slightly older meadowy haggs. The tops of next year's cut might reinforce last year's fences, as well as make its own, and so on around the whole coppice.

The woodsman managed the animals in the coppice, both to control and to encourage them. In the first four years, deer might devour and destroy the resprouts. Fencing and hunting kept them out. (Today, when deer are a serious problem, Fordham has hired skilled marksmen to cull the herd.) In later stages, however, the same animals helped control bramble, so he let them in. Noticing how a mammal liked to live, a thoughtful woodsman might create invisible highways. Every coppice is crisscrossed with rides, open pathways that give access to the cants. They are a barrier to the dormouse, who prefers to stay off the ground, passing from tree to tree. (Bushy tailed and omnivorous, dormice are a sign of a healthy coppice wood.) The woodsman left one or two long branches on an ash or oak or hazel, to bridge the ride aloft, giving safe passage to the dormice.

Like the plants, the birds tended to prefer one or two of the woodland stages. The tree pipit, white throat, dunnock, and yellow hammer thrived in early-stage coppice. The thicket stage, with its thick ground cover, attracted large numbers of nesting birds, including wrens, robin,

nightingale, blackbird, warblers (especially the garden and willow warblers), bullfinch, black cap, and chiffchaff. Tits and robins loved the later
pole stage. These were the chief victims of the cuckoo's cuckoldry. The
nightingale and cuckoo, the most frequent birds in British poetry, are
coppice lovers. The cut woods were a resource not only for fuel and tools
but for the imagination.

There are about 200,000 species of insects now in Britain. Half of
them depend on human-altered landscapes. About a fifth of these live in
deadwood, which though common in pollard woods, old orchards, and
hedgerows, is rare in the fells, the haggs and panels. Many of the rest,
especially the butterflies, delight in coppice. Adults of a species often
feed on the nectar of many flowers, but the larvae can feed only on one or
a small group of species. Without these flowers, the species cannot breed.
The Duke of Burgundy, the checkered skipper, and the fritillaries—the
pearl-bordered, small pearl-bordered, high brown, heath, and silver-
washed—are all declining with the loss of coppice. The fritillaries, for
example, depend upon the dog violets, except for the heath fritillary,
whose young can feed only on cow wheat. Both plants are found sometimes in rides, heaths, and meadows, but regularly and dependably in
new-cut coppice panels up to three or four years old. Many of the species
cannot disperse across wide areas of the land, so the rhythmic cutting
of coppice fells—cyclically renewing their favored habitat—is crucial
to their survival. When one fell grows too thick, another has just been
new formed.

For a thousand years at Bradfield Wood, people have harvested the
wood. In the act, they did not destroy the woodland. They made it stronger and more beautiful. Seeing it, I was more grateful for my plane trees.
They stood in a long line of revenants. They could be counted on. I might
relax and do my part to make them lovely and long lived.

MOTHER HAZEL

Hazel showed people how to coppice, from Scandinavia to North Africa. The tree was one of the first broadleaves to clothe the land after the Ice Age, spreading north from its refugia, following pine and soon competing with elm, oak, and alder, but preceding most other trees. Jays and magpies would carry the nuts north and the plants might germinate but never flower. As it warmed, flowers and fruits emerged, and hazel groves took root. Like the alder, hazel grew in thick stands with a natural multistem form, sprouting six, eight, twelve, or more times from the root collar, but unlike alder, hazel had a tasty and nutritious nut. The plant naturally sprouted again and again from the base. New stems of hazel might be only six years old, when the root mass beneath was two hundred.

In the Mesolithic, ten millennia ago, hazelnuts were a principal food. They are the most frequently found nut in the old hearths of Europe. They could also be eaten raw. By burning or cutting sections of woodland, people could keep the land sunny enough that the stems would bear their yellow early spring male catkins, their tiny carmine female flowers, and their clutches of acorn-sized nuts. The people learned that if you took a slender stem and stapled it to the ground with slender willow rods, it would sprout new roots, spreading the plant into new territory. They also learned that if you could break a few stems, even more stems would sprout back, each of these new trunks would flower and fruit, and they would begin to bear nuts about five years earlier than a hazel that had been grown from seed. The sections that you burned might also give back straight slender stems to make baskets and fish traps.

Hazelnuts often fall into the water, and some may have been transported to new homes along the streams. (They usually sink though. Norwegian kids sometimes tell which to eat by putting a handful in water. The ones that float are empties.) Fion mac Cumhail was the servant of a bard who fished for a famous salmon. The fish had eaten nine hazelnuts from nine trees that grew around a pool of wisdom, thus becoming possessed of all knowledge. If you were to eat this fish, you yourself would acquire its wisdom. Finally, the bard caught it. He gave the finny savant to his servant to cook, warning him not to take even a little bite of it. Accidentally, Fion burned his thumb on the juices in the pan. The wisdom went into him.

Maybe it was the hazel-fed salmon's knowledge that invented the sharp, durable Neolithic axe, a tool as different from its predecessor as a sledge hammer from a chain saw. With it, hazel became a principal instrument of culture. Whenever you cut it, it quickly resprouted, giving two or three stems for one. Seeing it repeat its multistem habit, people likely tried other trees: alder, ash, oak, birch, linden, spindle, rowan. Sure enough, even trees that typically grew only a single trunk would often grow back as multistems, just like the hazel. There appeared an industry of poles: some as slender as your finger, some thicker than your arm, the largest (and hardest to cut) as big around as a stockpot.

Home grew up around hazel. It made the slimmest and most flexible of rods. It was good to start fires, to make charcoal, to split for basketry, to use as the wood infill in wattle walls, to make woven fencing. It was the best binder in the whole Neolithic. You could twist and split it to hold the thatching on roofs or to make hedges keep their shape. You could tie the brushy tops into faggots to fuel the maltings. You could coppice it early when the pollen-rich catkins had just blown up, or coppice it late when the autumn-held leaves were still on the stem. In both cases, the cuts stems went to feed sheep or cattle.

The Celtic ogham alphabet called its ninth letter *coll* 𝍷𝍷, which means hazel. This symbol, a horizontal stem with four short rising branches, is as close to an ideogram as you will find in Western writing systems. It is a coppiced hazel.

With or without ogham, however, hazel wands were communicators. Magic wands were often made of hazel. Dowsing rods, for help in finding water, always were. Yeats's Aengus made a fishing pole of peeled hazel rod and with it caught a fairy girl. One of the stories of Tristan and Isolde tells how a hazel rod became a go-between. In this version, Tristan, learning that his lover, Isolde, the queen, would be passing along a certain road on her way to see the king, hid himself in a hazel coppice. Splitting a rod in four pieces, he inscribed his name on it and a message. One ingenious scholar had him also inscribe the ogham for hazel, joined to the ogham for honeysuckle, *uilleann* ⊐ . (Oliver Rackham reported in his study of Neolithic woven trackways that indeed the hazel stems often showed the marks of twined honeysuckle.) As the poem describes the two of them entwined like honeysuckle around a hazel stem, so the inscribed stick might have repeated the trope. Whatever it was, it must have been subtle enough to pass notice for all but Isolde, who, seeing it, drew aside from the procession, entered the wood, and met her lover there.

TO LAY A HEDGE

Those of us who cut wood for a living know that it is hard work and that by afternoon you may be pretty much on automatic pilot. I complained to a farmer friend that I was getting so old that when I pulled my foot out of a tree crotch where I'd wedged it, I got plantar fasciitis that took two months to heal. "Tell me about it!" he roared. He rolled up both pants legs and one shirtsleeve to show he was wearing braces on one elbow and both knees.

It will not do to romanticize the art of cutting wood. Still, it was and remains a remarkable and responsive kind of work. The more the hand learns, the more the brain knows, and the more the brain imagines, the more the hand tries something new. It is practical physics, joined to practical biology. One of the most common uses for coppiced hazel was to help shape hedges. The best of these living fences could stop a charging bull while simultaneously keeping a lamb or even a rabbit from shimmying through beneath. It had to be very strong and very thick.

There is evidence that the art dates at least as far back as 6000 BC. The word hedge itself has survived almost unchanged from the Proto-

Indo-European, always meaning fence. Hedge laying was already fully developed by 57 BC, when Julius Caesar noted a hedge that he encountered in what is now Belgium:

> The Nervii, in order that they might more easily obstruct their neighbours' cavalry who came down on them for plunder, they half cut young trees, bend them over and interweave the branches among them, and with the brambles and young thorns growing up, these hedges present a barrier like a wall, which it is not only impossible to penetrate but also to see through.

The military-minded Caesar may have mistaken for a fortification what was in fact a means to keep cattle in, not marauders out. Still, his report is testimony to the strength of the barrier. Wire fences began to replace hedges late in the nineteenth century. During the Great Depression, neglect of hedges led to their losing their form, a good excuse to change to the apparently cheaper wire. And at some point, the cash-cropping agro-businessperson began to realize that the damned hedge covered two acres for every hundred. Why should he not turn that additional land to make a profit? Between 1947 and 1985, more than 96,000 miles of hedge were grubbed up and thrown out. Hedge laying would have become a lost art by the 1970s, had it not been for those parishes and counties in England and elsewhere, where hunters wanted hedges for their steeds to leap in pursuit of the fox. Leicestershire, for example, where foxhunting is a leading pastime, is famous for having the best hedges and the best hedge layers. There, the tradition never died. When Ernest Pollard and his colleague wrote their wonderful book *Hedges* in 1974, there remained 620,000 miles of hedge in Britain alone. Later in the twentieth century, this man-made ecosystem acquired prestige for its diversity. Then, too, somebody bothered to calculate the life cost of a wire fence versus a living quickset hedge. It was found that over the fifty-year life of a hedge, before it needed to be relaid, the costs of keeping the living fence was less than that of buying, placing, and replacing barbed wire. (One nineteenth-century wire maker is said to have had his tombstone crafted out of wire, but now it has rusted away.) As hedge laying begins again across Europe, it is to these counties that people go to learn.

Hedging is a beautiful and a technical art. To lay a hedge, in accord with the ancient meaning in Old English, Old Dutch, and Old German, is to cause the plants to lie down, creating a fence. The billhook is the principal tool. There are still more than a dozen kinds of billhook, but each is a short-handled tool with a blade about a foot long and usually with an end that seems to bend back upon itself. It looks dull and bulbous—phallic, in fact—but it is actually razor sharp, at least from the handle along the blade and out to the fat distal bend. Some billhooks are bladed on both bottom and top, so the handle is the only thing that won't cut you.

Hawthorn is the most common hedge plant, blackthorn (also known as sloe) second, but almost any broadleaf plant can be used. You establish a row of five- or six-foot-tall plants along the future hedge line. Both the art and the science are in the stroke with the hook. Each little tree is called a pleacher. You support the pleacher near its top, while you bend over with the tool in your opposite hand. (This is why right handers usually lay left to right and left handers right to left.) The cut should enter the trunk at a height about three times the diameter of the stem, but who has time to measure, since you have hundreds of thorns to lay. It is a matter that, with time and work, the hand, eye, and brain make good. The cut must angle in steeply through the tissue, then flatten out along the stem, creating a thin strip of unsevered living wood called the tongue, stretching as near to the base of the stem as possible, without severing it at any point. The tongue needs to be thick enough that it will not break when you lay the thorn down to the 30–50 degree angle at which it will rest in the hedge. It needs to be thin enough that when you lay it down the bark does not split away from the stem, killing the slim tongue. The upstanding stump that your cut leaves in the ground is called the heel. The next cut reduces the heel, cutting it low at an angle that mimics the direction of the cut into the tongue.

Strength, decision, and delicacy meet in the stroke. Then, too, you need a little nick and tuck in the tops—light cuts to make stems easily bent or to remove unwieldy ones—to get one laid thorn to rest comfortably against its neighbor, and you must angle each a little toward the field side of the hedge, so that good light comes to the heel.

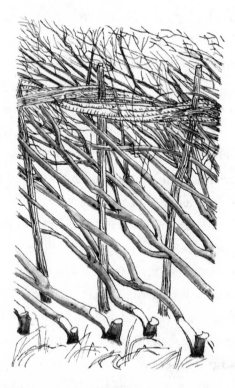

Pleachers with their tongues, stakes, and binders in a new-laid hedge.

Next comes the hazel. You need two sorts of coppiced rods, the first pile about 5 feet long and an inch and a half to two and a half in diameter at the thick end, the second about 8 feet long and no more than an inch thick. The first makes the stakes. A good hedge layer rests the thick end against his thigh and cuts a four-angled point with the billhook, revolving the stake as he cuts. (The trick is not to shave your leg, or worse, while doing it.) He knocks off the head of the stake to make a flat top. Many hedge layers even today use the old ell measure—from the elbow to the tip of the fingers—to space the stakes in the hedge, driving each in solid a little to the field side of the row. Again, the idea is to keep light coming to the pleachers and the heel. The long slender rods become the binders that join pleachers to stakes and hold the new hedge in place. Two by two, the maker twists the hazels, running them in front of and then behind and then in front of a set of stakes. He weaves one strand of the next pair back into the preceding braid and so on, making a thick twining rope of the 8-foot rods. The stakes and the binders make the hedge sturdy from the start.

Why so complicated? Most of us have clipped a modern hedge at least once. You can see that nowadays they just put the shrubs—privet or box or yew—close together, and then shear them into a single unit as they continue to grow. Nothing to it, especially with a gas or electric trimmer, though when you use hand trimmers, particularly the Japanese carbon steel ones, you can very much enjoy the act of shaping. But what cast of the primitive mind made these peoples of the past so fussy? Why did they pleach, why twine and plait the stems, and why make a fence out of hazel interwoven with a hedge of thorns?

It is hard for us who get most of our meat at the supermarket to imagine a time when the loss of lambs or the wandering away of a herd of cattle might have serious consequences for our lives and the lives of our families. We might be losing soup, meat, leather, wool, shoes, pants,

An often-sheared hedge, likely at least eight hundred years old, in winter.

sweaters, tunics, fertilizer, our stock in trade, and the potential increase of our herd. The escaped creatures might also end up grazing in someone else's fields, resulting in fines and restitution.

The point of a laid hedge is to be impermeable from day one. The strength and durability of the hedge will come from its sprouting. Some of the stems will rise from laid trunks of the thorns, but most will jump up from the heels. Over time, the hedge will become thick with living growth, so that an annual trimming—like the one we give a present-day hedge—will suffice to keep it thick and happy. It may be fifty years before it will need to be relaid. But it is the slant-laid living trunks and the frame of hazel stakes and binders that directs the ingrowth and that gives bull-proof stability to the hedge from the moment it is laid.

From the Neolithic until the 1900s, most of Atlantic Europe used laid hedges to keep its stock in bounds. From a distance or even from the air, you can tell an old hedge, because it is bendy, irregular, following the line of a stream or a slope, a dell or a trackway. In England, some of the boundary hedges that are drawn in the eleventh-century Domesday Book are still in place and still trace the same line on the ground. Such a hedge has been relaid many times and clipped countless thousands. Some are derelict, having grown up into rough open lines of trees and shrubs.

As Pollard and his colleagues showed, the older a hedge is, the more species of trees and shrubs inhabit it, adding very roughly one additional species per century, as birds dropped, squirrels buried, and the wind blew. An ancient hedge has likely at least acquired hazel, dogwood, field maple, serviceberry, spindle bush, and sloe. They might also take into their folds or even be interplanted with bramble, currant, cranberry, bilberry, moorberry, strawberry, pear, apple, medlar, viburnum, beech, oak, walnut, rose, crab apple, sallow, juniper, and pine. In the understory are dog's mercury and wood anemone. Not far southeast of London is a hedge that was catalogued in a Saxon charter. There is no dominant species in it, but it contains hazel, hawthorn, oak, two native roses, field maple, dogwood, crab apple, and two willows, ten species in all. Another old hedge near Salisbury has twelve species. By Pollard's count, then, those hedges are about one thousand years old and twelve hundred years old, respectively

Quickset is a lovely name. It refers to the hawthorns that are often the key plant in the hedge: thorny and thick. When I was a kid in church, they intoned each week, "He will come again in glory to judge the quick and the dead." I had a vision of God's hand grabbing us no matter how fast we ran away. Quick means alive. So the quickset in the hedge is not only the fast-growing, long-lasting plant, but also the hawthorn that is set there not as seeds or cuttings but transplanted as living plants. Many of the great nurseries now quick in Europe began by supplying quickset to the hedge-laying trade.

About half the hedges surviving in England predate the eighteenth century. The sixteenth-century agricultural poet Thomas Tusser—a worthy vernacular successor to Cato and Virgil—peppered his *Five Hundred Points of Good Husbandry* with hedge advice. Then, the quickset was either gathered or bought at market.

> *Leave grubbing or pulling of bushes, my son*
> *Til timely thy fences require to be done.*
> *Then take of the best for to furnish thy turn*
> *And home with the rest for the fier to burn.*

Hedge making often involved interplanting with other useful trees:

> *Buy quickset at market, new gathered and small,*
> *Buy bushes or willow, to fence it withall:*
> *Set willow to grow, in the stead of a stake,*
> *For cattle in summer a shadow to make.*

The stakes and the binders (called edders) were also often gathered in the course of other cutting:

> *In lopping and felling, save edder and stake,*
> *Thine hedges as needed to mend or to make.*

The practice was so widespread and so common that people took their names from it. All the Hayes, Hays, Hedgemans and Hawes, the Haigs and the Hages; the Hagelens, Hagemans, Haggarts, and Hagers; the Hagedorns, Hagles, Hagstroms, and Haglunds; the Haines, the Hainers, and the Hakes, the Haywoods and Hayworths, either lived beside hedges or made them. (Hay once meant hedge, as in the High Hay for a tall hedge.)

Then came the Enclosures, a movement that seized most of the common land in Britain, privatizing it and hedging it round. It was a jackpot for hedge layers and the makers of quickset, though a disaster for the millennial culture of the commons and the independence of those who lived by them. (Here first, not with the factory, is where the craftsman was turned into a laborer.) During the reign of Queen Anne (1702–1714), only about 1,500 acres were enclosed. Her successor, George I (1714–1727), presided over the seizure of almost 18,000 acres, but that was just the beginning. Under George II (1727–1760), almost 320,000 acres were enclosed, and under George III (the one who lost the American colonies), the total was almost 3 million acres.

Each privatized field needed a new hedge. This was the beginning of the reign of number and proportion, so you can tell an enclosure hedge from an old hedge not only by the smaller number of species but by the fact that the newer hedge is straight, measured corner to corner in furlongs (furrow lengths) or chains. Quickset, usually nursery bought, was the prime ingredient, with perhaps a little sloe mixed in. Where an old hedge bordered a road or wood, however, it was sometimes incorporated into the enclosure hedge. An enclosure-age hedge is more likely to add the spreading sloe, roses, ash, and elderberry. All may be cloaked with opportunist vines: bryony, clematis, bindweed, honeysuckle. Some vines are so common in the hedges that they take their common names from them: hedge feathers, hedge bells, hedge lily, hedge cherry.

The living hedge is a linear forest, on average about 6 to 9 feet high—with the occasional 30- to 50-foot pollard in the older hedges—and about 6 to 8 feet wide. The miles of this forest in 1974 in Britain alone would circle the Earth at the equator six and a half times. It is a remarkable product of human skill, imagination, and learning, in concert with Great Nature. Because the forest is all edge, it has a remarkable diversity of invertebrates, who attract an equally extraordinary number and variety of birds. In a healthy hedge, you will find 209 different species of insects and mites on the hawthorn alone, 153 on the sloe, 118 on crab apple, 107 on wild rose, 106 on hazel, 98 on beech, 51 on field maple, 48 on honeysuckle, and 19 on spindle. On the fruit of these sun-loving plants feed blackbird, song and mistle thrush, the fieldfare and redwing. (Cuckoo is the symbol of spring, as we have seen, as fieldfare and redwing are of the end of autumn.) Some both feed and breed; among the commonest are the blackbird, chaffinch, hedge sparrow, linnet, cuckoo, greenfinch, robin and wren, whitethroat, and yellowhammer. Pollard figured that if there is roughly one breeding pair of any species per hundred yards of hedge, then there must be about 10 million hedge-breeding birds in England.

In the United States, Louis Bromfield wrote about a small farmer in his neighborhood in rural Ohio, who unlike his neighbors in the 1930s had not ripped out the hedges to plant more corn. His hedges were far more basic than English ones, but they also increased diversity. Bromfield described finding the old man kneeling and peeping into the low shrubs of the hedge. When the farmer noticed Bromfield, he invited his neighbor to quietly see the young bobwhites almost invisible in their tiny nest on the ground. "They used to laugh at me for letting the bushes grow up in my fence rows, but they don't anymore," said old Walter. "When the chinch bug comes along all ready to eat up my corn, these little fellows will take care of 'em."

It was not only creatures that took sustenance from the hedge. So did people. The pollards in ancient hedges went for firewood, charcoal, and fencing, some even for shipbuilding. There are still tens of thousands of pollards in the old hedges of eastern England. Fruits and poles were also important. Edge hazel was coppiced for stakes and binder to make more hedges. Willow could be coppiced for basketry, fences, and clothespins. Crab apple and rose hips and blackberries made jams and jellies. Blackthorn gave its flavor to sloe gin. Elderberry was as good for jam as for wine.

Whether or not a living hedge is cheaper or lasts longer than a wire fence, whether the creatures living in the hedge are on balance better or worse for the crops in the field, whether diversity is better in itself or not. . . . Perhaps these nicely weighed matters of debate miss the point. The making, the maintenance, and the use of a living hedge require attention and response. A good hedge layer like Clive Leake has an intelligence focused not strictly on innovation but on seeing what is before his eyes clearly and responding in a way that helps it to go on. The phrase to "size up" in fact comes from hedge laying, for when it is time to re-lay an aging hedge, the skill of the maker is in choosing which stems to eliminate, which to choose as his new pleachers, and how low to cut them.

We would be better to focus more on acts and less on looks. Hedging puts us into the landscape intimately. It makes us pay attention. When we pay attention, we are repaid in many ways. Attention manifests itself in our activity, not simply in our reflection. The activity may produce only marginal benefits, but the attention multiplies these exponentially. My father always patted his plants; the biodynamic gardeners make elaborate and strange preparations using herbs, minerals, and cow horns, elixirs stirred a prescribed number of times in one direction and then in another. Who knows what outward effect these actions have, but *attention* is first, prior to what we do, which is always an experiment. The experiment without attention is usually counterproductive, regardless of its content.

We learn best in response to the living. The English philosopher Alfred North Whitehead thought that the condition of our intelligence in fact depended on the responses mediated by our hands: "There is a coordination of senses and thought, and also a reciprocal influence between brain activity and material creative activity," he wrote. "In this reaction, the hands are peculiarly important. It is a moot point whether the human hand created the human brain, or the brain created the hand. Certainly, the connection is intimate and reciprocal."

We live not in a world of things, but of neighbors. Each neighbor responds to the others. The real question is not "How can I become more efficient and show better numbers?" but rather "In what I am doing, am I a good neighbor or a bad?"

I said something like this to a friend, who replied, "Come on! We can't go back to the nineteenth century!"

"Yes, I agree," I said. "How about the twelfth?" If we are to get out of the dead end that our mastery of nature has backed us into, we will need to draw a much larger circle in time.

CAN YOU HANDLE IT?

The work in which head and heart and hand participate, at once, yields the only objective knowledge. It employs the ratiocinative capacity, the ability to discriminate and choose. It is driven by the wish to know. It is corrected, tempered and given form by work with the resistant materials of this world.

I saw José Ramón Juaregui make an axe. He talked about what he was doing. The sound of the metal in the forge gave him clues. The changing color of the metal did too. The number and kind and quality of the sparks that rose were important. When he took out the blank—the unworked metal—to hammer it, he set it at angles that took advantage of the deep pocket of wear in the center of his old black anvil. He had certainly measured the metal blank carefully before he put it in the forge, but the shape it took was made not by calculation and measurement, but by experienced perception. The size and shape of the tongs and the bits helped him eyeball the curve and volume of the head. He tried to explain how hard you had to hit the metal and just where, but words—even Basque words—failed him. The whole man had acquired this knowledge.

This I would say is knowledge of objective truth. It is not thinking. It is not feeling. It is the training of perception in the face of resistant materials. It is need and thought adjusting to the real. It is a new participation in the world of relationship, one through which a strange kind of flexible precision emerges unbidden.

In a nearby town lived a shepherd named Patxi Barriola. When he was fifteen, he first went up the hill to the shack and the fold, the *borda,* where he cared for a herd of about a hundred sheep. When he was younger, he had learned from his father and mother. He lived in the *chabola,* the one-room shack with its flat stone roof, for about eight months of the year. He decided every day whether or not the sheep would go onto the mountain pastures, stay in the closed pasture, or feed inside the fold. He cultivated ash trees all around the stead. Every year he pollarded some of them, only during a waning moon. He cut and dried the stems, to feed to the sheep on the cold snowy winter days inside the *borda*. If he needed to, he rooted a few cuttings and started new trees. In spring, he manured the small pasture with the winter sheep dung. His dogs managed the sheep. Each sheep had a bell whose sound was made by his herd alone. (The ironmonger made each shepherd's bells to a particular and unique length and girth.) He took the sheep down to a barn at the edge of town when it was time in March, around San José Day, for them to lamb, and brought them up again in May as the lambs became hardy enough to travel.

When I met him, he was eighty-eight. He had retired the previous year. He had spent seventy-three years at his job. He and his wife sat in their kitchen/living room with a big wood stove and a large television screen. I asked him if, in his working life, he had grown tired of the same routine. He seemed not to understand what I meant by "routine." "I was happy there," he remembered. "Really happy. No radio, no TV, no nothing." He paused and looked into the fire. "What a good place it was," he continued. "It was a good life. It fitted me." It was not routine work to him, but a way of life that never stopped bringing him into the real.

We still have this kind of knowledge—we can drive a car at 80 mph without a crack-up and make the coffee measuring the water by its heft in the pot—but we seldom value it. Yet for most of the world in most of human history, this way of knowing was a crucial part of every person's daily life and work, no matter how exalted or how mean their position. It was creative work.

My stepson recently helped me learn to sharpen my Juaregui axe. We set it up in the shed on an old worktable that I inherited from the last owners of our house, who very likely had inherited it from the previous owners. I had always wondered what the unusual wooden clamp on the forward edge of the table was for, and why there was a little wooden knob protruding from the table edge about two feet along the front side, three inches below the top. When we put the axe head in the clamp, it all came clear: the end of the handle came to rest on the knob, leaving the crescent-shaped axe blade in the jaws perfectly vertical and solidly stable.

Our sharpening tool was a disc about the size of a hockey puck, sized to fit comfortably in the palm of the hand, with a coarse side and a fine side. The coarse was about 120 grit, the fine about 600. Jake looked for the right angle to the bevel. "Tilt the sharpener until the little black line disappears," he said. (The line marks the shadow gap between blade and sharpening tool.) Then he began with a very light circular motion, using the coarse side, the edges poised on his fingertips. "Just a little heavier than the weight of the tool," he said. He was repeating what he had learning in studying restoration carpentry. I tried it too. After a couple of passes, we put our thumbs very lightly on the summit of the blade. It was rough and furry to the touch: the burr created by the metal that the sharpener was scraping off. We switched to the other side of the blade and repeated the circular passes. The burr moved over to the other side. My wife had given me a cellphone microscope for Christmas. We took a shot. It showed the burr perfectly. Cool! we shouted, almost in unison.

After shoving the burr back and forth a few more times, we switched to the fine side of the sharpener. Now the furry feel began to disappear. Same action: light circles up and down the blade at the no-black-line angle on each side. It was hard to make the motion smooth, even and rightly angled. As with measuring the coffee water by heft, the skill will come with practice. To finish the blade, we switched to the very fine 1200 grit of a Japanese water stone that I use for sharpening my pruners. Jake ran his forearm lightly over the axe blade. It shaved his hair. We took another cellphone shot. The edge was as smooth as a baby's bottom.

The highest-tech thing we'd used was the camera, and we could have done without it. An even better way to measure the results of our work was with a log. I happened to have a dozen trunk rounds I'd cut from a fallen ash. We set one up on my maple chopping block. It took a moment to get used to the short beech handle of the Basque axe. When we did, we saw the real results: one swing, the log was split, another and the split was split. It was like cutting pats of butter.

People still often used the phrase "Can you handle it?," meaning "Can you manage to do what you have set out to?" Axe work is the source of the saying. Before World War II, axe heads were not sold complete with axe handles. The buyer made the handle. There was thus a verb—"to handle"—which meant to cut, shape, fit, and attach a handle to a head. "Can you handle it?" originally meant "Have you got the skill it takes to make a well-balanced axe handle and securely attach it to the head?" It was a challenge but also a graceful measure. It didn't take a PhD or a million-dollar grant to get the intellectual and physical chops to do this work with supple skill using the resistant materials of this world. It was a small piece of objective knowledge, using head and heart and hand.

SPACE INVADERS

I still had not learned how to prune the young plane trees at the Metropolitan Museum, but as I plunged into the Neolithic and the long past of coppice and pollard, I began to feel more comfortable with my ignorance. A hundred generations of pruners had had to learn by responding to the trees. I was happy to join them. If you are modest and give the trees a chance to answer, they all counseled, you will be all right.

While I was working on the planes and the lindens, I often took breaks in Central Park, which surrounds the museum on three sides. Although it looks natural, the park is every bit as choreographed as my pollards. I loved walking among the great trees—the huge lindens, the elms, the red oaks, the sycamores—but not a stone's throw south of the Metropolitan's façade, I came upon a colony of invaders whose insouciance and insistence dramatically increased my faith in sprouts.

You have to admire invasive plants, whether they are native or from across the seas. They love disturbance, and they flock to it. Give them a nasty soil or a neglected corner, and they are on it like flies on an unwashed dinner plate. But who would think that they could set up shop in the exquisitely designed, produced, and maintained natural forest effects of New York's Central Park?

I might never even have noticed them, if not for a group of kids. In the middle of a school day, a dozen boys and girls were playing at the bases of elms, beeches, maples, pines, serviceberries, and lindens in the lawn hollow just south of the museum. They were forming, breaking, and re-forming playgroups, as kids do when left to themselves, and discussing important matters like the color of socks and how much a given boy had raised his voice. They gravitated through the big lawn trees to the inside edge of the lawn, where it turned briefly and narrowly to woodland. Their footsteps shushed and sussed in the carpet of fallen leaves. Two knots of kids were gathering piles of bark, lichen, moss, witch-finger twigs, and curled brown leaves. At the bases of trees, they turned their treasures into lean-tos and little rooms. Fairy houses, I thought, unbidden.

Seeing a largish older gentleman approaching her charges, a young teacher with a middle European accent appeared at my side. She politely asked what I thought I was doing. I explained that I love trees and take care of them for a living, and that I was interested in these trees and in how the kids were playing in them. I asked her what they were doing there during a school day.

"This is their forest period," she said primly.

"Recess?" I asked.

"Not exactly." She seemed shy to admit that this was an assigned class period, since it was just woodland play.

Suddenly it dawned on me. "Are those fairy houses?"

"Yes," she replied, and for the first time she smiled.

"Are you from a Waldorf school?"

Her smile widened. "Yes. We are right across the street on Seventy-Ninth Street. The Steiner School."

We both laughed. It was the fairies that had broken the ice. My mother-in-law, wife, and stepson had each gone to a Waldorf high school. They had heard from their friends who had attended a Steiner elementary school how many and how frequent were the gnomes and fairies who helped them to learn things like grammar and the multiplication tables. Famous among them, for example, was the "Carrying Fairy," who helped carry over numbers from the ones to the tens to the hundreds columns. When the students got through eighth grade, however, they often ended with the exultant chant "No more gnomes!" Meaning that they had outgrown such things.

These six-, seven-, and eight-year-olds had not. They were delighted with their fairy houses and pleased that playing in the woods was a regular part of their school day. So was I. On the excuse that I wanted to look more closely at the trees, I followed them into the woods, into which by this time all but the most timid had strayed. Their teacher came along, discreetly.

I was about to ask some inane question of an otherwise-occupied young one when I noticed something funny. There were clearly some venerable elms here, each as thick around the middle as a tractor tire. From their slightly mottled bark, not as tightly interwoven as nearby American elms out on the lawn, I guessed these were English elms. I looked at the big notched fruit decaying among the leaves. Right. English. There were also some old Sargent cherries, some underplanted hollies and serviceberries, a bunch of old failing ironwood, and a few struggling crab apples. Standard-issue Central Park trees. But everywhere some stem had fallen, up had popped another tree. There were dozens of them, all slender and sky-reaching among the larger older trees, some as tall as a stop sign, others taller than a four-story brownstone. Some were so close to one another that I could not walk between them. I expected this behavior from Norway maples or from black locust or ailanthus, but from a venerated elm?

I looked at the twigs of these young invaders to confirm what they were. Each had small, sharp-pointed buds, and the one at the end was curved and set at an angle, like the come-hither finger of a Marilyn Monroe. Unquestionably, these volunteers were elms. Not American elms! I thought, Certainly not. I had never seen it happen. But how could it be the English? This species had been widely planted in New York as a park tree, but I would have expected them to be even more polite and decorous than the Americans. I was dead wrong.

Two little girls were standing beside me. "What are you looking at?" one asked. "Yeah what?" the other chimed in. I had been bent over looking for root flares on the smaller elms.

"All these little trees," I said, and touched three or four of them. I pointed off through the woodland. "All of them, I think, are the children of this big one."

I was amazed. They were not. "Of course," said the boldest. "We knew that." Her friend nodded.

"Well, I think it is wonderful," I added. "I love it that they have made a home for themselves."

"So do we." The friend nodded emphatically, raising her chin up to where her forehead had been and bringing it down to rest on her sternum. The excitement done, they went back to house building.

I kept walking and looking, and I fell in love with these trees, not least because they had frustrated the neatnik park keepers. Grub out an ailanthus? That is fine. But remove the children of the venerable English elm? That would take planning and debate. Or perhaps indeed they had never noticed. If not for the children, I would not have either.

English elm is the most mutable of trees. It is such a master of disguise that it cannot even keep its own name. In every parks department manual, you will find it referred to as *Ulmus procera*, but in England, where it comes from, the species has been subsumed as a type of *Ulmus minor*. Easy for them to say, but there are hundreds, if not thousands, of types of this species, and indeed, it is a question whether the word species ought to apply to these trees at all. R. H. Richens, the great student of elms in the British Isles, found twenty-seven different village types in Essex alone. Oliver Rackham identified twenty-nine different clones on only forty acres of ground in Essex. Some had hairy leaves, some smooth; some double toothed, some single toothed and some hardly toothed at all; some had long leaf stalks, or short stalks or just a whisper of a stalk; some were tall and slender, some spreading, some low branching and some high; some had bark like lines of Japanese writing, others like the imprint of a circuit board.

The English elm is a champion root sprouter. It gives suckering a good name. In fact, as Rackham noted, it has almost given up sex, preferring to create a clone and then let it spread. Single genetic individuals may spread half a mile or more from their mother. My pipe organ set of tall young elms was every one a root sprout. I had been surprised to find so much English elm fruit in the leaf litter in autumn, since the tree fruits in spring, but few even germinated, never mind created new trees. Looking for the root flares typical of a seedling tree, I found none. Instead, I could almost trace the pattern of the parent tree's root growth by the spots where new trunks had come up.

Occasionally, however, a sexually produced and genetically distinct seedling does survive. If it prospers, it may become the source of a new, widespreading clone with novel traits. The occasional seedling survivor accounts, over time, for the tremendous variation in shape, size, leaf, and bark, as each new clone makes thousands more like itself. Elms, like the people who have loved and spread them—the leaves are the most nutritious of fodder, along with ash, and have even been used as human food—become endemic each to their own hometown.

Change and clone, seed and sprout, vary and repeat. This remarkable perennial pattern may at least in part explain why Dutch elm disease has not eliminated the English elm. Instead, there are repeated outbreaks. Elms suddenly disappeared from the English landscape during the Neolithic, about five thousand years ago. The disease may have been the reason. People with their new Neolithic axes may have pollarded or coppiced the elms. The pheromones released by the cut stems may have attracted the disease-carrying beetle. Pollen archaeologists have distinguished two more elm declines during the Middle Ages. In the middle and later part of the twentieth century, another outbreak began. The ability of the tree to try out and spread ever distinct varieties may be the secret of its ability to bounce back.

The elm is also matchlessly sneaky. I once had to protect the roots of one growing on a street in Greenwich Village. A new stoop was about to be built, which we needed to guide around the existing roots of the fifty-foot-tall tree. There were at least a dozen major roots spread out under the sidewalk, but we were able to find a way to preserve almost all of them. Whew. A month later, I got a call from the general contractor. "Can you come look at this?"

"Look at what?"

"Well, it's a root," he volunteered but would say no more.

When I got there, I saw they had excavated along the entire front wall of the house and down into the basement behind. As I had instructed them, they had wrapped exposed roots in burlap and were keeping them wet. Everything looked just as it should.

"What's up?" I asked.

The GC pulled the blue tarp off the excavation, and I could see down about 10 feet to the base of the old foundation, which they had removed on the street side. I followed a root that I had thought ended against a retaining wall near the house edge. In fact, it had dived down to the base of the retaining wall, gone under it, reached and passed through the bottom of the stone foundations, and ended up thirty-five feet away, beneath the basement stairs. Why it had gone there, I had no idea, but it must have found some goodies—probably a spring of water. What questing persistence!

The English elm uses its spreading root system to spy out new terrain. In a woodland, the roots spread freely among those of other trees. No new elm rears its head where the other trees are growing. They are lulled into complacency. Then, when a storm removes another tree or part of a tree, light strikes the forest floor. There, the elm root exults, and up comes a root sprout. Before the plants around can even react, the new elm is already established and growing happily, because it is still fed by its mother. This was exactly what had happened among the fairy houses south of the museum. A crab apple declined, an elm came up. A Sargent cherry stem failed, an elm came up. In this way, the English elm can take over an entire landscape. At Ross-on-Wye in England, elms growing in the churchyard finally sprouted and grew up inside the church. Now, *that* is prayer.

I thought for a moment of the fairy houses. It is our habit to imagine fairies as the little people of mythology, beings who might use toadstools for tables, but the Irish did not always see them so. The *Sidhe*—pronounced *shee*—were fairies thought to be about eight feet tall and faintly luminous. Their name means "the gentry." The slender young elms in the park are certainly tricksters like the fairies, and tall and straight like the *Sidhe*. They were not exactly luminous, but the children with their offerings of fairy houses made them so for me.

A WALK IN THE
TWELFTH CENTURY

On the second of October, 2016, I stepped into the twelfth century. I had not expected to. Traveling to learn how people once cared for their woods, I was going for a hike to find what I hoped would be at least a few ancient pollards, but the parking lot was full. Murua is a little town in Álava, not far from the city of Vitoria in the north of Spain. There was space under the oaks to park about two dozen cars. Each was taken. Someone had set up a large pop-up canopy tent that covered six or eight more spaces. The oaks to either side had been pollarded until half a century ago. The regrown sprouts were gigantic, each more than eighteen inches in diameter. The trees were lovely. My pique at the lack of parking was mitigated by the sight of them. Here was what I had come to see, and even if a mob of picnickers had decided on the same end, I would not be denied my pleasure at seeing these magnificent trees.

At last we found a spot by pulling onto a mound of cinders just off the street. Hard to say if it was legal or not, but two other cars had landed up there beside us. We started back through the lot to find the trail that we had been told led into an ancient woodland. There were people of all ages dressed mainly in postmodern hiking gear—that is, in bright colors. Here was an apricot Windbreaker, there a red-striped polo shirt, a deep green button-down, a yellow vest. A couple seemed to be with their teenager with Down syndrome. Three men sat together under the tent top on a bench. They did not look at one another, but appeared to be talking together. A man in a light orange windbreaker signed with an acronym, stood beside them, holding what appeared to be a staff covered in a yellow cloth sheath. It occurred to me that the three men were blind. Three more people were getting out of a car, or rather two people were. The third was unable to walk, so he was being helped by his friends into what looked like a tubular aluminum wheelchair. Only there were no wheels.

Toward the trailhead, there was a single large pollarded oak. It rose straight up twelve feet to a pair of shortened lateral branches. When last this tree had been cut—perhaps two-thirds of a century ago—the parts had been smaller. Now the trunk was thicker than the diameter of a truck tire, and the big lateral branches the diameter of car tires. The tree looked very much like a caduceus, its two laterals representing the twin arched wings, but instead of twined serpents on the trunk, it had several dozen branches of many different ages and sizes rising from the arched tops into the sky. They were by no means neat. They wandered and bent looking for light and air, appearing to jostle one another, like flames arrested by a photograph. Deep, serpentine fissured rivers of bark flowed up and around the stems.

What a gesture! If you cut off all the stems now, the tree would likely die back, but when they were only ten or twenty years old, they might have been harvested for firewood or to make charcoal to fuel iron foundries, or lime or pottery kilns. Ten or twenty years later, you could have done the same thing again, and so on indefinitely. The trunk and wings— the body of the caduceus—might have been kept for decades for a different purpose. If you were to do the laborious work of harvesting the tree down to its base, you would have had a pair of fine frame members for a boat, or a cruck post and beam for a barn. And if there were enough sun on the stump, it would very likely have sprouted again, and so a new tree might rise, root, and become a pollard in its turn.

We passed under this tree, following the road. Few could have called the thing beautiful, at least by any canon of beauty since Keats, but if it were ugly, it was bulldog ugly, which is possibly closer to real beauty anyway. I looked forward to more of these on what now seemed a very worthwhile woods walk. I looked ahead, where I could see three or four more pollarded oaks lining the roadside. As I was sizing them up, four people walked past in single file. It was the guy in the orange windbreaker, and the three following him were the three blind men. They held onto the first man's staff, which it turned out was an aluminum pole that he had telescoped out to more than eighteen feet long. He led them confidently at a good aerobic pace, the four talking back and forth in short bursts as they went.

They rounded a bend in the dirt road. We went after them. Without warning, I stepped into the twelfth century. Around that bend was not a respectable scattering of roadside pollards, but a forest of them, hundreds stretching out to either side. Some had burls at the cuts, some were wide and sedentary, many were narrow and rising. There were hollows in some of the trunks and stems, others were apparently completely intact. Some had been cut to two or three laterals from which gigantic branching sprouts arose, while others had normal branch patterns but with each branch pollarded like some kind of enormous flowerless bouquet. For the first time, I felt in my bones and saw with my eyes that pollarding was not some occasional trick that they performed in the old days, but a way of life.

In the twelfth century, long long before that, and all the way until the end of the nineteenth, people in the more settled lands around the world did not walk out of their houses and into a forbidding forest, but into woods that were worked and managed, places they knew as intimately as they knew one another. They were the source of fuel, food, building material, fertilizer, medicine, musical instruments. There, they formed an active, millennial relationship to nature that was not destructive but regenerative. It was good both for the people and the trees.

Now, it was like walking through a forest of upraised hands, each with impossibly long and impossibly twisted and impossibly vari-numbered fingers. I kept wandering off one edge of the road or the other to touch the trees, to prove that they were no illusion. I could imagine an autumn in 1145 when half the village was abroad in the woods, taking out their rations of winter wood. One family might be harvesting to restore a wattle and daub wall. Others were just gathering firewood. Neighbors were hauling their sticks to a lime kiln, where they slaked the lime that would paint their houses, disinfect their interiors, and fertilize the next year's crops. Another family was harvesting willow wands cut back just last year, so they were still thin and whippy. These would become fences and screens near the house and in the garden. Others were building a pile of cut branches, covering them in earth, dropping fire down a central chimney, and beginning to make charcoal. Still others were on the edge of the woodlands, cutting year-old ash sprouts to be winter fodder for the sheep. The *curandera* was among them, gathering bark, fruit, and herbs to make the medicinal drinks that would be kept at the bodega.

While I was distracted, two charioteers came up behind me. As they passed, I recognized the man whose friends had been helping him into a chair. Now, that chair was mounted on a large single wheel, and the two friends pulled it along, like twin brightly caparisoned draft horses, holding on to aluminum poles. There was another, identical setup, again the walkers pulling for one who could not walk. All six waved as they passed, headed up a gentle incline. A pair of the pullers suddenly sped to a trot and jumped their charge over a hump beside the road. They all laughed.

I followed them. To my left appeared a trunk that I judged to be about thirty feet off the trail, but it could not possibly have been as large as it seemed. I suspected it was two or even three trees. As I approached I saw a family wandering this way and that beneath the tree. Two little girls were dressed in white, their mother in pale blue, their father in black. Each had a plastic shopping bag into which they were placing thumbnail-sized nuts, pale brown and striped, exactly the color that in a horse is called chestnut. In fact, they were gathering beneath a single chestnut tree, with eight huge pollarded branches, and a trunk more than seven feet broad.

The European chestnut held in Europe and the Near East a position even more important than its American cousin held in Appalachia. The wood of both species is resistant to decay, and so was favored for fence posts, for sills, and for other applications that alternated wet and dry. In Europe it was the preferred wood for vine props, and whole woods of chestnut were coppiced for this use. The nuts were eaten roasted and even made into flour. (In Appalachia, until the blight, chestnut gathering was an important source of income for people fortunate enough to have them.) The foliage was excellent fodder for all domestic animals.

We were all so deep in the pollard wood that no other trees could be seen in any direction. Most were oaks, but there were beeches and chestnuts as well. The couple with the Down-syndrome son walked by. The young man held a few beechnuts in one hand. He was rubbing the convex side with his thumb. I tried the same trick. It was a pleasure to feel the smooth curve of the nut.

Along the road verge beneath the oaks, I kept finding autumn mushrooms growing out of the leaf litter. A few were recognizably boletus, with a white bulbous stalk and a humus-colored cap, a very sought-after edible. They were selling by the kilo at the market in town. One mushroom had a tall white cap, whose pileus hung low like a flapper gown. It was the lamppost of the fairies. I suspect it was a death cap, in the genus *Amanita*. Some mushrooms under the beech had overlapping smooth round caps the color and sheen of aluminum. A column of deadwood on a trunk had a pendant of brown turkey tail.

As I walked on, a man with a large mustache came striding purposively from the opposite direction. He was wearing a T-shirt and had on big boots. He carried a staff. He looked like a liberated office worker, which indeed he was. He stopped to talk. Retired from accounting, he had now lived three seasons on the mountain. He was discreet about where his house lay, since he may well have appropriated an abandoned place in the woods officially belonging to someone other than himself. His business in the fall was to gather wild produce. He showed me a canvas backpack stuffed with boletus mushrooms. I said I had seen a few right near. He said he knew the spot well, as he had been gathering in this area for more than a decade. Off he went at a brisk walk, like a hunting dog, casting to right and left. I saw him pick one of my boletus on the way.

At last I came over a rise where the magic stopped. Beyond was a cleared space, edged with conifer plantation.

I started back. A third aluminum chariot passed me, still outward bound, with its pleased rider and equally pleased beasts of burden. Two more groups of the blind passed, holding lightly to their poles. The road became thick with a variety of couples and small groups, at least one of whom in each had a physical disability. The members of one of the groups were signing to one another.

As I walked, I passed again into the ancient forest, and I thought about the enormous resourcefulness of trees—and not only of trees, but of the people who had lived among them. They had worked out together a way of living that had given to both what they needed. Keith Basso, an anthropologist who has studied Apache storytelling, reported that young

Along a road lined for more than a quarter mile with ancient pollards of oak, beech, and chestnut.

Apache living in eastern cities would say that they were "being hunted" by stories their grandmothers had told them. Through most of my life, I have been hunted by a phrase that appears often in the Psalms and in the Christian liturgy: "Let us worship the Lord in the beauty of holiness." Seeing the woods and the walkers and riders, the line jumped to mind.

It occurred to me here that that beauty was not in any one thing, but rather in the meeting of things. It arises where individuals become more the more they give. The trees and the people who pollarded them had this loveliness. So did the people who gave to one another what each possessed, in the name of moments to be created together. A friend of mine told me a saying among Crips: "Nothing about us, without us." We cannot do things for others, but we can do things with others. The twelfth century of which I had my momentary vision was not just the trees, but the people in the trees, a vision of companionship.

BOAT WOOD

There is a woodland near the public pool in the small town of Etxarri-Aranatz in northwestern Navarre, about forty miles from the port of San Sebastián. It is called the forest of Sakana. It has been decades since animals grazed there. As a result, the ground is overgrown with brambles, weeds, and bracken, and thousands of young volunteer trees—hawthorns and the invasive American red oak—compete for light on its slopes. No one notices it. The people are just on their way to the pool.

Out in the scrub, however, are dozens of old oaks. If you look closely, you see that they have grown with a consistent and unusual habit. Perhaps they are a different species? Most have a crown with two prominent leader branches, one going more or less straight up and the other stretching out nearly parallel to the ground. Occasionally, there are also forks with two rising leaders, like the semaphore formation for the letter "U" or two arms raised in triumph. Furthermore, the trees seem to have grown far apart from one another—maybe as much as fifty feet—as though their outstretched arms had been meant to fend off rivals. Some of the trunks are straight up and down, but others have grown in a gentle

In the woods of Sakana, an oak pruned in *ipinabarro* style to yield knees as ship timber.

S curve, responding perhaps to their position on the slopes and among the other old trees.

If they are a new species, they should be christened the *ipinabarros*, which in Basque means "Let's leave a few branches on the tree." That is what these trees were called. They are in fact quite ordinary European oaks, *Quercus robur*. Their semaphoric shape is the result of pruning, of the response of the oaks to the work of men. "There is no forest in my whole country that is not humanized," said Álvaro Aragón Ruano, the great student in Spain of the relationship between people and trees. He started listing them: the *chopos cabeceros* in Aragón, poplars pollarded for straight wood to build houses; the *pendolones*, evergreen oaks near Salamanca, pruned and shaped like apple trees to give plenty of low branches to cut for charcoal and with twigs and leaves for the pigs and cattle; the beeches whose pollard branches fed the foundry fires in the town of Leitza (see page 142); the oak pollard *carrascos* in the Sierra de Guadarrama near Madrid; the *dehesa* oaks of Extremadura, which gave charcoal, cork, and ink; fed the pigs, and sheltered farm fields; pollarded ash for sheep fodder; coppiced chestnut and hazel for barrel hoops.... They were the common landscape of the world until the twentieth century. It is simply that almost all of them have been forgotten.

The *ipinabarros* at Etxarri-Aranatz were just as much a *dehesa*—a forest farm for feeding livestock—as the oaks of Extremadura, two hundred miles to the southwest. Young trees were severely pruned, either by selecting the needed branches on saplings and suppressing the rest, or by heading back a young tree and selecting the few sprouts that grew back in the desired directions. The small number of major stems were then pollarded every eight to twelve years, leaving one rising stem on each major branch to reach higher into the sky. The small branches went to make charcoal, and the charcoal went to feed the ironworks for which the Basques from early in the Medievum were famous throughout Europe. Good grass grew in the sunny spaces between the widely spaced and much thinned oaks. Every summer, herds of sheep arrived from as far away as La Rioja—more than ninety miles south—to graze on the pasture among the *ipinabarros*. For thirty days starting on San Miguel's

Day, September 29, the grazing was restricted to pigs who fattened on the falling acorns. All the animals went to market on the Basque coast, from which ships took their fleece or their hams to the rest of coastal Europe.

Some oaks were simply headed back and allowed to sprout many new stems. The *ipinabarros*—the "leave a few branches" oaks—had another purpose. The boats that brought the products of the country to the rest of the known world were themselves the products of this forest. "*Ipinabarros*" were what the people who cut the trees called them, but it was illegal to write a contract or a royal decree in Basque. When the princes wanted more boats, their minions commanded the foresters in Castilian: "*Dejarán*," they wrote, "*horca y pendón*." It was a characteristically graphic expression in Spanish. *Horca* can mean simply "fork." The word *bandera* or *punta*—"flag" or "tip"—might also be used. *Horca* meant a large upright, often lightly curved stem. The word *pendón* meant "pennant," one of those cloth banners much longer than it was tall, often in the shape of a triangle, which fluttered from a castle's turret. In this case, it described a large branch trained to grow almost at right angles to the trunk. The general idea, then, was to make by your pruning a few strong vertical branches and a few almost horizontal ones. Perhaps the double meaning of *horca*—it also meant "gibbet" or "hanging tree"—was not meant to be lost on the royal subjects, who might be tempted to disobey.

The charcoal makers certainly saw no reason to do this elaborate form of pollarding, but the boatbuilders did. In fact, they could not get along without it. To make the frame of a large merchant ship, they needed a great number of stout curved timbers, *curbatones*. The knees that stabilized the hull structure had to have grown with a deep bend that was almost quadrangular, the *pendón*. The long curved futtocks, the rib cage to which the planks attached to make the skin of the ship, needed to be upright with a gentle curve, the *horca*. Sometimes, as in the Y-shaped floor timbers that accommodated the rising of the floor aft in the hull, the ship makers needed a double *horca*, which indeed resembled the double tines of a pitchfork. For the all-important sternpost, which held the flat stern to the rest of the boat, they had to have a very big *pendón*, at least 18 inches in diameter, at least 15 feet long on one stem, and maybe 8 feet long on the other.

The Sakana *ipinabarros* were at once agricultural and industrial. They fed the sheep and the pigs, they provided charcoal, but first and foremost, they created boat wood. Between thirty and ninety years after they had first been pollarded, the oaks were harvested to build the ships. There is even some evidence that in order to get nearly identical pieces for the repetitive use in a hull structure, the *bosqueros,* or foresters, tied down branches, guiding them to get just the angles they wanted. The inherent architecture of *Quercus robur*—Rauh's model among the twenty-four possible forms of trees (see page 43)—also helped the men produce trunk and branch combinations of a stable and dependable shape. The oaks and the men worked together.

All that had been forgotten by the 1960s. The oceangoing, far-trading, whaling, and cod-fishing Basques had turned their backs on the sea. The town built the swimming pool and tolerated the nearby woodland as it filled with thorns. Then, in 1978, marine archaeologist Selma Barkham and her colleagues had found almost intact on the sea bottom a 250-ton whaler, the *San Juan*. It had been about ninety feet long, capable of carrying a thousand barrels of whale oil or salt cod, and it had gone down in a blow when it dragged anchor in 1565. Dendrochronology showed that its wood had come from the Sakana *ipinabarros*. It was not found in the harbor at Pasaia, near San Sebastián, where the ship had been built, but about 2473 miles northwest, near Saddle Island in the Strait of Belle Isle, at Red Bay, Newfoundland.

Timber by timber, the Canadians brought each piece of the boat to the surface, studied it, measured it, and sent it back to its cold silt bed. In the process, they also found the remains of three whaleboats—the launches in which the sailors chased the whales—the oldest European clothes and shoes ever discovered in the New World, and whale oil barrels with their hazel hoops. The archaeologists found two more sunken whale ships in the same bay. In so doing, they resurrected a forgotten period of early modern history, and showed how a new kind of ship first came to be built.

More Iberian ships visited Terra Nova for whales and for cod than ever carried gold and other booty from the Indies. For almost all of these ships—whalers, cod ships, Indies traders—the Basques were in charge of both the building and the sailing. (In every port in Europe, you wanted a Basque pilot for your boat.) Some say they had reached the New World before Columbus, and although no documentary evidence has surfaced to substantiate that claim, they were certainly at least on his heels. The Basques were after fish, not gold. Salt cod was a mainstay food all over Europe, and by the sixteenth century most of it came from what would later be called the Grand Banks of Newfoundland. The word *bacalao*, which the whole world uses when it buys dried cod, is simply the way to say cod in Basque. When a ship had made several rounds of the North Atlantic fish trade, it might be retired to the warmer and less rough Indies route.

The greatest shipwrights of the sixteenth century were not the English or the Dutch, not the Portuguese or the French. They were the Basques, who lived and still live in the elbow of Europe, where southern France meets northern Spain. They are a people of unknown origin speaking a language of unknown provenance. It is likely that they are children of the union between indigenous Mesolithic hunter-gatherers and incoming Neolithic herders, before ever there was either a France or a Spain. What matters to them is not the nation-state, but the lay of the land, a narrow coastal plain cut with river mouths backed by wooded mountains that in contrast to the rest of Spain are continually green. The whole Basque coast, from Bayonne to Bilbao, is only about eighty miles long, but in the 1500s, it contained at least fifteen shipyards. The builders turned out twenty ships bigger than 100 tons each, per year. It took about four months to complete an average *nao,* the old Spanish for *nave,* or ship.

The Basque country has been a contested region as long as there have been records of war. Julius Caesar fixed the boundary between Hispania and Aquitaine that would become the division between Spain and France. (There is a mention of the Romans defeating a force of Saldunas in the *Gallic Wars.* The word is Basque for "cavalry.") The Vikings found it a fertile place to raid, especially when the pilgrims' road to Santiago de Compostela provided a steady stream of victims. The French and Spanish fought over Basque country for thirty years running during the Renaissance. Napoleonic France invaded Spain through it. Defeated Republicans fled into France by way of it at the end of the Spanish Civil War. Through it all, the Basques remained where they were, and they remained emphatically Basque. They built the finest ships of the sixteenth century, helped change the way boats were built, and did so by means of these woodlands of *ipinabarros.*

The most generous impulse of human beings is the wish to exchange. Its dark side is the lust to have more than your neighbor, and indeed to control what your neighbor can have at all. Out of a tradition of fine carpentry and careful consideration, this people built new kinds of ships to trade with all of Europe and to bring fish and oil from Terra Nova. Not one of these boats was an eagle of the seas, although the king of Spain pressed them into service for his wars. (Many of the ships of the Spanish Armada were built on the Basque coast.) The shipwrights wanted the boats bigger not to hold cannons and soldiers, but to carry more casks of goods. They were among the first to make the difficult transition between the old lapstrake style, where the skin of the ship was first nailed together with overlapping planks, and the carvel style, where a strong broad frame came first.

A Basque carpenter knew what his wood could and could not do. One month, he might make a house, the next a rowboat, the next an altarpiece, the next a whaler. Everybody wanted the ships to carry more cargo and therefore earn more. Even an ordinary seaman did well out of a successful trading voyage: typically one-third of the proceeds were divided among the sailors, and they were likely to be better fed at sea than they would have been on land. The sailors from Spain ate wheat, biscuits, bacon, beans, peas, bacalao, sardines, garlic, olive oil, sherry wine, and cider; the seamen on the French Basque boats ate even better, adding eel, butter, and beef. Basque sailors never got scurvy, because the hard cider they quaffed three times a day was rich in vitamin C.

The wood for the ships often came from municipally owned forests, so when a new ship was made, the nearby town prospered. The price of the wood meant more money for the town fathers to build a bigger church or to improve the always difficult roads. Since a church was not only for worship but for every kind of public meeting, market, and celebration, everyone had an interest in maintaining and expanding it. The carpenter put his mind, heart, and hand to the task.

There is an ancient saying among the seagoing peoples of Europe: "If you want to learn to pray, go to sea," to which some added "If you want to learn to sleep, go to church." One can imagine that a carpenter dreaming through Mass one Sunday at his parish church might have conceived the analogy between the structure of his boat-to-be—a *nave* or *nao*—and the nave of the church in which he pretended to be wide awake. He had built both kinds of naves, the one that floated and the one that stood. There had always been a loose analogy between church and ship, since Christian iconography envisioned the church as a ship in which all of the people rode to heaven. What if he looked more closely into the analogy and made it into structure?

The owner was bothering him to fit more cargo in the new *nao*. What, he must have thought, if I treated my ship nave like a church nave? What if I built a sturdy frame, buttressed against all kinds of twisting? What if I clad the three- or even four-storied frame with planks, just as I clad the church with stone? What if I used for the building of the ship a system of proportional measures like those I use for laying out nave, chancel, and sanctuary?

Suddenly, he really was awake. He sat up so straight so fast that people around him coughed and looked studiedly away. *"As, dos, tres,"* he mumbled, hoping it would pass for a prayer. *"As, dos, tres."*

"One, two, three."

Let my house—I mean, my ship—be one unit across the beam at its widest point, he thought. Let its keel be twice that unit. Let its whole length from stem to stern be three times that unit. Now, I must sit in the sea, not on the land. I need to be rounded and stable in the waves. I need to have a strong neck like a cod. And like that bacalao, I need arcs from top to bottom and from front to back, so I can breast the waves without breaking. If I do these things, I can make a deep hold with three stories, like a house, and the crossbeams of the hold itself will help stabilize the shape.

Mass had become very interesting indeed.

After church, he was late for lunch. He was out in the yard, sketching in the dirt with a shepherd's staff.

So, he said to himself, I know the widest breadth amidships and the depth of the hold I want if I am to carry all those barrels of goods. From these dimensions, I create a master frame, the centerpiece of my strong bacalao skeleton. By making a series of arcs and lines—the widest arc, the arc of the bottom, the arc of the sides, the line of the floor, and the line of the top deck—I can create a mold with which to mark the central master frame. Then, by shifting the mold to accommodate the narrowing and rising of the fish body, I can make a series of arcs and lines that will mark for me the dimensions of at least the most important frames fore and aft of the master frame.

He was dizzy, and had not yet had his cider. They were calling him from the dining table.

The boat would be based on frames, not planks. It could have internal floors and ceilings, so that there were three separate decks to hold cargo. The central dozen or so frames would be worked out directly with the mold, and they would be joined one to another with mortise and tenon to lend greater stability in the middle of the ship, where the mast was tacked and where the greatest forces would come. (When heeled over for cleaning or repairs in the drydock too, it was this section that bore the brunt of the ship's mass. Behind and ahead of these crucial frames—the *maderas de cuenta*, or calculated wood—each frame would have to projected using the mold, the *maderas de cuenta*, and the builder's eye. But it could be done, it could be done.

Now, he could go in, eat his dinner, and raise a toast to a ship shaped like a cod that could carry a thousand barrels or more. It was all thanks to his wandering mind at church. Perhaps without knowing, he had indeed been learning to pray.

To make this imagined ship, he needed a tremendous quantity of wood, and the crucial part of it needed to be large and curved, to make the bacalao's spine and ribs. When finished, the ships would be rated at 200 to 500 tons. (Tonnage is a measure of how much cargo volume the hold can bear.) Each hundred required at least 4300 cubits of wood, or about 6000 linear feet. Fortunately, his cousin was a *bosquero*. Together, they examined the municipal forest at Sakana. There were already a decent number of oaks with forks that could make good ribs, futtocks, floor timbers, stem- and sternposts. If the idea caught on, however, they would be making many more than one of these ships. They would need to design the ships to fit the wood and the wood to fit the boats.

To build the bacalao-shaped ship, the local people needed to organize. An owner hired a carpenter. The builder went to the *bosquero.* The forester found some of the wood already grown, but he also began a steady program to make new wood. He started new oaks from acorns, trained them in the nursery planted them out, trained the young as *ipinabarros,* took a few harvests of charcoal from them, and after thirty or forty years, he could cut them for a new boat. He also found young and resprouted oaks, cutting them to *horca y pendón*, and so shortcutting the time to harvest. The building and the woodsmanship both called for skill, practical intelligence and consistent planning, as well as the training of apprentices to continue the work. (It necessarily took more than one generation.)

To fund the work, an owner joined with outfitters, who would take his finished boat abroad to make money with it. They both borrowed from lenders at what may now seem exorbitant rates of up to 30 percent. "*Prêt a grosse aventure*," it was called in the French Basque lands: "loan for a big gamble." As a backup, some of the world's first insurers underwrote the cost in the event of disaster, taking a 15 percent stake. The same carpenters built seamen's chapels on high points overlooking the Bay of Biscay, so the wives could pray for their husbands and sons, looking out over the seas that had taken them, and the husbands and sons could direct their prayers and hearts toward those same high chapels. As they left port, the chapel was often the last thing that the sailors could make out on land, and the first thing they could see on their return.

The change in the boats was both revolutionary and traditional. It was accomplished by carpenters, each of whom had learned from his father or teacher—usually one and the same—the way to turn wood into structure. Nothing had changed, except the context. By dreaming with a wider eye, they had transformed the way men went to sea. Still, the process was idiosyncratic, always incorporating the apprentice's learning.

It became customary to make the new boats entirely of oak, but the *San Juan,* like many older boats, had a beech keel. She was nothing special as a new-style boat, just one of the hundreds of *nao*s built in the sixteenth century in the Basque country. At three decks and 250 tons, she was small to average in size. Beech had the advantage in Basque country of being easily available and when it was in forest situations of growing straight. It took a straight, unpollarded trunk to make the keel. Beech was also an excellent wood to carve. And carve the builder did.

Viking boatmakers had been called stemsmiths, because the carving of their keel and prow was the central fact from which the rest of the boat emerged. Half a millennium later, the builder of the *San Juan* still acted like a stemsmith. The keel was almost fifty feet long, cut from an eight-ton trunk. In the center, it was shaped like a capital T, but as it stretched forward and aft, the builder had carved the garboards—the first exterior planks—right into the keel. For those runs, the keel has a cross section like a capital Y. The first "planks" there were in fact built into the keel. On the forward edge, he carved the keel to angle it up toward the stem. In short, the carpenter envisioned the whole boat and constrained its construction in the shape he gave to its first and fundamental piece.

A contract for a cod-shaped *nao* ran no more than three hundred words. They had to be in Spanish, but as it happens the writer occasionally needed to borrow a Basque word, for want of the equivalent in Spanish. Thus, in order to say that the carpenter was responsible to make the entire ship, the contract specified, "You will complete the ship from the keel to the *albaola*." The latter was the very top edge ceiling piece all around the boat. It sealed the joints between futtocks, hull, and ceiling, so the water ran off and not into the holds or the frame. It was elaborately crenellated, like the battlement of a castle, the top of each third futtock slotting neatly into the pattern. It, too, was a masterpiece of carving.

Between the two named pieces, the whole of the new ship had to rise. The frame pieces—the three layers of futtock that made the cod skeleton, the knees that stabilized it, the floor pieces that made a firm bottom, the enormous stem and stern pieces—all had to be found among the *ipinabarros*, felled, hewed in the woods to their rough final shape, ox-drawn to the river sides, and floated down to the building site where the river ran into the sea. There were ninety-six each of first, second, and third futtock arcs, and more than sixty knees. From the same woods or from another nearby where the oaks had grown in tight groups to make them straight trunked and little branched, the fellers took whole oaks to the base, then pit-sawed them tangentially for the planks, stacked them, loaded them, floated them down the river, and took them to the boatyard at Rentería, where the work was about to get under way. Some of the planks were thirty feet long or more.

All the wood was cut and used green, which made it easier to shape at the site but liable to twist as it dried. The work began in late winter, partly because it was easier to see the needed shapes and lengths when the leaves were down, but also because the trees were dormant and the low temperatures kept them from drying and shifting quickly. Still, there was pressure to get the work done quickly. Fifteen or twenty fellers and sawyers worked together in tight woods; maybe thirty or more fellers and hewers among the more widely spaced *ipinabarros*.

Only when both kinds of wood were on site could the work begin. The keel, keelson, and stem and stern pieces set the dimensions of the frame. The three levels of futtocks—placed one atop the other—made the skeleton. The knees stabilized it fore and aft and side to side. The planks—not lapped as in the medieval boats but butt-jointed one against the next up and down and side to side—formed the skin on the outside and the supports for the decks on the inside.

Although the *nao* depended for its capacity and stability on its strong skeleton, the frame was not completed before the planks were applied. Rather, the building went on stepwise, in rhythm. Teams of framers and *clavadores,* or nailers, followed each other through the boat.

Indeed, sometimes one team would go down the beach to work on another *nao* and return later to continue on the first when the other team had knocked out its part. The framers began by placing the floor timbers and the *maderas de cuenta*, from which the rest of the hull would be projected. Then they started by placing the first futtocks in a section of the ship. The nailers followed, using iron nails to set the long thick planks in place, and setting sleeper planks on the inner face, both to hold in place the first futtock tops and to create a support for the decks to come. On the first pass, they used only iron nails. Later, they would return to place oak treenails. The latter expanded into the holes and stabilized the all-important connection between planks and frames.

On these boats, the planks really were part of the frame. It was they that gave the fore and aft stability to the rising ribs. Indeed, the three levels of futtocks that stretch from the floor timbers to the *albaola* were not joined butt to butt. Instead, they overlapped one another at each level. They were called floating futtocks. Only the inboard sleeper and the outboard plank held them in position with respect to one another. The effect when you see the frame in process is of a thousand intricately woven tuning forks held together by horizontal lines of tongue depressors. This made the initial structure a little tenuous, but when the planking was done, it was a stable and a flexible frame.

One thing the makers took pride in was their adze work. If you have ever held or used an adze, you know it is a heavy and somewhat awkward tool. The blade is set at a right angle to the handle. You stand on the wood and cut between your feet. A saw opens the grain, tearing the fibers; an adze can close the grain, making the wood repel oils and stains and resist the invasion of marine worms. A good adzeman left a mirror finish on the surface he cut, as smooth as could be accomplished with a plane. All the futtocks, knees, and planks were adzed smooth on each of their exposed faces. Heavy though the tool was, it left a delicate edge, like a face that has just been shaved.

Almost half a millennium later, in Pasaia, the same port where the ship was built and using wood from the forest at Sakana, the same woodland that gave it its *ipinabarros,* a small group of historical-boat builders are making the *San Juan* again. They call their project *Albaola,* for that finely carved sill that was part of the old contracts, and also *"Itsas Kultura Faktoria,"* a sea culture factory. They started in 2013 and were supposed to be done in 2016, to celebrate the European Union's declaration of San Sebastián as that year's "capital of culture." Easier said than done.

Making a boat that was part of an intricate culture, handed down from generation to generation, is not as simple as pushing Save on the keyboard. *Ni mucho menos.* The first issue was the wood. There are those ninety-six curved first futtocks, each with a radius of about twenty-one feet. The builders went out to Sakana and to other pollard woods nearby. Although hundreds of years had passed, the shapes were still visible. It looked as if it would not be easy to find the pieces, but not too difficult either. Sure, they would be a little larger than they might have been in 1564, but that would simply mean a lot more sawing and adzing. The trouble was first one, then another, then a third, was rotten at the core.

Even where the wood was intact, it had often long since grown and lost branches, leaving knots that weakened the stem, or developed shakes, cracks that reduced its stability. "If the carpenter of the *San Juan* looked at what we are using," said Mikel Leoz, one of *Albaola*'s leaders, "he would be horrified. 'This is shit!' he would say. 'Get rid of that one.

And that one! And that one!' He could pick and choose. He had good wood. Ours is second or third quality." The pollard forests are almost gone now. Using the last remnants is like trying to make a lamb stew out of week-old roadkill.

It took the original builders only four months to make the first *San Juan*. The *Albaola* project had three years. Surprisingly, the greater time frame made the work harder, not easier. A large number of people working quickly to achieve the end certainly must have given the project a spirit of camaraderie, but that was not the reason for the speed. Green wood moves as it dries. The *Albaola* carpenters found out to their cost that if they set up a section of futtocks and left it alone for a month or two, when they came back, they would find that their straight line of square timber tops was no longer straight, no longer equal in height, and each piece was no longer square but a nest of drunken rhomboids.

How had the original builders avoided this warping? By working fast. The nailers came right after the framers in a come-and-go rhythm, not just to get the work done and the boat in the water but to keep the wood in line. When you nail a plank and a sleeper to the top of a course of futtocks, it can't go anywhere, not up or down or out of square. The intelligence of the making was not only in the design and the materials, but also in the teamwork and the timing. From start to finish, each person had a job that mattered.

Itsas kultura. Sea culture. The builders at *Albaola* may not have finished on time, but they have begun the work of remembering. It is a hopeful sign. They have shown that not in the ancient past but teetering on the edge of the modern world, it was still possible for people to give and take with the woods around them, without degrading either. It was not just raw materials and labor that built the *San Juan*. It was a way of life that embraced woodlands, river, ports, carpenters, the open sea, the whales, the cod, and Labrador.

Soon enough, the Spanish king would demand the ships for war. Soon enough, the Little Ice Age would bring early ice to Red Bay, trap ships for the winter, and change the migration patterns of the right whales and the bowheads. Soon enough, the Dutch would figure out a way to make ships cheap and dirty and sail them using convicts, ending Basque preeminence in trade. Aragón Ruano thinks that the surviving *ipinabarros* should be preserved and treated with reverence as though they were cathedrals or castles. It is a good idea.

HILL GIRT

Wrong exit? From six smooth lanes to two rough ones, then a steep bend and a turn sharp right. The road did not quite end, but the track that went on mirrored the undulation of peaks, ridges, and a steep-sided canyon edging a small stream called Erosoleku, as though the route had been laid out by sure-footed donkeys. In late September, it turned suddenly cold in its shade. How could any town at all be in a place so tight, so precipitous, so barren? The road went on for six or seven miles, and we were about ready to decide we had gone wrong, when a square stone house appeared on the right, and then another. The land opened in front of us as though we were coming out of the neck of a funnel and into its cone.

A place was there indeed. The road wound into it. A right turn led up a steep hill to the church at the top of town. Above it stretched grass green pastures so steep that were you to fall from the top of them, you would likely roll straight to the bottom. And likely go on rolling. You would pass the old and much used battlemented church, lurch into the main plaza of Leitza, only distinguished from the rest of the town by the fact that it is almost flat and its tall walls have space for Basque graffiti; roll down around the bend past the village's principal monument, the public laundry that has been there since time immemorial, and past one of the two *hostals*, run by the three generations of the family that live on the second floor; careen onto the main street again and carom off the bread and pastry shop with its fine handmade wooden clock showing a bear and a tree with the hour and second hands branches, a clock made by the owner of the store, who said he was a woodworker but got married, had kids, and, well, he needed a steady income. His chocolate rolls were big and sticky, and conversation at his place in the morning washed back and forth between Spanish and Basque. You could then barrel straight down the street keeping left, bounce off the *jakatea*, the restaurant where the wife ran the kitchen and husband did the waiting, past one hardware store, a furniture place, a post office, two cafés, two markets, two banks, another *hostal* at the crossroads, and land up at the bottom of town among the buildings of the factory where they turned plain paper into wallpaper and fine endpapers for books.

You have just rolled through all that there is of downtown Leitza. The whole township embraces about twenty-two square miles, or 14,000 acres, of which less than a tenth is the urban core. "The rain in Spain stays mainly in the plain," said Professor Henry Higgins in the movie *My Fair Lady*, but that is a lie. The rain in Spain falls mainly in Leitza, about 2000 millimeters a year, or 79 inches. In late September, when most of Spain south of here is yellow and dry, Leitza is every shade of green. It rains without a moment's notice, a little or a lot, and at any time at all, but seldom too much at once. At night rain pounds on the roof, with a sound like river rapids. In the morning, the sun rises. At ten a.m., a brief shower falls. If it is this steep and this wet, how come I see no gullies? How come so little erosion has occurred? One reason is that trees on the steep slopes were pollarded. Because the tree trunks and roots remained alive in the ground, resprouting, and because shepherds maintained unbroken pasture grass on the open lands, there is little or no soil erosion, even on the steepest slopes.

The town had been dying in the 1950s, when they talked the paper factory into opening here. There were a little more than fifteen hundred people left. Now there were more than three thousand. The schools were full of children, and so were the playgrounds. Every open space in town was laid out with a dense complicated vegetable garden, with several kinds of pole beans, many more of kale, and tomatoes and salad greens. It was autumn, and the late tomatoes were tented in hooped plastic covers. The walls of many houses were painted with whitewash, but the windows were all edged with quartered gray blocks of stone. From each balcony spilled a surprisingly orderly blanket of bright red, yellow, or blue pelargoniums and petunias. It was as if all the housekeepers in town had hung out their flower rugs to beat the dust from them. In disused corners and the back edges of buildings stood piles of logs, not cut wood, but whole tree trunks. Beside them were stacks of firewood split out of the balks. Oak, ash, beech, chestnut. What were they doing there?

There exists a fine map of the township of Leitza. It was researched, designed, laid out, and made by José Miguel Elosegui in 2014. It is as clean and detailed as a USDA quadrangle map, the sort that we used to carry to keep from getting lost in the backcountry. It's an eight-fold map, about four feet high by three feet broad when fully open. It takes a dining room table to hold it. It is both an accurate topographical survey and a detailed road map. From its size, you would think it a map of Spain or at least of the whole Basque country, but it is simply a map of Leitza. The scale is about 3 inches to 1 kilometer.

The whole sheet is dense with names and symbols. It is a well of deep memory. Towers with twin feet are lime kilns. Tiny green phalli leaning to one side are hunting blinds. They are small elevated shacks that line all the hilltops and ridges, the favored place to hunt pigeons on their autumn migrations. There is a lottery to see who gets which blind, three hunters to a blind. There are more hunters than blinds, and everybody knows which are the best ones. (Prior to the lottery drawing, you may see an unusual number of men in church.) Accurately drawn steel-windmill forms are wind turbines. Red rectangles with a little black rectangle beside them are sheepfolds. Blue water drops are springs, blue rectangles water troughs. Lightning bolts in a circle are local electric-generating plants, many of which once supplied small-stream hydroelectric power to different parts of town, each serving a hillside. Black crosses in a circle mark sites that were iron forges. Warehouses are gray rectangles; houses and farmhouses are burnt-umber rectangles.

There are hundreds of names on the map. Ridges and peaks get names; creeks get names; hillsides and springs have names; valleys and passes have names. And almost every house or farm or *borda* (sheepfold) bears the name of the person who occupies it. There are eight ridges on the south edge of the township and each is named in its turn: Aldatzegi, Ipuru, Egiestu, Egimearra, Egiaundi, Isastiberde, Zurlandua, Egiluzea.

I had never met before a landscape so intimately known and named. Elosegui and his wife have known it a long time. When they first arrived in the 1950s, she had taught school in Gorriztaran, the prosperous farm valley in the southeast of town. The worthies had just installed an electric center, a water-powered generator in a shack about the size of a chicken coop, which gave the people on the hillside power enough to last until early evening. Then, they brought out the candles. A new school had also just opened, which meant that the kids of the district now had to walk only forty-five minutes each way to school rather than the two hours it took to go to school downtown.

Unfortunately, when the school had first opened, the Spanish government had sent teachers who spoke no Basque. (During the forty years of

Francisco Franco's dictatorship, it was officially illegal to speak Basque.) Imagine walking almost an hour to meet a teacher with whom you could exchange only a few intelligible words. José Miguel's wife indeed spoke Basque, and she had a flair for communicating complex concepts to her young farm kids. To explain a thermometer, she boiled milk for them. They watched as the milk expanded, occupying more volume the hotter it got. "That is just like what happens inside a thermometer!" she explained. Of course, the children often came in tag teams, a boy one day and his big sister the next, their little brother the third. Things could get a little muddled. When she asked on a quiz how a thermometer worked, one bright lad wrote, "The thermometer is full of boiling milk."

Leitza had the usual twentieth century: roads came, cars came, wars came, factories came. Once when I was there, a pan-European feminist bicycle tour roared through town to cheers in the public square. At that season of the year, you heard the chain saws in the woods all day long. But there is one thing that Leitza has not done. If you hold up the map of the township, almost three-quarters of what you see before you is owned in common by all the neighbors. *Leitzalarrea* (literally, the pasture of Leitza) and *Haritzaunde* (the garden of oaks), more than sixteen of the twenty-two square miles of the place, are *bienes communes*, or common goods.

No wonder there are so many names on the map, since each place has been lived in, polished, and passed on. In the map's legend, the two smallest pica sets of names refer to *"paraje"* and to *"lugar."* Both translate as "place," but they are different. A *paraje* is bigger, explained José Miguel. "It contains at least a few *lugares.*" (Wanting to explain how out of the way and tiny our hero's home was, Cervantes began *Don Quixote* with the words *"En un lugar de La Mancha"* or Somewhere in La Mancha.) On José Miguel's map are noted two nested kinds of place in a space where we from another world would likely not put any name at all.

But much of what is best in our world comes from the one that persists in this mountain valley. The logs lying along the house walls in the middle of town are harvested from the commons by common right. A forester apportions what can be harvested each year. Each parcel amounts to five tons of wood. The rights are distributed in an annual lottery, and the winner of a section is responsible to cut and to remove the wood. When you enter the lottery, you pray to win a parcel *up*hill from the road, since it is easier to roll logs down than to drag them up. Where other towns make much of a soccer star or a battle fought nearby, Leitza remembers its laundry and its world-champion axe cutters. The woodland weaves the life of the town together, both in the present and in deep memory. The relationship between people and trees is intimate and active.

Right beside the square is the ancient laundry, the town's one tourist attraction. The signage is attractive, and the accounts of the laundry's use precise and detailed, a note of pride in each paragraph. It is a stone-walled enclosure, open to the air above, the walls pierced with large open windows. Inside is an elliptical basin punctuated on its raised edge with fifteen smooth, rectangular stone surfaces, each angled into the basin at a pitch that makes scrubbing easy. Beside each is a ledge for the wash bucket. The housewife put the dirtiest clothes—usually the sheets—into the bottom of the bucket, then the more lightly soiled things. On top of the clothes went a filter cloth. Onto the cloth she poured a few cups of ashes, made from the stems of pollarded beech and ash trees, sprinkling bay leaves on top. She poured hot water into the bucket through the ashes and the leaves. The ash created a slurry of potassium carbonate, the bay left a pest-repellent perfume. The hot solution soaked for hours, renewed once or twice with more hot water. Then, she released it into the common basin through holes in the bottom of the washtub. The wastewater would be either reused for someone else's clothes or taken away for other house-cleaning tasks. The clean sheets and clothes were set out on the grass of the steep pastures to dry and whiten in the sun.

By the old Plazaola railway station, right beside the paper plant, you could take a slight right turn onto a small dirt road that led out of town into *Leitzalarrea*. Almost immediately, pasture began. At the second hairpin turn lay the remains of a lime kiln. There oak and beech pollards had supplied the wood to turn limestone into quicklime. The kiln was a masonry structure with a chimney above and cooling chamber below. In the middle, you stacked a layer of stone, then a layer of wood, then a layer of stone, as many layers as could fit. Gorse and heather brands were used to start a slow fire. For five days, the fire had to burn slow and steady. The minders worked in shifts to keep it going. At the end, they began to clear out the ash and pull down the quicklime, cooling it and bagging it. It might be mixed with water and glue to make the whitewash for houses, or it might become a pH-raising fertilizer for farm fields. It was a cleaning agent and disinfectant. It went into the mix in the forge to make iron and the kiln to make glass.

Farther up the winding track, the verge was lined with young ash trees. All of them, when I was there, had just been pollarded. They were worked on a one- to two-year cycle, because the shepherd wanted their leaves for fodder more than their wood for heat. "You can always find a *borda*," said José Miguel, "by looking for pollarded ash trees. Each one is surrounded by them." The *borda* was the key to a way of life that has produced abundant sheep in northern Spain for at least three thousand years. It was a small stone barn built into a slope, so that you could access the top floor from the uphill side and the bottom floor from the downhill. It had a broad double door at either end. One end led into the enclosed winter pasture, the other into the larger landscape. Beside the *borda* was its hut, the *chabola*, where the shepherd stayed beside his sheep. This hut was a simple one-room rough-stone house, with a wooden door and a bench in front, but the roof was made out of broad flat stones. It could not be made with roof tiles like the *borda* itself. A tile roof on a human dwelling signifies ownership, and the *chabola* too was part of the commons, not a private holding. The shepherd and his family might say they owned the shack, but they did not own the land it sat on. They could not sell it or give it away. For nine months of the year, the sheep were at the *borda*, either in the fenced winter field or in the surrounding open pastures. They came down to the home farm in town at San José's Day in March for the lambing, then climbed aloft again.

In much of Spain, even in other parts of Navarre, the flocks went a long distance to summer pastures, often on the limestone bowls of mountaintops, where the grass was fresh. The shift rested the home pastures and gave the sheep a cooler place to pass the warmest months. In Leitza, however, the heights were near the town, and the system so finely tuned that it was not necessary to go far away.

The rhythm of grazing and strict pollarding of ash trees kept the sheep lands of *Leitzalarrea* perennially productive. The preservation of thick-rooted native grasses on the hillsides—*Agrostis capillaris, Agrostis curtisii, Festuca nigrescens, Potentilla erecta, Jasione laevis, Gentiana pneumonanthe, Danthonia decumbens*, and *Nardus stricta*—prevented erosion. The very wet climate, with regular rain and fog, prospered the grasslands. The seasonal movement of sheep from one area to another and the limited number allowed on each pasture by the commons law gave the land regular rest.

Ash trees were the perennial fodder crop whose winter use further rested the grass. When you harvested the young stems, the trunk and branches of each tree survived, its roots holding the soil on the steep hills. Each tree might survive for hundreds of years. Whenever the shepherd needed a new ash, he rooted fresh twigs in spring.

Here was responsibility in the etymological sense. The word comes from the Latin *responsum*, meaning "answered" or "offered in return." The system was not immune to abuse. Pastures might be periodically burned to keep off shrubs and thicken the grasses, but too much burning hurt the grasses, and erosion followed. Overgrazing had the same effect. Interestingly, efforts to improve the pasture by planting improved fodder, fertilizing, and watering it have also increased erosion. But when you followed the rules of the commons, the landscape remained intact, with its full productive capacity. The townspeople took from it, but at the same time offered in return. In the *Ordenanza de comunales*, the Law of the Commons, one provision states that in lieu of paying a fee to use the land, you might do *auzolan,* service for the common good. One form of *auzolan* was to manure the common pastures.

The one-year-old pollard stems of the ash trees were cut in October

Close-up of pollarded ash with one-year-old stems, ready to harvest for sheep fodder.

while they were still green and stored in the upper story of each *borda*. They were pushed down to feed the sheep from Christmas until March. When you see the one-year wood just before it is cut, there is a strange beauty to the attachment of each three- to five-foot-long sprout to its parent stem. Each rises from what looks like the nipple of a breast, and each can be imagined as a spurt of green milk, arrested in the moment of its emergence. A few sprouts may be left on the tree to reach two years of age. These grow to longer than six feet and are stiff enough to stand upright. In every vegetable garden in town, the poles support the beans.

It was the season of fruit: apples, chestnuts, acorns, beechnuts. Sheep were on every hillside. Cattle grazed in a park among the picnic tables. Along a narrow stretch of twisting road, with steep drops to the west side, the cattle went in single file, picking up the fallen chestnuts. Uphill stretched a long green pasture, bordered by trees, mainly beeches, and all pollarded at about six feet high. The road wound up into a forest entirely of beech pollards. Here, Leitza got wood and charcoal for heating and for making glass and firing pots, but it also got the charcoal for a major medieval iron industry. By the thirteenth century, there were sixteen iron foundries in *Leitzalarrea*.

To have a foundry, you needed water, iron ore, and wood for charcoal, all in close proximity. Each foundry was located on the slopes of the commons to take advantage of this confluence of necessaries. The beech and oak pollards throughout *Leitzalarrea* yielded the wood, which was converted into charcoal. The ore was heated over the charcoal, until the slag separated from the iron, which fell into collecting tubs at the base of the foundry. The waterpower was harnessed with a waterwheel made from the wood of oak pollards, and used to drive hammers that shaped the molten mass. From this industry came nails, swords, knives, and axes.

In the Basque lands, the axe was a country man's main tool. He used it for cutting, for hammering, for shaping, even for hoeing. *Aiskolaris*, the sport of axe cutting, in part kept the tradition alive.

It is a serious sport. In training, an axe cutters runs twenty or thirty miles per day, works out with weights, and spends the balance of the day practicing his cutting. He will do this for two or three months, seven days a week, leading up to the contest. Until the 1970s, the Basques were always world champions of this sport. They used axes made in Leitza or in nearby Urnieta. These had a carbon steel blade folded in the forge over a soft iron poll. In 1976, some Australians showed up with steel axes that had been industrially made in Manchester, England. They handily won the trophy. Not ones to stand for a pointless tradition, the Basques switched to the Manchester blades and won it back. The Urnieta maker studied the English tool, and he now makes an all-steel axe for the competition.

Way up on top of *Leitzalarrea*, you could look out west into the province of Guipuzcoa. It was the same country of mountains and steep slender valleys, but the change in the landscape over there was dramatic. The Guipuzcoans had adopted modern forestry in large parts of it, cutting out the native trees and substituting fast-growing conifers, a cash crop. There, 70 percent of the land was privately owned; here, 70 percent was owned in common. Those Guipuzcoan hillsides were furry with the even deep green of conifer plantation; the pastures were few and look barren. So it was not the uniqueness of place that made Leitza. It was the way that people treated the land. It was in large part the careful maintenance of the commons.

While José Miguel Elosegui and I were looking out, a pale green pickup truck rattled up behind us. Out climbed the brothers Esteban and Patxi. Both had the stocky build and broad chest that many Basque men share. One had thinning gray hair, the other was balding. They were both wearing rugby shirts—one striped green, one orange—with jeans and cross-track shoes. Each man was more than seventy years old, though neither would say just how much more. As younger men, they had been farmers and foresters. Patxi was an axe cutter who had won the world championship almost fifty years before. They had agreed to show me the speed and skill of competition axe cutting.

They pulled out a beech log from the truck, huffing and smiling. It was about twenty inches in diameter. Then they hoisted out a long box.

"What's that?" I asked.

"The axes," Esteban replied.

He opened the box. Four axes were nested inside, each in its own niche. They then nailed four pieces of two-by-fours to the bottom side of the log, and set it in the levelest piece of ground they could find.

"How do you sharpen the axes," I asked.

"With stones," replied Esteban. "The blades must be sharp enough to shave with."

To show that this was not a metaphor, Patxi held the axe he was hefting near the poll and gently ran the blade across his left forearm. One pass left it smooth, his gray-blond hair glistening as it fell.

Patxi jumped up on the stabilized log, spread his legs wide, and started to cut between them. He cut on the exhale. The huff of his breath and the whizzing of the axe head sounded together. The notch of the kerf was peculiarly made. One side was very steep, almost parallel to the log's cross section, the other was at a very wide angle. I noticed that the effect of this shape was to launch the wood cut with each blow out of the kerf and onto the ground. That way, he wasted no time clearing the notch. He cut rapidly and steadily, but without hurry. In about a minute, he stopped, handed the axe to Esteban, and they changed places. The brother started the same rhythm. A minute later, Patxi was back in the saddle.

In under three minutes, the log fell neatly in two pieces. Watching this, I understood for the first time how it had been possible to make a world out of such hand tools. A small pollard cut would fall off in two blows. Even the rib of a ship, cut from a curved piece of oak twenty-four inches in diameter, might be reduced to its ship shape in a couple of hours.

Esteban showed me the line of the cuts in the kerf. There were only a pair of little ridges that showed how two cuts were made at a slightly different angle. "Those are the mistakes," he said, with a smile. "Those are mine." The rest looked as though it had been cut with a chain saw, two single smooth faces that were the result of maybe four hundred blows. This was skilled axe work. The two seventy-plus-year-old men were not even winded.

Few people were left to learn the skill now, but it has survived into the twenty-first century. When you looked across at Guipuzcoa and then back to the pollard mountain on which we stood, you could see that the modern change was not inevitable. One could choose relationship. One could choose responsibility. One could choose the commons. One could choose a life where head, heart, and hand might work in concert. It was not a Romantic or a nostalgic dream. It was an enterprise like any other, and maybe it was worth the hard work.

THE COMMONS

In my generation, almost every person with a liberal education had been taught two phrases. One of them was "paradigm shift." It had been coined by Thomas Kuhn in his *The Structure of Scientific Revolutions* (1962). It was a comforting thought, usually taken to mean that smart people could always completely change the way they thought, revolutionize everyone's lives, and keep the miracle of progress going. The other phrase was "the tragedy of the commons," which came from a 1968 article of the same name by the ecologist Garrett Hardin, itself based upon an English economist's 1833 essay, which had coined the term. The idea was that every individual, following his own self-interest, would seek to put more animals on a common pasture, so destroying it. To be fair, Hardin regarded this as an argument for declaring natural resources to be common resources and so preventing their ruthless exploitation. His only error was to call the exploitative way "the commons." I said the phrase to a well-educated colleague, referring to Leitza, and he responded, without letting me finish my sentence, "Ah, the tragedy of the commons!"

In Leitza, at least, the commons was not a Hobbesian free-for-all, but a carefully and exactly delineated compact. The 2015 revision of the *Ordenanza de comunales* defines who can have what common rights, how they are apportioned, what price or labor may be attached to each, and what will happen if someone ignores the law. The law covers nine legal-sized, single-spaced pages.

Common land is subject to all the same pressures of greed, of scheming and finagling, of nepotism, of good-old-boy favors as is any other system of land tenure. Also, as Inaque Iriarte Gona showed clearly in his *Bienes comunales y captilismo agrario en Navarra, 1855–1935*, the fact that particularly in the mountainous northwest of Navarre more than 97 percent of the land was held in common well into the twentieth century did not mean that the commons was an egalitarian paradise. The people who had the larger herds tended to get the better pastures, and you could horse-trade some rights on land you did own—the trees on your property, for example—for more rights on the common pastures. The well-off tended to remain so, but the poor never froze or starved. As Martin Luther King, Jr., said of the 1964 Civil Rights Act in the United States, "It may not change the heart, but it can restrain the heartless."

When in 1855, the newly aggressive national liberal government in Spain decided to assert itself, it did so with typical bluntness. It decided to imitate the English and seize the common lands. What the English had euphemistically called "the enclosures"—where lands held in common or by religious institutions were taken for private sale—the Spanish called frankly the seizures: the *desalojamientos*, or literally, the "throwing off the places." Paradoxically, however, where the English enclosures largely succeeded in privatizing the land, the Spanish, at least in Navarre, largely failed. Local authorities were reluctant even to answer the required questionnaires, and when asked questions about what land was commons and what was in private hands, they often said that they just weren't sure.

In part, this response was intentional obfuscation, but in the main, it was an honest admission that the existing system of the commons was enormously complex. In most places, the municipality ran the commons, but in some it was instead managed by neighborhood associations. There might even be common rights on royal lands, since the kings of Navarre had given the rights to pasture, water, and wood on their land in order to attract settlers, and many of these rights were still presumed. Sometimes, a common right was only for the people of the town, but sometimes for the whole province. To this day, any citizen of Navarre has the right to take his sheep to summer pasture in the *calizas* atop the Sierra de Urbasa.

Not only that, private land might have commons growing on it, and commons might have privately owned things growing on it. The grass growing on privately owned land might be used as commons. (In return, the owner might get more rights to take his animals onto other common lands.) On the other hand, a person whose house adjoined a fern patch—fern paved the floors of the winter *borda*—might harvest the fern off the commons for two years running and then assert his right to keep taking that fern for the future. If you planted trees on common land, you might have a private right to them. *Suelo y vuelo* was the shorthand for this confusing situation. Just because you had a right to the ground (*suelo*), you didn't necessarily have the right to what rose from it (*vuelo*), or vice versa. A parcel of common land might have three different people with three different rights on it: one who got the trees, one who got the ferns, and one who got the pasture. Some of these rights were subject to annual allotments among all residents. Increasingly—particularly as municipalities and the provincial government grew and required larger budgets—rights on the commons might be auctioned for a set period and the proceeds divided between the municipality and the province.

One of the central government's arguments for the seizures was that they would allow a more rational use of the land. But where the preservation and use of the land is concerned, perhaps rational use is not always the best use. At the beginning of the twentieth century the Spanish historian Joaquin Costa argued that agriculture, pasture, and forestry were better held in common, since only in common could they respond to nature with a suppleness that would allow both communities and their land to prosper. (Hardin would not have disagreed, I think.) The complexity of the system put a brake on rapid change and gave the common owners a chance to consider well what a given use might yield.

REMEMBERING THE FUTURE

At the Metropolitan Museum we are working to keep our trees young. We prune them to preserve them in their youngest stage of life. In Leitza and at Burnham Beeches and at Epping Forest in London, Helen Read and her colleagues are caring for ancient pollard beeches, some more than five hundred years of age, seeking to make old trees young enough to last, though she works with them in the third stage of their life, when they are growing down.

Read takes seriously Aragón Ruano's notion that these ancient, much used trees are monuments as important as cathedrals and castles, perhaps more so. In my native California when I was a boy, we learned that our hero John Muir regarded the groves of giant sequoia and redwoods in the high sierra and the coast ranges as cathedrals. They looked primordial and untouched, but in fact were the result of thousands of years of Indian craft and care (see page 207). The amazing groves of ancient beech trees in Europe—principally in England right in and near London, as well as in northern Spain and southern France—do not look in the slightest untouched. Their smooth gray trunks divide into huge rising fingers of wood that shoot straight up fifty or sixty feet into the air. They are forests of upraised hands, showing very clearly that they were cut and used by humans for hundreds of years, then let go to grow these astonishing ash-gray moon shots, but they are cathedrals just as surely as the sequoias are. Not only that, but these ancient trees even in their decay are the habitations of hundreds of beetles, pseudoscorpions, flies, lichens, mosses, and other creatures that once inhabited the wild wood, and now live nowhere else but in these ancient trees. Muir succeeded in making the big trees a stop on every tourist's itinerary. Why shouldn't these pollards be too?

The beeches are as seriously threatened as the big trees. When they were forgotten and let go, they began to grow in a way that cannot help but destroy them. Huge stems attached at the base to old cuts must in the long run fall apart in wind and storms, and sometimes even with-

Ancient beech pollards in a drawing by William Blake's disciple Samuel Palmer.

out these. Often, they cracked apart at the bole, or bolling. That is the place—usually six to ten feet above the ground—that they had last been cut during the early 1800s. Read must bring the trees back into relationship to people, if they are to survive, and even more than we do in front of the Met, she has no pruner to guide her, because she is doing something that has never been done. We can look to the past; she must look to the future.

More than half a million people visit Burnham Beeches, on the outskirts of London, each year, and almost as many go to Epping Forest. To preserve the trees is not only to help keep the visitors unharmed, but to make sure that they see before their eyes an alternative to the world they inhabit. There was a time when people did not devour things, crumple them up, and throw them away. It is a way to remember a possible future, when we will again live in the way the people lived among the beeches.

Burnham Beeches was and is a commons. It is open to everyone. It has been so for at least the last eight hundred years. In the past, the locals had rights to grazing and to pollard firewood. They might also have made charcoal to burn bricks. Once there were 3000 pollards of beech and oak here. The last firewood cut may have been as much as two hundred years ago; the last regular grazing stopped around 1920 (though they are now beginning it again). When Read arrived here in the 1990s, there were about 957 pollard left, but they were falling apart at an alarming rate. What was to be done?

The first thought was to cut the trees right back to the bolling, a cut one or two centuries old, and so let them start over again. But how to make the cuts? Alex Shigo, the American pruning visionary, had taught that a proper pruning cut was right to the parent limb, leaving no stub. The pruners decided to try that. And, although it is shade tolerant, beech does not grow well and does not regenerate branches when it is in deep shade. Many volunteer trees had grown up around the old pollards and were shading them out, so logic dictated that the new trees should be removed, opening up the beeches once more to the light.

The results were disastrous. Trees cut back to the bolling sprouted well the following year, but thereafter they rapidly declined and died. The "proper" pruning cuts removed the many dormant buds that typically lived in the stub just beyond the parent limb. And when the surrounding trees were removed, opening the beeches suddenly to the light, their bark scalded and the trees declined.

The pruners had to try to think like the trees. If a tree had been living on its erstwhile sprouts for two hundred years, it was a poor idea to remove its livelihood all at once. Instead, they began to remove only a selection of the older stems—maybe a fifth of them—and to take them back ten or fifteen feet, but not all the way to the bolling. To keep a good supply of dormant buds, they learned, it was almost always best to leave a long stub on each cut stem, at least a foot and a half. They made sure all the while to leave active smaller branches with plenty of leaves, young sprouts to draw up the sap from the roots. After an interval of ten to fifteen years, if the trees responded well, they cut them deeper.

In releasing the beeches from the shade, they also went more modestly. Calling it "halo cutting," they gradually pulled back the volunteer trees from around the ancient ones, sometimes only topping a volunteer, not entirely removing it, in order to bring light in gradually, a little at a time.

At Epping Forest, Jeremy Dagley was working the same way. Together, they have dramatically reduced the rate of tree failures. At the same time, they have started large numbers of new beech pollards. Read aims for a thousand new beeches, because no matter how well they care for the ancient trees, eventually those older beeches will go. The arborists play the role of the commoners, cutting new trees to begin the cycle again. For the new trees as for the old, modesty and response are the watchwords.

They will cut out the tops and one or two aggressive branches, wait for the tree to reply, and then cut again.

For Read and Dagley, the trees become their teachers. They have to be patient, responsive. In 1996, C. S. Holling and Gary K. Meffe wrote an essay in the journal *Conservation Biology* called "Command and Control and the Pathology of Natural Resource Management." In it, they showed how, in many different realms—in fire suppression in forests, in monoculture farming, in flood control dams, in the floodplain of the Mississippi River—the effort of human beings to impose their will upon a complex natural population led to disastrous unintended consequences. Likewise, the insistence upon making the trees look exactly "right," quickly, led to dead trees.

In 2003, Read was on a tour of Europe to look at its ancient pollards. She sought models to help her care for the trees at Burnham Beeches. When she got to the Basque country, she was overwhelmed. Beeches, oaks, chestnuts, ash, willows, alders, poplars, and more, all had been pollarded in profusion. Thousands and thousands of them still survived. Leitza was her paradise. Beech pollard was the staple crop, seconded by oak and chestnut. More than half the forestland was beech, maybe 5 percent was oak and chestnut. She met José Miguel Elosegui and his wife and the other people in town who cared about the woodlands.

The last of the Leitza iron foundries had closed sixty or seventy years prior. Since that time, most of the beeches had never been cut. Their rising stems had grown as thick as Doric columns. Many had failed in storms. In no uncertain terms, Read told anyone who would listen how important they were and how endangered. She spoke of their cultural and historical importance, of their crucial role as an ecological niche, of their beauty and fragility. "Before Helen came," remembered José Miguel Elosegui, "we didn't value the pollards. She opened our eyes." With José

Miguel's son, the forester Miguel Mari Elosegui, and a few people sent from the town council, they decided in 2005 to start pollarding again.

How should they cut the trees? At first, they followed the counsel of Miguel Barriola, who had distant memories of making charcoal in his youth. He had recalled that when as young men they had pruned the stems, they took them right back to the place that they had been cut before—that is, to the bolling. From a nest of Doric columns, they created what looked like the upthrust fist of a giant. They did the work in the waxing moon for beeches, in the waning moon for oaks. This was the timing that according to traditional wisdom got the best result.

A man named Gabriel Saralegi was there from the beginning, pruning the limbs with his sharp Urnieta axes. "We cut them way back at the beginning," he said, "just as we cut back hard the ash and the chestnut that we still pollarded." The response was good at first. When Read returned with a group of English arborists the following year to help with the work, she was troubled by the deep cuts. It was just what they had first tried on her London beeches. The Leitzans worked together with the English arbs but were puzzled by how little the English cut—sometimes taking off only fifteen feet from the top and sides, rather than thirty feet or more. They dubbed the cutting *"estilo inglés,"* English style. A group of young Spanish arborists from an association called Trepalari joined the party. Soon the three units were working together on a regular basis, exchanging traditions, experience, and hope.

At the end of 2017, they met again in Leitza for a conference that was properly dubbed, by Read's colleague Vikki Bengtsson, "a meeting of pollard geeks." There were talks, and there was fieldwork. Over the last twelve years, they had learned a great deal about how to restore the old beeches. Though the Basques still liked deeper cutting, they all agreed that it was important to leave some smaller leafy branches on the pruned tree. It was also good to leave "eyes," the closed wounds where small branches had previously been pruned, since these often had many dormant buds around their edges. For the same reason, they had learned to cut leaving stubs of branches or even natural tearaways. It was crucial to make sure that all the newly cut branches had access to sun, but not to suddenly expose them. In Leitza, said Miguel Mari, they now worked annually, adding a few more trees to the restored group each season. Of those that had been cut, seventy were doing very well, thirty were fair, and eight had died. The eight were distinguished by too deep cutting and too much shade. Likewise, as they began to form new pollarded beeches—a new generation eventually to replace the old—they needed to keep the new trees in the sun. Otherwise, the trees responded poorly.

In the field, two Trepalaris did the second cut on a beech that had first been pruned in 2007. One of them learned that when you cut with an axe, you have to be able to plant your feet and swing your hips, not so easy in the top of a tree. Samuél Álvarez, with his modern saw, danced around at his rope's end, pulling back branches by fifteen feet or more and leaving long tearaway wounds, which made it look as through the branches were sticking out their tongues. This was the polar opposite of Shigo pruning. It was a thing learned from thousands of years of culture, not only from nineteenth-century science. "*No es mutilar*"—It isn't mutilation—read the T-shirt one of the Trepalaris wore.

The effect of the pruning could be seen in the cross section of one branch that the arborists had just pruned. Its inner growth rings were so tightly packed they had to be cleaned and polished to even be counted; the outer ten rings—formed since the last cut—were bold and wide, each with as great a radius as all the inner rings combined. The latter represented the first fourteen years of the branch's life, when it had languished in the shade of other branches. The growth increment of the annual rings had been tiny. After the first cut seven years ago, the branch was released from the shade. It had grown like gangbusters, putting on large growth increments and very wide annual rings.

There had been twelve years of great practical study, like the learning of a shared language. The arborists had spoken in saw, and the beeches had answered in sprout. But why do it? Why spend all this time, energy, and intelligence on an old and superseded practice on trees that were already more than half dead?

Someone said that every civilization reaches a still point. The progressives can't go forward, and the conservatives can't go back. One demands continual advance, the other longs for yesterday. Both seem more than a little crazy. They growl and lunge at each other, like two packs of dogs in a small back alley. In that situation, the saying goes, you must use that stagnant point as the center and draw as large a circle as you can around it. That circle reaches much farther back in time, well beyond the short memory of the conservatives, and much farther forward, well beyond the sanguine hope of the progressives.

That, they say, is what opens the imagination and allows a way forward. It may be that a nuclear disaster, a pollution implosion—a third of the untimely deaths in the world are now from pollution—or both will occur, and then we will need desperately to know how to pollard again. God willing, no such thing will happen. Even if we never need to cut trees again as once we did, the larger circle draws on the well of deep memory. Burnham Beeches, Epping Forest and Leitza rise to the surface. We may not do exactly what they did for the reasons that they did, but they give us the power to imagine new ways to act like that. It is no longer a commons for wood or grazing, but a commons for the imagination.

THE RHYTHM OF TREES

The Guinea savanna of northwestern Sierra Leone contains both rain forest and tall grass savannas. In the savannas, woodlands run in crooked lines and patches along the rivers and creeks. The dry season lasts from November to February—dominated by hot dry winds off the Sahara—and the rainy season from May to October. The trees have mainly compound leaves. Each leaf with its many leaflets looks like a fronded fan, meant to cool you in hot weather. It acts as a cheap, throw-away branch. Some, like the orchid tree, are named for flowers as lovely as the catalpa's. Others yield food and medicine. *Dialium* and *Anisophyllea* grow to sixty feet or taller with straight trunks and long stems, so they are favored in building. Southward in the savannas the trees dwindle. The tall grass plains burn fiercely every year. Here, in a difficult place—the land of blood diamonds and of the Revolutionary United Front (RUF) insurgency—a coppice agriculture used trees to tell time. The rhythm of tree growth marked the farmer's years and kept the harvest constant.

In the late 1980s and early 1990s, the anthropologist A. Endre Nyerges studied Kilimi, a little corner of the savanna country that has since been made into a national park. About five people lived in each square mile of the land, roughly one-sixth of the average for all of Sierra Leone. Infant mortality was so high that people did not name their children until the babies survived the first few months.

The story of the founding of what was then Kilimi's principal village was itself a tale of woe. The founding chief, a warrior called Gulu Burai-rai, had crossed the river from Guinea, four generations prior. He had been tired, so he had taken off his war shirt and lain down to rest among the trees and the termite mounds. (Five-foot-tall termite mounds are a prominent feature of the landscape, like tiny ranges of mountain peaks.) When he arose, he found that the termites had devoured his shirt. For some reason, this made him want to stay there. He called his wives to him, and there they settled down.

That he had *kashkili*, or good sense—the mark of a leader in this land—was evident from the fact that four generations later the village was still there. More or less. In fact, it had recently been abandoned for a generation after a fire, and then rebuilt. Nyerges reported that he was told about and saw evidence of eleven different villages in Kilimi that had been abandoned within living memory. There were, when Nyerges studied, twelve active villages in the area, containing about six hundred people in all. Almost as many settlements had been abandoned as were intact. The ability to attract and keep people at a place was a real accomplishment in the sparsely populated savanna.

An elaborate social web was meant to help do the job. Being a founder or related to a founder allowed you to own the best land. If you were an elder male in that position, you were likely to be thrust into leadership. (If a younger brother showed *kashkili*, he might end up in conflict with his elder. In such cases, the younger would likely have left to found a new habitation.) Men and women both had their jobs in the fields. Although nominally inferior, women were the ones who controlled peanuts, the main cash crop. Men prepared and planted the fields for the subsistence crops, mainly rice, sometimes interplanting sorghum, millet, tomato, maize, chili peppers, okra, and sesame seed.

The elders used marriage to bring new workers to the village. The same old men were typically also the imams and the letter writers for the town. They controlled knowledge as well as land. They spread the story that an unmarried woman couldn't go to heaven and that a husband's prayers were necessary. At the same time, they organized the coming-of-age ceremonies for young girls as public spectacles to show off their talents and beauty. Shortly after, the girls were expected to marry.

The young men frequently came from elsewhere and were required to stay in the village once they were wed. They were almost always in a fix. They borrowed from their own parents to get the dowry to marry the girl, and once hitched, they owed the bride's parents and the new town what was called "bride service." In other words, they had to work in the fields. All they controlled were their bodies and their sweat. Doubly indebted, they could easily become disaffected. (A bride sometimes would return to her parents if the husband were behind in his service.) When the RUF and other insurgencies came into the area, they often found these rural young men to be willing recruits. Those with *kashkili* soon went off to found their own towns. It was a recipe for social fragmentation.

Nonetheless, in this difficult land, *kashkili* included a rare benefit: a way of farming that did not degrade the fragile land. Perhaps indeed *because* of the knife-edge of poverty on which they lived, the Susu peoples here found a way to get their staple foods perennially. They used the savanna trees as timers to tell them when to plant and when to leave be. Every fifteen to thirty years, a farmer cut down a patch of forest, planting rice and the intercrops in the opened dirt. That year, the farm bore fruit. Then it returned to forest. When the trees had reached their former height, it was time to cut again. And again. And again. In the plots he studied, Nyerges found coppice stumps that had been cut and recut at least three times, leading back to the beginning of the twentieth century.

Late in the dry season, usually in January, a *somoi*, or men's work group, started the new farm with a prayer. Then they cut the trees. leaving the stumps at waist height. They began with the small ones, those about two or three inches in diameter, cutting with machetes. In the next few weeks, they used axes on the larger sizes, although the biggest trees permanently remained. A good axe crew could cut trees up to about a thirty-six-inch diameter. The oil palm and a large *Nauclea*, related to the guinea peach, were usually among the trees that were kept. The one yielded palm oil, the other a large leaf in which to wrap foods like kola nuts for transport. Some larger old trees of coppice species were also left, their seeds reseeding the wood's floor. The coppiced stems became posts and wattle for houses or poles for fences, or the wood was used for cooking.

In April, before the rainy season began, the farmers burned the cut stems, leaving a black unsightly tangle. Unlovely as it may have looked, the cover of half-burned stems on the site preserved soil texture and prevented erosion. The ash fertilized the dirt. "You didn't walk through these fields," recalled Nyerges. "You climbed across them." Rice and intercrop seeds were broadcast into the massy black mess, giving them a start on the weeds that would jump up once the rains began. With short-handled hoes, the work crews lightly covered the seeds, twisting and bending to find their way among the burned stems. As everything grew up together, the farm looked more like a midden. The farmhands weeded once—pulling, not rooting out the weeds—but that was all. Tomatoes twined on maize, on sorghum, on cut trunks. Vigorous, tillering pearl millet fought it out with grassy sesame seed. Carrots, chilies, and okra staked out the periphery. Blue-eyed wandering Jew, purple witchweed, yellow nutsedge, Asian spike sedge, goat's beard, young man's trousers, cogon grass, Indian crabgrass, jungle rice, and about three dozen other weeds wound among them. The best sites were on bottomlands with a high water table, so no additional water was needed. No fertilizer was applied, since the woodland had spent the last two or three decades enriching the soil.

In the classical rotation, the farmers harvested most of the crops at the end of the season, picking their way through the tangled, tumbled field. The chili peppers were ripe in the second year. Thereafter, the land was left to the woods. In the first year after harvest, the trees had only just resprouted and weeds were everywhere. Three years later, the new canopy was more than fifteeen feet tall. Mona monkeys occupied the rising spring. Understory plants began to be shaded out. At seven years of age, the plot had a closing canopy twenty-five feet tall. After fifteen years, the trees had reached thirty feet and the canopy was fully closed. Green monkeys, chimpanzees, sooty mangabeys, and Guinea baboons lounged and leapt among the trees; warthogs roamed the understory. At this stage, sometimes the trees might be cut again. In the longer fallow, the woodland reached fifty or even sixty feet tall. Black-and-white and red colobus monkeys appeared. Finally, the farmers cut again.

Far from destroying the forest and extending the grasslands, the Susu preserved and restored the woodlands while getting the food they needed. Indeed, because villages were not permanent but shifting, the people even contributed their own towns to the woods. Fire was often the cause. The ferocious annual burn of the savannas sometimes overtook the towns. "The brush fires were everywhere," remembered Nyerges. "You found yourself running down a trail with the fire licking at your elbows." Villages might disappear in the flames.

It was a disaster, but not an unmitigated one. The human shit, the wooden houses, the middens, the kitchen gardens, the fabrics, the thatched roofs, all went into the dirt from which they came. The house walls and fences, which were made with poles cut from the coppice forest, also returned to the land. It took about a hundred poles to make a single house, and thanks to termites, the structure lasted only about seven years, even in the absence of fire. On these abandoned village sites, new forest sprung up quick and thick. A restored town usually appeared not on but near the old site. The elders thus remained near the place of the ancestors and founders, but also took advantage of the help the old place gave the woods. A village thus could turn into a farm.

At Kilimi, the Susu not only preserved the forest, they restored it, and Kilimi is not the only place in the African savanna where this regeneration agriculture has occurred. (Nyerges thought of calling it "phoenix agriculture.") The Sudanian savanna belt of southwestern Mali, for example, is drier and the fires fiercer than those in the Guinea savanna. There, some farmers use thirty-year fallows called *jaban*.

In 2008, Paul Laris decided to compare tree growth on the *jaban* and on nearby unfarmed forest. Typically, the long fallow farm would be cropped for three to five years, then let be for thirty years. The results were striking. The unfarmed area was a mixed bush, its patches of mainly multistem trees and shrubs interspersed with perennial grasses. The *jabans* by contrast were full of tall, straight-growing trees, often three or four times as tall. There were twice as many species on the fallows as on the unfarmed forests. In the former, trees sprouted evenly over the landscape, while in the latter, the tallest trees crowded the places where the dirt had been thrown up in termite mounds. Farmed and unfarmed land experienced annual burning, but the removal of perennial grasses and the hoeing and working of the ground on the farm plots both lessened the intensity of the fires and increased the number of young trees and the spread of their root systems. One local *jaban* owner expressed astonishment that the scientists were surprised by this effect. "Of course," he said. "Farming always makes more trees grow."

Like all human activities, however, these regenerative ways are deviled by temptation. A person may easily exchange love for power, the right thing for the thing that promises quick security. As Henry Nouwen wrote, "It seems easier to be god than to love God, easier to control people than to love people, easier to own life than to love life." In the wooded savanna, giving in to temptation meant shortening the fallows, to get more wood faster, to harvest more, and to allow for planting cash crops. The long fallow on the Sudanian savanna is becoming less common, and shorter fallows lead to tree loss.

In Sierra Leone, Nyerges thought that the coppice system as he studied it had been a corrective response to a previous period of rapine about five hundred years prior, when incoming Mandé-speaking tribes exploited the savanna woods not only for farming but for iron smelting. The Susu were known for their metal craft, and when Portuguese traders began to ply the African coasts in search of captives to turn into slaves, the Mandé-made iron bars were a first-rate trade item. The ships would stop in Sierra Leone, pick up slaves and iron, and sail on up the coast, trading the bars for more slaves and for ivory. (The first ship to sell slaves in the New World was a Portuguese vessel, in 1520.) The exponential rise in demand for slaves and for iron may well have tempted the farmer smiths to over-tax their land, coppicing too frequently and degrading the forests.

In the 1990s too, the *kashkili* of the elders was sometimes not a match for greed inflamed by insecurity. Both leaders and followers had their part in the temptation. There was not too little land in Kilimi. There were too few people. Anyone who cleared a farm (with permission) effec-tively owned it, but much of the work was done by work groups. The male groups were called *somoi*, as we have seen, and the female groups *kile*. They started and ended work with a song, the anthem of their gang. They sowed and weeded to drums. If a person came late, they might get a mock whipping; if slow, they might have a verse composed to celebrate their sloth. It was a hard life, but not a dull one.

The trouble is that there was too much work for all that the elders planned. Starting in the last decades of the nineteenth century, the Susu grew not only their subsistence crops but cash crops, newly introduced from the United States: chili peppers and peanuts (or groundnuts, as they are called in Kilimi, because the fruit is borne on the roots). The first of these was worked into the normal fallow system, as we have seen, but the peanuts need separate planting and far more weeding and care. Also, the groundnuts disliked the low wet ground that is favored by the rice.

Because the ground was already cleared and because the crews would need to weed for the peppers anyway, some elders decided to extend growing on the fallows into a second season, sowing peanuts in among the chili peppers on the land prepared and worked one year prior, then cleared and burned a second time. The *kile* did this. The second-year preparation was often too much for the stools of the coppiced trees. When their sprouts were knocked down by new cultivation, they did not return the following year. Instead, perennial savanna grasses and other open-land scrub extended their roots into the growing space. When the plot was abandoned, it was now savanna, not woodland. Furthermore, when the land chosen to farm was not the low wet fields that subsistence rice prefers but the rain-fed uplands that the peanuts favor, there was a risk that rice yields would be lower—in a poor year, disastrously so. As a final insult, there was now a cash market for Kilimi wood, to fuel fires in the capital city of Freetown, removing the old wood that feeds the dirt. To pay their debts, to remain big men, to give the orders, the elders might take risks with everyone's lives.

The way we treat the land is the way we treat each other, and the ways of humans to each other are as ecologically important as a water table. Wrong behavior ruined both people and the land around them. Jeremiah wrote, "How long will the land mourn, and the grass of every field wither? For the wickedness of those who live in it, the animals and the birds are swept away, and because people said, 'He is blind to our ways.'"

When the elders misbehaved—just as when the smiths sold iron to buy people—it both degraded the land and reduced the security of those beneath them. But their juniors were not slow to follow suit. Indebted, overworked, and powerless, the young men in Kilimi sometimes got permission to farm young fallows near the village. Here was land that had been cropped only five or six years before, not even halfway to its minimum fallow, but it was near enough to home that they could work it when their other tasks were done. (Many fields were an hour and a half walk, or more, from town.) The crops grown on this land were predictably sparse and poor. Worse, the premature working let the open savanna plants get the upper hand. It is no wonder that these men were ready recruits for the RUF, who promised freedom, reform, wealth, and a new way of living, though they actually provided hunger, warfare, looting, and rape.

Temptation degraded both land and people, but during the time Nyerges studied Kilimi, about two-thirds of the plots were still maintained in the traditional long rotation. After that time, the RUF swept over the savanna, along with AIDS, Ebola, and the struggle to control and exploit alluvial diamonds. The wealthy West had mainly been concerned with how to extract the maximum resources from the lands without much care about how it was done. One group of fighters in many conflicts were private contractors hired by a corporation or by private investors.

Then the World Bank arrived, followed by philanthropists, intent on helping the savanna's people. They provided money to forward an ambitious goal: "to develop 100 new crop varieties in five years, so farmers can double or triple yields within 20 years." They wanted nothing short of an

African Green Revolution. What a change from the previous years! It must have made the Susus' heads spin, but it is as easy for well-meaning as for ill-meaning outsiders to misunderstand the African land.

In 1948, an expedition from Cambridge University had gone to study moist forest sites in Nigeria and Benin. They were looking for virgin forest. The Nigerian Forestry Department had sent them to a mature climax forest in Benin, but as soon as the researchers put a spade into the dirt, they turned up bits of pottery, charcoal from hearth fires, the remains of villages, all deep in the putatively pristine forest. "Most of the land, which now carries some of the finest forest in West Africa," wrote P. A. Allison in 1962, "has been farmed at one time or another during the past few hundred years." It was a surprise to the researchers, who had believed that farmers were the ones who had destroyed such virgin forests.

The experience of the Turkana, four thousand miles east of Kilimi, was emblematic of how far from helpful outside help can be. After a year in college, early in the twenty-first century, my stepson, Jacob, had the chance to spend time in a small Catholic mission in Turkana. This region lies in northern Kenya, near the borders with Somalia and Ethiopia. It took two days to drive over almost roadless terrain to the mission. After hours in the desert, they approached an immense turquoise lake. On its shores stood a modernist building that would not have looked out of place in Oslo. "What the heck is that?" Jake asked. He had been told the lake was home to ten thousand crocodiles and not to get too close to any because they were fast on land as well as water. He was ready for the reptiles, but not for this product of European largesse.

In 1971, a Norwegian-government-sponsored aid project built a plant to freeze fish from Lake Turkana—where hundred-pound Nile perch are as common as the crocodiles—and also built a road to the nearest city, so the fish could be distributed. The whole package cost about $22 million. Unfortunately, the amount of electricity needed to run the plant each day was as much as was then produced in all of the Turkana region. The generators to make it actually happen would have made the fish too expensive to buy or sell. Not only that, the tribes in the local area were resolutely herders, not fishermen, and they did not see why they should change. "It's 100 degrees in the shade here!" said Jacob. "What were they thinking?" They were thinking like Norwegians, not Turkana.

When he reached the mission, on the other hand, the aid they offered was almost invisible. The fathers had a well and ran a vegetable garden. If people asked about it, they showed them what they grew and how. If they asked about the well, they pointed to their vintage truck, fitted with a drill rig. It occurred to the Turkana that with a well of their own, the women would not have to spend half the day hauling water. "Yes," said the fathers. "We can dig you a well. How many goats is it worth to you?" They haggled and came up with a price.

Father Mark Lane from Brooklyn was with them one day when they went to a village to dig a well. He told the story in a homily. After a jarring ride over roadless country with sparse grass and scattered acacia trees, they came to the place. The head men were there, and so was a herd of goats. The fathers counted the goats. They came up about two dozen short. "No deal," they said. "Where are the goats we agreed upon?"

The Turkana men hemmed and hawed. It had been such a bad year, such a dry year, the intertribal raids had been worse than usual, they just couldn't come up with quite that many goats. Surely, the fathers understood.

One of the priests called to the trucker who was erecting the drill rig on the truck's back. "Stop," he said. "It looks like these people haven't got the price." The man started to lay the rig back down in its place in the truck bed.

"Hold on!" said one of the Turkana. "I thought you were here to help us."

"We are," said the father. "But we need you to pay the price."

Father Mark said that at the time he thought, The guy is right! What are we doing charging them in goats? They are poor and drought stricken. If they haven't got a few of the goats so what? But he said nothing.

Sure enough, before the hour was out, the missing goats appeared and were exchanged. The rig was erected again, and the digging commenced.

Later, Father Mark and the other priest discussed the price. "I had to make them pay it," said the priest. "Otherwise, I would not be treating them like my equals, like fellow human beings."

Modesty and honesty are important in dealing with people who have long traditions of caring for their own land. The Turkana revere their sparse but critically important trees. The most important is *Acacia tortilis*, the umbrella thorn. Urban Kenyans and some foreign aid workers accused the tribespeople of destroying their sparse tree cover by overgrazing, by feeding their stock on pollarded branches, by cutting down trees for firewood and housing. In recent decades, laws have been passed prohibiting the Turkana from pollarding the trees for stock fodder or for burning.

The people do not use wood but dung for burning. They know the value of the trees that are the only shade in a hot dry land. They pollard the trees to give the cattle and goats crucial feed at the end of the dry season, but they are confident (and right) that the trees will sprout back. Indeed, the corrals where they keep the stock safe overnight become a nursery for new thorn trees. The animals that have fed on acacia pods, either on the trees or in the cut fodder, drop seeds robed in dung into the night corrals. There the seeds sprout prolifically and grow quickly. Thickets of acacia in the landscape often mark where corrals once were located.

Real help comes from living with people, helping them to make their lives steadier, not by prescribing progress for them. In the 1960s, an outside group introduced oxen and plows to work lowland areas in central Sierra Leone for rice and other subsistence crops. It seemed that oxen on heavy swampland would reduce the total labor needed, both for planting and for weeding. Then, the aid workers went away. More than two decades later, an anthropologist returned to see what had become of the project. "It's good to see you!" the people cried. "We have repaired these plows again and again, but now we need to buy new plowshares!" They were still living as they had lived, singing their songs, marrying and dying in their own ways, but with less worry about a shortage of labor.

Maybe it is time that helpers learned from the rhythm of trees. A cut tree is not a dead tree, but a tree that is coming back again. It times planting, restores savanna, fertilizes ground, and gives villages structure, medicine, and food. If you want to help, why not build on the *kashkili* that is already there?

STANDING AND SITTING

From the Bronze Age until the end of the twentieth century, Norwegian farming depended upon pollards, but as the turboprop came in to land at Sogndal Airport in the western fjord country, I wondered how anyone could farm there at all. From the air, the landscape appeared to be composed of blunt-topped mountains whose steep sides plunged straight into sapphire blue water. Most of the mountains had patches of autumn snow on the high couloirs, remnants of the previous winter. There were still several active glaciers, caused not only by the cold climate but also by the short winter days and the quantity of snow on the heights. There were houses and barns in places that looked impossible to reach without rock climbing. Only a third of Norway is below 1000 feet above sea level, and almost a fifth is higher than 2500. As the pilot made his approach, he descended to a level where a fjord was several thousand feet below. The airport's mountainside rose up suddenly to meet him, so in the end, he did not descend to the tarmac at all. He simply pointed in the right direction and pulled in, like a city dweller finding a parking place. Who could farm such a place?

The Gulf Stream and the prevailing west winds off the water make the Sognefjord a much less unwelcoming land than it seems from the air. It is almost as warm as coastal New York in the winter, as long as you are in the narrow zone on the hillside between the water and the heights. Up high and down low are colder, sometime dramatically so. Near its western end, where it joins the Atlantic Ocean, the 127-mile-long Sognefjord is the wettest place in Europe, though at the eastern end only a quarter as much rain falls. Microclimate is not an adequate word to describe the way the weather changes from one place to another in western Norway. "Picoclimate"—the prefix means "one-trillionth"—might be better. A few hundred yards from where you stand, the temperature may be 5 degrees colder. Yet in this unlikely and churningly changing landscape, people who in the main could neither read nor write created the most intelligent way of farming that the West has ever known.

The Psalmist sang, "Truth will spring out of the earth, and righteousness look down from heaven." It does not at first blush look like a description of farming. Perhaps in scholar and clergyman Eugene Peterson's colloquial translation of the Bible, called *The Message,* it is a little more understandable. He makes it, "Truth sprouts green from the ground, right living pours down from the skies." When I asked Ingvild Austad, the great student of traditional farming in western Norway, why a few farmers still insisted upon the old pollard-farming ways, she had several clean, precise-scientist answers. One was the brother and sister farm. It was often the oldest son who took over the farm from his parents and the oldest daughter who cared for the parents as they grew older. When the elders died, the unmarried children wanted things to stay the same as they had always been. Farms run by children's children almost always modernized. Austad paused. Then she said, "But what a lot of these farmers told me is that it was for religious reasons. This is what God wanted them to do."

It doesn't sound like a credible or testable hypothesis, but it may indeed be precisely what the farmers were aiming at. Truth, in biblical terms, is not a gold star on your notebook. It is an honest relationship between persons and the world around them, giving results that mirror an honorable intent. The prophet Isaiah made an equation between sprouting and farming on the one hand and right living on the other: "For as the soil makes the sprout come up and a garden causes seeds to grow, so the Lord will make righteousness and praise spring up before all nations." Right living was a response to God's gifts.

In western Norway, a farm was not a place but an itinerary. The words *stolen* and *seter*, standing and sitting in old Norse, appear again and again in the names of farms. There are people and pasture grasses with the two words in their names. Lars Grinde farmed *Grindeseter*, or Grinde Farm, as had his father and his father's father, but the farm was not named for them. Rather, they took their name from the farm, as had uncounted generations before them. Grinde Farm, on the heights above the Sognefjord near present-day Liekanger, has been farmed continuously since the Bronze Age.

Ingvild Austad has studied Lars Grinde's holding for four decades. When I first visited, it was a wet day. We looked at the few, less steep places where Lars grew his cabbage, his potatoes and his grain. We saw the sloping pastures where he grazed his cattle and his sheep at the home farm. Western Norway depends upon its animals. Without them to convert green plant energy into milk, butter, cheese, meat, manure, leather, and wool, it would not have been possible to live here.

We were walking along a narrow sheep track in an infield pasture. The fjord stretched away from us five hundred feet below. Austad pointed to elms, ash, birch, and other trees, lower on the slope, that had been pollarded every five years, until Lars became too old to keep them. Now they were growing tall with many stout branches. One had fallen over in a storm. When we started down the hill to examine it closely, my feet went out from under me. I slid a man's length down the hill like a ballplayer sliding into home plate. Austad expressed alarm, but when I got up, she chuckled. I had a brown stripe on one leg from the top of my socks to my thigh joint. If you don't stand or sit on a farm in western Norway, you may well fall, because not very much of it is flat.

To make a living, the farmer had to range each year from fjord-side— the *fjora*, the land between the tides—to the highest mountain valleys. It was very much like the vertical economies of Neolithic Europe, harvesting an entire landscape from its depths to its heights. Indeed, many students now extend the continuity back to the Mesolithic, when there is the first evidence of the dung of grazing animals and the appearance of cereal grains. It is very likely that what evolved in western Norway harmonized the gatherer economy with the beginning of the agricultural way of life. In this landscape, both continued well into the twentieth century of our era.

Each farm depended on the exact possibilities of the given land. Standing, sitting, walking, digging, cutting, stacking, drying, storing, the family walked with their herds from sea level to 2500 feet high during the course of the year. At the fjord, you might harvest seaweed to fertilize the cropland, and you certainly caught fish for the table. At night, the herring fishermen were often abroad. They lit the water to attract the fish. You saw the crisscrossing of shining points of light across the dark scrim of water, the stars overhead. Before electrics, they used torches. The fish guts and the fibrous bones went into the potato, cabbage, or cereal fields.

The main farm, however, was seldom located right at the fjord. Starting at about 300 feet elevation and up to about 1000 was the place for the *heimseter*, the home settlement. In the picoclimate of this furrowed landscape, the shape of the surrounding mountains affects where the sun comes. In some places, because of the size and shape of the facing peaks, direct sun disappeared in October and did not come back until April. A few hundred feet west or another few hundred up the hill, the sun might make her appearance twice as often. Elevation was only one factor in choosing where the main farm was to go.

Still, the middle elevations were almost always the warmest. The sun never comes straight down in these northern latitudes. It always hits the ground at an angle. Thus, if you were standing on a steep middle slope, the sun's rays might come straight at you. Cold winter winds flow down the steep mountainsides, so the land at the water is almost as cold as it is on the heights. Where the water was salt, it did not freeze, but lake water did, so it was even colder in the freshwater lowlands. You harvested by the water, but you did not want to live there.

The sun pointed right at the best place to settle. Before the land reforms of the nineteenth century, most farms had a cluster dwelling place, where seven or eight extended families might live together. It amounted to a small town. All had holdings on the named farm. In the old days, the nearby fields were divided into strips and shared out or traded among the group members. Each was a private holding, some for crops and gardens, some for grazing cattle, sheep, and goats, some for hay, and some woodland, almost all of it pollarded.

You couldn't make a living on the main farm alone. Had the farmers stayed only there, they would quickly have worn down the land and the woods. Instead, every year they followed the green as it spread up the hillsides in spring, then back down in autumn. Sometimes, in April, they would even put the sheep and goats in a boat, rowing them down the fjord to the first patches of grass growing on a sunny isle or on the opposite side. Each farmer had at least two farms, and most had three or four: a main farm, a spring farm, a summer farm, an autumn farm.

There was often a fixed date upon which they would plan to set out from the main farm, but the weather was so changeable that in fact most waited for other cues. In one place, they looked for a snowfield to divide into three parts, while in another, they went when a snowfield took the shape of a swan. On one farm, they waited every year for a particular avalanche. They called it "the cow avalanche." Lars Grinde waited on his animals. "They knew when it was time," he said. "They would just start out." Because a farmer kept each sheep for a decade and each cow for twice that, the old hands in the herds knew where they were going and felt the moment to go.

If you tried to force an early date, things could go ill. Once at a settlement named Bjerganne, the farmers wanted to get off the home-farm fields fourteen days before midsummer. One reason to take the stock aloft was to keep them from ruining the growing crops or eating down the hayfields. There were no fences. If it were an early year for the infields, there was a temptation to get the animals away sooner. That year, they set out for the summer farm, but had to spend a whole day clearing snow at the river, so the cows could cross. "We never tried that again!" they said.

The spring farm helped. It was a way station, often on a plateau just a little up the valley, a few hundred feet higher than home. The farmer looked for a place that had grazing and where at least one field might also be mowed. (It couldn't be too rocky or too steep.) The cattle and the sheep would feed in the meadows through the late spring. There might be trees that could be pollarded, or there might not, depending upon sun, stone, and slope. The spring farm was near enough home that you could come down in the evening, carrying the day's milk with you. There it would be consumed or made into longer-lasting butter and cheese. At Lars Grinde's spring farm, they stayed overnight, milked the cows in the morning, brought the milk down, worked on the home farm for the day, and went back up to milk the cows in the evening. After the animals had gone up to the summer farm, men from the main farm would hay the spring farm meadow, storing the fodder in a stone or a wooden barn. In winter they would come up with sleds to bring the hay home.

The summer farm was different. Hold up your arm in front of you. Point it at an angle toward the ceiling. Hold your palm open facing upward. If the home farm is at your elbow and the spring farm where that big vein they take the blood from dives too deep to see, your open palm represents the summer farm. High and far. It was half or more often a whole day's walk from home. The people who kept it lived there for most of the summer—from four to ten or twelve weeks, depending on the location and its picoclimate. They were women and children. The women and girls milked the animals and made butter and cheese. The boys watched over the grazing herds.

Anestolen. Frudastolen. Boystolen. Standings. Places where the cattle would stand to be milked and where the sheep would stand around grazing. A summer farm was seldom on an exposed slope. It was in an open bowl at the head of a valley with the peaks cupping up around it: rock, rock, rock, and grass, a river running through it. Pollarded birch forests lined it, though you had to be careful cutting birch. If you overcut it, it did not respond. (The wood is crucial to feed fires to make cheese. If there were none, people had to bring their own peat or wood.) The bowl kept the animals with their child herders in place and in sight, and it brought water to the standing, not only for drinking and cooking but to keep the milk cool. You can still see where a pool in the creek was pent with stones to hold the crocks. Spreading out below might be fields or even a tarn. It could be very rocky ground, subject to avalanches in the winter and the spring. The view focused down the valley, sometimes to a bend in the range, sometimes to the fjord twenty miles distant.

Life was closely organized on the summer farm. The habitations had two rooms: one for sleeping and resting, the other for work. The business end of the hut had a chimney and a stove, where the women made the butter and the cheese. Nearby were one or more sheds for the animals. On the cow side, sticks leaning against the wall made separate stalls. On the sheep side, there was a common pen with a sunken area to collect the dung. Both cow and sheep manure was swept up and stored in another house. Later, it would go to the main farm as fertilizer. If there was enough season and enough land to mow, there was a barn to store the hay.

Every summer farm was a meeting place. Different holdings used the same high valley, and their houses, barns, and sheds were mingled, in the rocky places that were no good for grazing. (They didn't put a building where an animal could feed.) Here was where you got to spend time with neighbors whom you might otherwise seldom see, except to say good night or to wave across a deep ravine. Here, too, came friends of the family or younger sons who had gone off to Bergen or to Christiana or later even to Minnesota, and who were home for a visit. During the week, it was just women and children, but on Saturday and Sunday?

We like to think that modern life created leisure and so made the weekend. Before the blessed five-day week, life was not only nasty, brutish and short, but also a constant round of backbreaking work. The women and children on the summer farm indeed were not at leisure. They had as much work to do as when they were home, but it was a different place, with more and different friends. During the week, the women had a chance to be alone. There was time to sit and talk, to compare notes, to sing, to tell stories among themselves. And on the weekend, the whole world came to them.

I asked Lars Grinde about going to his summer farm, *Steinsete*. He smiled, hummed a tune, and held his arms in front of them, rocking as though with a partner in the dance. Every Saturday, one man with a horse had to go up to the summer farm to collect the butter and the cheese, bringing it back to market. It appears, however, that many men accompanied the horse. It is likely that more troths were plighted and more children conceived on the summer farms than after the more famous Midsummer's Night bonfires in western Norway on the twenty-third of June. (The Norwegian landscape painter Nikolai Astrup painted these bonfire dances many times, and some of them show on the edge of the reveling a solitary pregnant girl, her hands on her belly.) The women made tangy sweet summer farm food, like *setermat*, out of the yellow whey left over from their work and mixed with smoked salt meat and blueberries, or *ystingsoll*, out of sour cream, cottage cheese, whole milk, and prim. They walked and talked while the moon rose. The young people who had moved away got to know their old friends again. They sang songs derived from the cow and goat calls, high-pitched songs that could carry across the whole bowl of the mountain valley, or danced to a fiddler's tune. (A good fiddler sometimes claimed he had learned to play from a waterfall. He might sacrifice a ham to the white water as thanks.)

On Sunday afternoon, the men and their horse wound their way down to the main farm. The women went back to work and the kids to watching the animals. Perhaps it was they, twenty-five hundred years ago, not we in the twentieth century, who invented the weekend. These were not rare events. Before the end of the nineteenth century, there were seventy thousand summer farms in Norway.

In late August, the land cooled. The green faded down the valley. By early September, there might be fresh snow on the peaks. They brought the animals down, often again to the farm they had used in the spring or sometimes to a separate autumn farm for two or three weeks, and then back to the main farm. It was said to be bad luck to move the animals up to the summer farm on Saturday or Sunday—likely because it would have meant missing a weekend—but it was good form to bring them down on a Saturday. The whole valley rang with the sound of a hundred lowing cattle and several hundred belled and bleating sheep. (The latter still come down through the paved streets of Leikanger, leaving a trail of dung.)

The main farm threw a party. Homecoming. The fiddlers were out again and the singers. The same people who had mingled on the summer farm were together one more time before they went their separate ways to prepare for the oncoming winter. Likely, not a few had paired off over the summer, so for the first time they would be going home together. When people look for the origin of American homecoming parties at high schools, colleges, and towns—usually centered around a football game in early autumn—they might look way before the nineteenth century. . . . Maybe the fourth or fifth century. BC. Summer vacation. The weekend. Homecoming. These are not the fruits of modern wage labor or liberal democracy. They are impulses of the human heart as old as the summer farms, at least.

For all their intelligent transhumance and all their sensitivity to the picoclimates of western Norway, however, these ancient farms could not have lasted a decade without their trees. Only about a tenth of the land in this country can grow crops or pasture. No matter how carefully you harvested and stored and from how many farms you cut grass hay, you could not cut enough to last the winter. About a sixth of the land was woods. Ash and elm were the most common trees near the fjord. Everywhere else, it was the birches. Linden was also to be found, along with oak, willow, alder, hazel, juniper, rowan, and aspen. Some had special uses: linden bast—the stringy inner bark of the tree—was used to make rope. Hazel was coppiced and split to make barrel hoops. Oak went for shipbuilding, for house posts, and for watertight barrels. Juniper was selected for tall single-stem plants that made the best fence posts and hay drying racks. Young alder, birch, and willow stems made a rough-and-ready twine to knit bundles. But the indispensable use of trees was for what they called *laufkjerv*: leaf hay.

In Norway, the rest of Scandinavia, and the whole northern world, broadleaf trees were pollarded and coppiced on a short cycle of four to six years. Alder, willow, and sometimes rowan were coppiced, cut straight to the ground. The rest of the trees were pollarded, started with a heading cut at six to eight feet above grade and then trained to grow outward with scaffold stems that could be cut back in rotation perennially. The stems were allowed to get almost as big around as a man's arm, which kept a high ratio of leaves to wood. (On a longer rotation, you get more wood, fewer leaves.) Some of the farmers cut the branches in late summer, while the leaves were green and still nutritious. Others lopped the smaller, leaf-bearing stems off the big ones. They gathered clutches of them under their arms, bundled and tied them with whippy rowan or birch twigs, and dried the bunches on poles, trees, or racks. On some farms, they built the bunches into rain-shedding concentric stacks of two or three hundred bundles.

Nowadays, Lars Grinde used a bow saw for most of the cutting, and some other farmers used a chain saw, but for thousands of years the main tool was the leaf knife. Even before metal tools, a sharp-edged stone hand blade could be used for the same purpose. For this reason, it was possible to feed leaf hay to the animals in winter hundreds of years before it was possible to use a metal scythe to cut grass hay. A good sharp leaf knife could get through an arm-sized stem in four good blows. "*Tuk, tuk, tuk, swsh*," said Lars Grinde, suggesting the rhythm and sound of the cutting. I have used a leaf knife. It is about the size of Captain Hook's hook. It extends your hand in a short thick comma of sharpened iron. The main way to get hurt on the farm was to drop a leaf knife and try to catch it, or to fall out of a tree while you were holding one.

The average farm holding in western Norway had six to ten cattle and calves—until recently, the small native breed *vestlandskyr*—twenty-five to thirty sheep or goats, and a horse or two. It took between 2500 and 3000 bundles of leaves to keep them fed through the winter. A good family team could cut, make and hang 50 or 60 bundles per day, taking 15 or 20 from each tree. They took the ash first, then the elm, then the other trees. The daily yield was about 100 pounds of ash or 200 pounds of elm. It took almost two months to harvest the leaf hay. For fourteen days, they dried it, and then it was stored in the barns.

There were small woodlands on rocky piles of scree and other unfarmable places, but most of the trees were along the edges of fields and meadows. The hay harvests went hand in hand. First, the reapers brought in the early grass hay, then pollarded the trees for the leaf hay, then in autumn took the second harvest of the grass. The haymakers worked barefoot, digging their toes into the sod on the steep meadows. To get the fodder in, different farms often shared their labor, even if it meant crossing the fjord.

The cutting of the trees stimulated faster and thicker meadow growth. Typically, groups of trees were pollarded in succession, year by year, so there were five different states of regrowth. A novel ecosystem of invertebrates, fungi, lichens, and other creatures inhabited the trees as they regrew. Where trees had recently been cut, the pasture grasses grew thicker and quicker, not only because they got more light where the branches had been cut back but also because small dying tree roots— the roots retrenched when the trees were pruned—contributed organic matter to the soil. The grasses were grazed twice in the season, so they had the manure, as well as the feet of the animals, opening up the sod. Early grazing kept down the most aggressive grass species. Furthermore, because the stock grazed in pastures from the high mountain to the fjord, they ate a diet of both mountain and valley grass species, carrying each of them up and down the mountain as they went, distributing them with their manure. The meadows on the farms were thus rich in species from all elevations. As happened in virtually every place in the world where pollarding or coppicing were conscientiously practiced, the result was a habitat of greater, not lesser, diversity than the untouched land. The pruned woodland edges promoted a wide range of species, both under their shade and in the pastures at their margins.

Meadows beside pollards were more productive. One third to one half more grass hay came off a field surrounded by pollards than from an open meadow or from one where the trees had never been cut. The grazed and mown fields with their edging of trunks and stone walls were a delight to look at. We are taught the Anglo-American ideal of a garden of lawn and trees is a novelty, but it is likely that it is actually a distant memory of such ancient wood pastures.

Leaf hay and grass hay. Both were heavy to carry on your back, but that is what every farmer had to do. It was not so bad going downhill, though you might well slip and roll, but it was hell going up. Usually, the carrier would sit down on the slope and sling a rope of linden bast and twisted twigs over his back. People would pile the hay against him, gathering it tight with the rope, the end of which they handed to the carrier over his back. Then, the trick was to rise. You had to plant and twist on your left knee, then spin up into a standing position. Ingvild demonstrated, but without the weight on her back. When you were up, you were generally looking straight uphill. Not an encouraging sight. When metal wire became common, it must have been a delight to rig a sky line that could ride the hay uphill and downhill through the air.

Hard as the work may have been, there is no more beautiful farmland in the world than the infields of western Norway as autumn comes on. The pollarded ash stretch downhill toward the fjord like broad-shouldered giants. Fences made of old straight ash poles from the pollarding of former years run in ranks across the steep meadows, each fifty feet long or longer, and each completely covered with panels of drying grass. (A large farm might have four hundred of them.) It is almost as though the grass-rug merchants had hung out their wares for the giant trees to look at as they promenaded, a fjord-side version of the bookstalls and stamp merchants along the Seine in Paris. Stacks of leaf bundles stand twelve feet high, made of concentric whorls of leaves. Other bundles are hung to dry on new pollards, on ash or elm stakes, on piles or rough gray boulders, or even on the sides of barns. It is easy to see why this land is said to be full of supernatural beings. All of them look alive.

During the winter, the animals would get grass hay in the morning, leaf hay at noon, and grass hay again in the evening. Only the sheep and goats got alder, since its leaves gave an acrid taste to milk. The sheep also got birch, hazel, linden, bird cherry, and even oak. The cattle ate elm, ash, goat willow, and rowan. Elm and ash were most nutritious, and the stock liked them best. The farmer tended to keep them for last, feeding the alder, birch, willow, and other species first. A saying kept in mind the relative virtue of the main fodders:

Animals get fat on elm.
Get fed on ash,
Survive on alder,
Starve on willow.

Leaf hay was a mainstay. It had more protein, more sugar, and more vitamin B_{12} than did grass fodder. In Sweden in the nineteenth century, when the counting mania began, it was calculated that the sheep and goats across the nation ate 191 million bundles each winter. Still, leaf hay alone was sometimes not enough to get through the winter. There were other ways to call on the trees for help, without destroying them. One was to pluck the leaves from elm and from ash in later summer. In the first two years after pollarding, you had to leave the trees alone. During the third and fourth years, you might harvest the leaves just after they had made most of the food the tree needed but before they began to yellow. The leaves were dried in bags and fed to the animals in the cold season. Even if the leaves were left until autumn, they might still be harvested or at least raked up to use in the barns for bedding.

In later winter, as the buds swelled on the ash and particularly on the elm, there were two other sources of food. Some trees were not low-pollarded by topping. Instead they were left to grow to fifty feet or more in height. The intrepid climbed them in February and March, lopping the young stems off large branches. They called it *ris*, or shredding. It made the pruned trees look like immense bottle brushes. The sheep loved the fat buds. On different elms, people might leave the branches alone but harvest strips of bark. Mixed with water, this *skav* made another late-season food for sheep and goats.

In western Norway, the farmers created and maintained this way of life for at least four thousand years. In 1981, there were only fifteen farmers in the middle Sognefjord still harvesting leaves, and they collected only a few hundred, not a few thousand, bundles each year. Many of the old outfields had been turned into spruce plantations, a government-subsidized venture that gathered strength through the 1960s. Most of those who still harvested did so only for their sheep, thinking it better for the animals' health. With feed concentrates, fertilizers, and improved breeds of everything, it was hard for a small farmer in the middle of nowhere to find a market for his goods.

Over in Kussalid, above the Fordefjord, Kare Solhaug was a young man trying to make the old ways new. He had about a hundred sheep and a hillside full of ancient elm pollards. Some were as much as three hundred years old. When he started to cut them again, many had been let go for thirty years. Some died, others fell over. He has been moving young elms up the hill and planting them in the pastures as replacements. He still harvested the leaves on a five-year rotation, but he did not hang them out to dry.

Solhaug had an old wood chipper about the size of a refrigerator on wheels. "Maybe this year is the year it dies," he said, patting it gently. He hauled the chipper up the hill behind his tractor. Instead of laboriously cutting and binding the cut stems, he threw them all through the chipper. Five days of work the old way fit into one mechanized day. The chipped branches went into the barn, where a big fan labored to dry them. When we visited, it was a very windy day, what they call back in the Sognefjord community of Laerdal a *lauftorkinvind*, a leaf-drying wind. Solhaug wished he could order up this wind every time he cut.

In the winter, about 20 percent of the fodder for the sheep came from these leaves. They plucked the leaves out of the mass of the wood, leaving the chips behind. In spring, he used the chips for bedding during lambing. It was not as efficient as feeding concentrates, and it was hard work cutting and chipping, but he said that the sheep love to pick through the mass to get the leaves. And he liked to do the work. Just as he left some of the elms large—"all the same size is boring"—so he stuck to pollarding. It kept him interested, deeply connected to his farm.

Solhaug is not the only one trying to remake a landscape of grazing ecology and leaf hay. In West Sussex, a former farm on the Knepp Castle Estate is now beginning to use grazing animals—cattle, pigs, sheep and even deer—to once more make diverse landscapes composed of dynamic edges between woodland and pasture. Even in the United States, the idea is beginning to take hold. In Maine, with its long winters, the Maine Organic Farmers and Gardeners Association (MOFGA) sponsors classes and conferences in leaf fodder and wood pasture.

I asked Lars Grinde what was his favorite job on Grinde Farm. "Pollarding," he responded without hesitation. You can see it in his trees. He thought about which way the branches would go, and he cut them to make shapes that at once made the best leaf-bearing and that were beautiful in every season. A lot of sculpture is not half so good. He used a particular word to describe the "liking": *hyggelich*, a word that translates literally as homely, but that means a thing that is pleasing and lovely in an absolutely everyday way.

Once, in New York, I was approached by an artist. She told me she was having trouble with some trees she had used in an installation. I swallowed. This did not sound promising.

"Here," she said. She handed me a photograph. She had somehow managed to hang half a dozen red maples upside down in the air, their roots in containers over their heads, their crowns hanging down. The cross between a trapeze rig and a steel mill that had made this possible was an ingenious device, and the trees were certainly both alive and upside down.

"What is the trouble?" I asked.

"Well," she said. "It's obvious, isn't it? The bottom of the trees keep trying to grow upward!"

I looked at her with my mouth half open. I wondered if this was actually some kind of performance art in which I was the unsuspecting straight man for a macabre comedy routine. I could see no one with a camera nearby, though perhaps she was wearing a wire.

I said in measured tones, "You cannot expect the crown of a living tree to grow downward. In order to live, its leaves must find the sun." It was hard to believe that a person of such obvious intelligence did not know this. I believe I suggested she might put mirrors on the ground beneath the crowns. The tree might at least get some of its light from the reflection, but I doubted it would really keep the trees from trying to grow back upward.

While I was walking along a line of Lars Grinde's pollarded ash trees bending down toward the Sognefjord, I thought how beautiful they were, and the inverted red maples came unbidden to mind. This farmer had not set out to make an installation. He had to feed his sheep in a place that was challenging and to live in the presence of his days. But what he made in the course of that work was orders of magnitude more beautiful than the ass-upward maples.

INSTRUMENT OF LIGHT

If you haven't got an instrument,
then play as best you can
upon the instrument of light
that fills the whole sky.

Miyazawa Kenji

Not far from Lars Grinde in the western fjord-lands, at the turn of the twentieth century, lived Nikolai Astrup. He grew up in the town of Alhus on Jolster Lake and lived all his life on its shores. He changed a precipitous hillside into a terraced farm, and he painted his family's work and life there. I stumbled upon him because he drew and painted pollards. I became obsessed with his life. He is Norway's most beloved landscape painter. Astrup, like Grinde, lived in the presence of his day. He conceived plans for his farmwork and his paintings, put his heart into their doing, and learned from his hands as he made them. Dirt, rock, plants, pigments, and canvas were his materials, but it was the light of western Norway that gave them life. In one sense, he was a rare creature,

Nikolai Astrup's drawing of a woodland of pollards on a rocky slope.

but in another he was exemplary. He showed how head, heart, and hand can make a full life out of unexpected materials, and how the difficult love of a place and its people can transform a person.

Astrup farmed to feed his family, and the family, the farm, and the mountain landscape with its pollards were what he captured in the light. In this, he closely resembled his contemporary Miyazawa Kenji, half a world away in northern Honshu in Japan. (Likewise, I had stumbled upon Miyazawa when I looked at coppice forests in Japan.) Both men considered farming a primordial art. At once poet and teacher of agriculture, Miyazawa wrote a poem in which an old white-haired man, with a stroke of a hoe, taught the farming teacher how to sow red turnips. "What brush stroke of ink painting, / what fragrance of a sculptor's chisel," he wrote, "could be superior to this." When he wrote a poem of praise and challenge to a student who played the bassoon most beautifully, Miyazawa commanded the boy to learn to play upon the instrument of light. In other words, his art was not the fruit of its practice alone, but of a fully lived life.

At the age of twenty-six, Astrup fell in love with Engel Sunde, a fifteen-year-old local farmgirl. All of the Jolster district was scandalized when they wanted to be married, not because of the difference in their ages—in those days fifteen was not considered too young to marry—but because of the difference in their classes. Nikolai was the son of the Alhus priest, an upper-crust civil servant like the teacher and the sheriff. (Norway's is a state church.) Engel was the daughter of a farmer, not a mere cotter—a sort of sharecropper—to be sure, but still a whole social rung lower than a civil servant. Astrup's family was particularly troublesome. "I was just about done for when I met her," he wrote, "and I owe it to her that my vitality flared up in me again, and the 15 year old girl, who followed me without fearing rumours, also gave me back my faith in human beings again, and why should I not marry her, despite the rumours and the talk in the family?" They were married the night before Christmas Eve, 1907.

They moved to the remains of a cotter's farm, called Sandalstrand, reached only by a precarious flight of stone straight up a steep slope. The long stairway was about as wide as the average doormat. When you walked up or down it, you had to keep your feet together, or you would fall off. The first time Astrup climbed the steep stairway, he noticed that if you dropped something, it rolled down the hill until it fetched up in the alders at the lakeside. The last direct sun hit Sandalstrand around the first of October. It did not return until the middle of March. There were two small houses on the property, but the rain came in the roofs.

The first thing they needed was a way to get home. Astrup carved a three-turn switchback path from the lake up to the cabins, wide enough for a horse and a cart, and gentle enough for them to get up without losing their breath. Part he dug into the hill, part he supported on stone and dirt foundations. It took a year to build it. Three fast streams came through the property. He dug deep channels for them and made bridges over the path to prevent erosion. He dug out a pool by the place where he planned a barn, in order to keep milk cool.

For his family's private gathering place—he called it the Grotto—he pollarded a linden and a willow, training the sprouts to cover the flat terrace at the back of which he installed a fire pit in the hollow beneath a rock. Nearby were a pair of goat willows that he twined together when they were young, so they grew up in a strange embrace. Below the houses rose tall birches that made the family think they were living like birds in the treetops. "In spring," he wrote, "it is lovely to have the windows open here, and hear the song thrush outside in the treetops."

He planted extravagantly, both to feed the family and to keep the steep slope from eroding away. His first nursery order contained 451 fruit trees (apples, sweet and sour cherries, blue, Victoria, and Mirabelle plums), 611 berry bushes (raspberries, black currants, red currants, gooseberries), 100 rhubarb plants of ten different varieties, and 500 vegetables. He might have fed an army of frugivores, if not for the beast he called "the devilish hare." Of the hundreds of fruit trees that he planted in 1914, not more than 50 were still alive a decade later. The price of this purchase amounted to a tenth the cost of the whole property.

To present this botanical menagerie to the sun, he built almost two dozen terraces on the slopes above and behind the houses. The tallest terraces rose almost thirty feet from the land beneath them. Others made small fields a mere five or ten feet above their neighbors. Into a small terrace on top of the tallest hummock, he built a cold frame to start the vegetables. Dynamite, dirt, stone, and three years' hard work put them into shape. He did not like bare stone walls, so he clothed the retaining walls with sod, each tranche held in place with posts driven through peat blocks. It was not simply an aesthetic choice. Astrup appears always to have been thinking of the sun, not only what it could give but what it might take. He reasoned that covering the walls with grass would reduce erosion when the torrents of spring came at last, and that the clothed undergirding of stones would shift less in the freeze and thaw. He edged all the terraces with berry bushes—currants and gooseberries, chiefly, tough stringy bushes that sent out explosions of clinging roots into the erodible edges.

One of Astrup's greatest interior paintings at Sandalstrand shows Kjokkenstova, what was for years his family's main house, on Christmas morning. A young daughter—the couple eventually had eight children—stands on a backed wooden bench leaning over a table filled to overflowing with colored fruits. The window behind frames the table and the lake beyond. It is a spacious and encompassing picture. Looking at it, you

Looking from the fields above the dwellings at two of the three principal houses at Sandalstrand and Jolster Lake below.

would never guess that it showed almost the entire inside of the house. Here was a microcosm of the family's life. They lived in a mountain-enclosed land, with a short growing season, using tiny growing plots, and in a very small community, where neither of them fit the expectation of what they were meant to do and be. More than once, Astrup wrote to friends that he would give it up and move away, to Denmark or to somewhere even more cosmopolitan, but he never did. Almost grudgingly, he wrote, "I have become fond of this farm, where I have taken on so many heavy tasks."

Ingeborg Mellgren-Mathiesen, a fine garden maker working to restore the Astrup property, said, "He never called Sandalstrand a garden. It was always 'the farm' or at most 'the farm garden.'" Astrup delighted in the contrast between the huge red-stemmed leaves of his many rhubarbs and the delicate white flowers of the cherry trees, and he painted them, but he was equally pleased by the food that they produced. His aesthetic pleasures were woven together with the work and the fruit of his days. The outdoor paintings at Sandalstrand often show his family on the terraces, making rows in the vegetable patch, planting seeds, cutting rhubarb, harvesting mushrooms.

They waited and waited for the coming of spring, when at last the sun would shine on their faces again. In 1921, Astrup wrote to a friend, "We are living here on the 'shady side' of the lake—and when after almost half a year's absence the sun begins to appear—then we move into a permanent sunfilled yearning for the 'other side' of the lake, where people have already long been living in the sun's magic above the thawing slopes and snowy mountains, while over on 'this side' we are in shadow all day long—or maybe just get a glimpse of the sun for a couple of minutes each day." They would walk down to the beach and touch a little of the snowmelt along the thawing shoreline, just to assure themselves that it was really happening. "We begin to think that we too here in the shadow side will finally have spring—the air is full of catkins—you feel that spring is coming as through a cobweb of branches . . . the rushes are already sprouting—and even the old alder trunks have enough sap to bleed one last time."

Spring brought holy beauty and a hard day's work. The change was explosive. Everywhere in fjord country, one of the first signs of spring came not to the eyes but to the ears. Sun high on the slopes started the melt. The short, steep-tilted streams and waterfalls—quiet in the gray of winter—woke up and thundered. Everything had to be done at once. Fields had to be manured with what the animals had made in the barn over the winter. The pollards had to be pruned. Cabbage, potatoes, beets, turnips, radishes, swedes, carrots, lettuce, onions, peas: the seed had to be sown or the seedlings that had been started in the cold frame mound set out, the potato eyes cut and planted. Gooseberry and black currants on the terrace edges had to be checked, pruned, and replaced if necessary, before erosion could start. Lambing ewes filled the barn. Winter damage to the fruit trees had to be pruned. The raspberry terrace and its two hundred plants had to be tended to and pruned. Damage to the big path had to be repaired. The roofs had to be weeded. The perennials like rhubarb had to be checked to make sure they were sprouting and perhaps dosed with just a little spare manure. It was not a gentleman's farm.

The coming sun woke the land so quickly it seemed miraculous. Astrup wrote Per Kramer in the spring of 1920, "Everything was changed in these two days—the apple trees were almost fully sprung, and the cherries and plums in full bloom, rhubarb leaves got twice their size in just two days." He suddenly had not only to plant and tend the farm garden, but to paint it. "Motifs were everywhere," he wrote. "I didn't know where to start painting." Every year, it must have been delightful and utterly exhausting.

Rhubarb if any was his favorite plant. His first nursery order included

100 plants of ten different varieties, including the immense-leaved Chinese rhubarb and the popular cultivars Victoria and Monarch (both still available today). He asked for one cultivar that he claimed grew only in the king of England's garden. A great painting shows Engel in a print dress picking rhubarb. She and the red leaves fill the canvas, a delicate white flowering cherry to their left.

The marriage of an artist and a farmer was a strange one. Both sides of society looked askance. Not only that, the fact that a priest's son had become a painter and a farmer and that he made and drank wine, where his father had never touched a drop, caused people to shake their heads. Out of that difference, however, the family created their place. Astrup loved to tinker. He confessed that he had the bad habit of crossbreeding plants to see what might come of it. (He had a fence-enclosed nursery terrace for the purpose.) Many of his creations died on the vine, but he was particularly proud of the cross he made between the Victoria and Monarch rhubarbs. This unnamed hybrid was the variety he preferred to use to make rhubarb wine. His wine was first popular among his friends, both those from the local community and visitors from far away. He began to give it to people for their wedding feasts, and soon it was in demand all over Jolster.

The Astrups shared produce with their neighbors, both giving and receiving. Even if only fifty fruit trees survived, the fruit and berry produce of the farm was far more than even eight children could eat. They gave fruit to neighbors. They propagated and gave gifts of plants. It became known around the lake that Astrup loved the old-fashioned Jolster plants, as did many of the farmers. When new drainage projects threatened the beloved marsh marigold, he got plants from the neighborhood and tried to keep them at Sandalstrand. When new improved swedes appeared, he championed the old flat ones, collecting them and growing them in his garden.

The Astrups designed village banners for parades and festivals. On one occasion, Nikolai was asked to design a wedding apron, the indispensable centerpiece of a fjord-land wedding dress. He complied, and he suggested that Engel print and make it. For decades afterward, the designs made by Astrup and created by Engel were a main source of wedding aprons in Jolster. From being the couple of a scandalous marriage, they became—through their wine and their wedding aprons—a part of almost every wedding in the district.

Head and heart alone do not cross the barriers of mistrust, but hands do. When they began at Sandalstrand, Astrup and Engel were ostracized. When he died of complications of lifelong asthma in 1928, the entire lake came to his funeral. Indeed, the people of Jolster paid for it.

MAKING GOOD STICKS

Just like a research library, the Phoebe A. Hearst Museum of Anthropology at the University of California, Berkeley, had its stacks. In the back rooms, behind the colorful, perfectly illuminated exhibits were fluorescent-lighted, floor-to-ceiling battleship-gray industrial shelves filled not with books but with almost every kind of thing that the California Indians ever made. Each artifact was numbered and, in fact, a photograph and data on each could be accessed online. But there was nothing like standing there among them. There were baskets, ropes, stirring sticks, poles, traps, bows and arrows, wooden pillows, hoop and lance games, snowshoes, boats, skirts, and coil after coil of the stems that the Indians used to fashion them all. It was a treasure house. It was clear at a glance that their lives had been every bit as rich as ours, only their home in the world had almost entirely been made of wood.

In one aisle, we came on some odd ceramic cones. "What are these?" I asked the curator, Natasha Johnson.

"Pots," she said matter-of-factly.

I stopped short. They look like ceramic top hats, minus the brims. They were perhaps the ugliest pots I had ever seen.

She guessed what I was thinking. "Most of the California Indians were not very good at pots," she said. "In fact, many didn't even try them."

"Why not?" I asked. "What did they use for storage? What did they cook in?"

"Baskets," she replied, with a tone that suggested how woefully ignorant I was.

"Baskets!?" I exclaimed. I thought that with my heavy wheezing and my chest cold I must have misheard her. "For cooking?"

"Of course," she answered. "They were watertight. They'd put in the finely ground acorn, add water, and throw in hot rocks or ceramic boiling 'stones.' The acorn boiled and could be cooked into a thick soup or a porridge, or rolled into biscuits."

She smiled gently, as though to encourage this knowledge to sink in.

The museum was located in Kroeber Hall, named for the anthropologist Alfred Kroeber, who had been responsible for the rescue of much of the material in the museum and who with his students and his acolytes had collected every bit of information they could about the indigenous cultures. But not an acorn biscuit toss away was the Bancroft Library, named for the noted historian George Bancroft, who had opined that the California Indians—who were derisively known even among us 1950s California kids as Digger Indians—had been stupid and lazy, "sunk almost to the darkness of the brute."

What was I to make of the fact that they had little or no pottery? (A friend of mine, when I mentioned this, asked, "I wonder what got in their way? Not enough clay?") And indeed what were generations of historians to make of the fact that they had no agriculture, nor when the white man first arrived did they show even the stirrings of a wish to grow crops? For many, these facts were prime exhibits to prove the Indians' stupidity and backwardness. They simply lived off the land, with no inkling of tomorrow. Pottery and agriculture would have been signs of advancement.

But there was another school of thought: What if the tribes had had no agriculture, because they hadn't needed one? Each small tribe had lived intentionally in a vertical economy—that is, a place where the people had at least two different landscapes to harvest, each with its own community of plants and animals. One was usually higher than the other, hence the name. It might be a seacoast and a hill range, a valley and uplands, low hills backed by higher ones. This stack of ecosystems yielded each group an unusually large variety of seasonally available plant and animal foods, medicines, and craft resources. This was true even in the deserts, where a spring of water harboring the native Washington palm tree centered a culture that branched out in the surrounding high desert hills. Who needs corn, beans, and squash? Early in his career, Kroeber had thought so, before Carl Ortwin Sauer convinced him that it was California's summer dry climate that kept Indians from growing corn. That California now annually harvests more than 700,000 acres of corn should put that notion to rest. Though the Indians might not have grown that quantity, they could easily have irrigated riverside fields.

The fact is that the California Indians created the most affluent hunter-gatherer culture that the world has even known. They did it over the course of twelve thousand years, and it was only a little long in the tooth when it was wantonly destroyed by the incoming Europeans. Kroeber counted one hundred Indian languages in California, 20 percent of all the languages then in North America, and on less than 2 percent of the land. There were no great cities and no great warlords. The average tribe numbered less than a thousand people, and there were more than 275,000 Indians living in California, a greater population density than anywhere else north of Mexico. There were indeed elites, who gave the feasts and directed the larger projects and were certainly not altruists and were often self-serving and corrupt; but in general, this enormous number of polities lived well with one another and with the world they inhabited. Their diet came from more than five hundred animals and plants. Acorns were a staple for many, and for coastal tribes, so were mussels and salmon. Deer was an important resource, but so was roasted grasshopper. Clover was their favorite fresh salad herb, but they harvested dozens of seeds, bulbs, and corms. In the desert, they had mesquite beans, yucca, Washington palm. If one food source failed, there were half a dozen more to back it up.

Baskets made the house a home. A photograph taken in 1930 by B. F. White shows a Karuk woman with her family's baskets. There are forty-one of them: some are small enough to twirl on the end of your finger, others are big enough to sit in, and none are the immoveable granary storage baskets that could fit a grown person inside. (They would have been very hard to bring to the photo site.) There were baskets for burden, to carry your nut or bulb or seed harvest or your family's goods. There were baskets to haul water, baskets for cooking, baskets to store food and medicine, baby baskets—two for each baby, one for newborns and one for later—and basket cradles. There were basket seed beaters to sweep the ripe seeds off the tidytips, the red maids, the wild oats, the popcorn flowers, the balsam root, owl's clover, goldfields, and fireweed; baskets to collect them in; and baskets to parch the seeds over the fire. There were baskets to winnow the fine-ground acorn, catching the good flour in its ribs and leaving the hunks to be swept back into the bedrock-pounding mortar with a soap-root brush. There were sifting baskets. There were basket trays and baskets to serve supper on, feast baskets for when the guests came. There were scoop baskets to measure out ingredients, and dipper baskets to get a drink of water. There were baskets to place on a sand bed to let the acorn meal leach, bottomless baskets to pen the flour

A Karuk woman with a selection of the baskets she had made for her household.

and keep it from blowing away. There were baskets for storing foods in the house and large baskets, often protected on stands under trees, for long-term storage. There were baskets for hats, baskets for cages, baskets for traps, baskets for fish weirs, and even basketlike sandals. Of course, there were also baskets to hold presents and baskets that were gifts themselves. A woman's bride price—paid to her family—was doubled if she was a good basket maker.

The women used shrub and tree shoots, herbaceous stems, flower stalks, and roots to make the baskets: sourberry and redbud, hazel, deer brush and manzanita, blue brush and willow, black oak and big-leaf maple, bear grass, tule reed and bracken fern, spruce and redwood roots. Seventy-eight different plants went into the making of baskets in California. This work—a deft and often intricately patterned weave of warp and weft that Kat Anderson in her wonderful *Tending the Wild* compared to the playing of a concert pianist—required an astronomical number of long straight stems, or "sticks."

Today, when an Indian woman goes out to gather materials, she says she is going "to pick sticks." It takes between 500 and 700 sourberry sticks to make a cradle board, 188 sticks of buckbrush to make a seed beater, 3750 deer grass stalks to make a medium-sized cooking basket, and 35,000 stalks to weave a forty-foot-long deer net. It could take 10,000 sticks to make half a dozen average baskets, and if there were twenty-five basket weavers in a given village, they would likely use more than 250,000 sticks each year. And this count does not even reckon with the sticks for other daily uses: for arrows, spears, harpoons, game pieces, fishnets, flutes, clapper sticks, cooking tongs, fire drills, hot-rock-lifting sticks, and stirring sticks.

Each stem, whether it was woody or herbaceous, had to be long, straight, unbranched, and flexible. A naturally growing, undisturbed plant produces almost none of these. Where were the weavers going to get enough such sticks for a single year, never mind for a thousand? Obviously, they would have coppiced them. Cutting low, they would have got back the next year exactly the sort of stems they needed. This was true for herbaceous stems too, since cutting back removed all the dead, diseased, and dying stems, leaving a clean base from which to sprout again. But how much labor would it have taken to cut the number of plants required? They found a better way.

The very first European visitors noticed it right away, though they had no idea what it was for. In October 1542, Juan Rodríguez Cabrillo, commander of the first European fleet to reach Alta California, saw what appeared to be wild fires burning up and down the coast near present-day Santa Monica. He named the place Bahía de los Fumos, or Smokes Bay. More than half a century later, once more in October, Sebastián

Vizcaíno, sailing coastwise on a mission to locate safe harbors on the California coast, observed continual burning in the vicinity of what is now San Diego. He reported that "the Indians made so many columns of smoke on the mainland that at night it looked like a procession and in the daytime the sky was overcast." Later land expeditions often found themselves short of fodder because as Father Juan Crespi repeatedly noted during the 1772 Portolá trek to what is now San Francisco, the Indians had recently burned the landscape, leaving nothing for miles that a horse or pack mule could nibble on.

A century later, naturalists suspected that the landscape they crossed had been formed by fire. John Muir commented on the parklike quality of Sierra woodlands: "The inviting openness . . . is one of their most distinguishing characteristics. The trees of all the species stand more or less apart in groves, or in small irregular groups, enabling one to find a way nearly everywhere, along sunny colonnades and through openings that have a smooth, parklike surface." The great California botanist Willis Jepson observed the same thing about the valley oaks in the Central Valley. Widely spaced, magnificently tall and wide, and of strong bearing, the valley oaks were so regularly spaced and the ground below them so clear that he called them "oak orchards." He despaired of ever detailing the history of their formation, but he wrote, "it is clear that the singular spacing of the trees is a result of the annual firing of the country."

Fire coppice. Who knows in what deep of time it was begun by the California Indians, and it stopped only when the white man prohibited it. It is now estimated that the Indians burned annually an average of 7,000 to 18,000 square miles, or about 6 to 16 percent of the state. These were not large, intense conflagrations, but slow and steady ground fires, and they likely comprised selected patches of the country, not wholesale swathes. The fires probably were set on the same patch every one to five years. Fire needs something to work on. Often, people had to wait a little longer than they might have liked to, because not enough plant material had grown back to support the burn. Usually, the fires were set in autumn, just after the harvest of coppice shoots, though they might be set in spring, if the intention were to suppress shrubs in favor of herbaceous plants. They might be set in open country, in chaparral, or even in oak or conifer woodlands.

The Indians were skillful fire managers. Not only did they consider wind, temperature, rainfall, and time of year, but they were also good at turning the fire in the direction they wanted, by piling brush along the desired path. They aimed their fires, often so that they would eventually reach another patch that had burned the previous year. When the fire reached that place, it found too little fuel and so burned itself out. Sometimes, they would burn from the edges into a center. When they did so, they were often not only opening the country and coppicing their basket plants, but also driving deer or rabbits, or roasting a few thousand grasshoppers. Lois Conner Bohna, a fine Chukchansi-Mono basket maker, visited the Martu in the Australian outback, an aboriginal people who still burn. "Seen from the air," she recalled, "their land looked like a patchwork quilt." She thought that her own Sierra foothills once looked much the same.

Getting long, straight, slender, and flexible fresh bear grass shoots, tule reeds, sourberry sprouts, and redbud sticks was not the only benefit of burning. It also killed unwanted plants in forest areas, stimulated mature trees to sprout from the base, caused a fresh crop of edible herbaceous plants like clover, stimulated the seeds of fire followers like redbud to bring new plants, increased the fruiting of nut plants like hazel, renewed the growth of berry plants, killed ticks and other pests, and attracted large numbers of game animals to feed in the tender resprouting land. Before burning, a place might show fourteen species growing as ground covers; after burning, the number jumped to eighty.

Early visitors to the Indian territories often noted the smoke and the burning. The second thing they almost always commented upon was the abundance of game animals. In fact, when I studied history in the 1960s, we were taught that the Europeans had come from country so exhausted that they wildly exaggerated the richness of the New World flora and fauna. When he stopped in San Diego Bay, Cabrillo reported, "There are large savannahs, and the grass is like that of Spain. . . . They saw some herds of animals like cattle [likely, in fact, pronghorn antelopes], which went in droves of a hundred or more, and which from their appearance, from their gait, and the long wool, looked like Peruvian sheep." Thirty years later, Sir Francis Drake agreed: "Infinite was the company of very large and fat Deere, which wee saw by thousands, as wee supposed in a heard; besides a multitude of Conies, by farre exceeding them in number." The French Comte de La Perouse thought the land of "inexpressible fertility," and a young boy who had come to live among the Yokuts wrote of "thousands of band-tailed pigeons in fights that would sometimes block out the sun." Otto von Kotzebue, the captain of a Russian ship in the far north of California, remarked, "An abundance of deer large and small, are to be met with all over the country, and geese, ducks and cranes on the banks of the rivers. There was such a superfluity of game, that even those among us who had never been sportsmen before, when once they took the gun into their hands, became as eager as the rest."

In fact, these accounts were not exaggerated, but misattributed. The abundance was real, not imagined. It was not, however, the fruit of a virgin land, but of a country that had been skillfully managed and maintained through the work of its human inhabitants for at least 2500 years. (I choose that number because it is the current estimate for the antiquity of intensive oak culture in California, though tending of the whole spectrum of plants and animal resources is far older than that.) The burning made a constantly changing succession of ecotones—edges between habitats—where a procession of different species lived and thrived. It took the already diverse resources offered by a tribe's vertical economy and increased them by an order of magnitude. It made the hunter-gatherer life as secure, healthful, and affluent as it has ever been. It was the opposite of current First World urban life. We get the smallest number of staple foods from a worldwide array of suppliers, with little concern for how those suppliers treat the land, and as cheaply as we can. The California Indians got as many products as they could from as near as they could whenever they were ripe, and spent their time (their kind of money) keeping their sources in good order and preparing to use them. Indeed, every tribelet had at least one legend that told how when the people stopped caring for and giving thanks for what they had, the human race was destroyed.

"Plants want to be used," said Bohna's aunt. "If you don't use them, they disappear." That did not mean you had to plant them yourself. A larger community was in charge of that. A Mono woman was asked if she ever planted oaks. "I'd be dead before they were grown," she answered. "Let the blue jays do the planting. It's their job." That said, every tribe that had acorns paid great attention to the care of their oaks. When a group of foresters and a Forest Service botanist went with Bohna to look at a thirty-acre grove of black oaks in the foothills, the botanist said, "If I didn't know better, I would have said this was an orchard."

"You hit the nail on the head," answered Bohna.

"Well, this can't be man-made," the botanist retorted.

"My mother, her mother, and her mother's mother lived here, and acorn was their main food," said Bohna. "The oak trees have been nurtured, have been cultivated since they were little. This was my great-grandmother's orchard."

Burning was key to the care of oaks, and it happened in the autumn of the year, just before the harvest. The fire had many purposes. Acorns infested with weevils and other pests usually fall before the main crop does, and the pests overwinter as pupae in the ground. The fire was an effective pesticide, turning the infested acorns to ash and heating the ground enough to kill the pupae. As a Shasta named Klamath Jack put it, "Fire burn up old acorn that fall on ground. Old acorn on ground have lots worms; no burn old acorn, no burn old bark, old leaves, bugs and worms come more every year. . . . Indian burn every year just same, so keep all ground clean, no bark, no dead leaf."

The burn did many other things. It culled the seedlings of unwanted competitor plants, like the bull pines that in the foothills now drive the oaks to grow too high, fighting for the light. It made more water available to the oak roots, just as happens in an apple orchard floor. It gave a small fertilizer boost to the roots. The burn had to be carefully controlled so it didn't damage the oaks—particularly if the grove was of the sensitive tan oak—but it was a good thing if the flames caused a few sprouts at the base of the tree. Basal black oak sprouts in particular tolerated rapid heating and so were prized as stirring sticks and rock pickers, for putting the hot rocks into the basket and taking them out.

Finally, fire cleared the ground for the harvest. Then came the knocking. From the ground or from a perch in each tree, someone would hit the oaks' branches with a stick, dislodging the almost ripe acorns and breaking the smallest branches. It was a form of rough pollarding, because the small broken stems would ramify and sprout back the following year, spreading the tree's crown and in theory increasing the harvest. (You had to be careful if you were knocking trees in the red oak group, since they mature their acorns in two years, not one, and you did not want to destroy the coming crop.) The acorns fell on the clear ground, where they could be harvested quickly. This was not just a matter of efficiency but of protecting the crop. Blue jays, woodpeckers, and pigeons also had a strong interest in acorns. An industrious scrub jay can grab four hundred acorns in an hour. The knocking also lightened the stems, making them less liable to break under winter snows. If you asked a participant why they were doing it, however, they may well have answered with what they had been taught: "Knocking wakes the tree." It was a way to keep up the community formed by the people and the oaks. In almost every place, before the new crop was eaten, a sample was offered ceremonially in thanksgiving.

Many living California Indians—Bohna included—claim that their forebears got a reliable harvest almost every year from their oak groves. "They call me a liar when I say that," she remarked with a frown. For one thing, the Indians often had more than one species of oak, so a poor year for one might be a mast year for another, but the important thing was the care. Untended, apples too are alternate bearers, with a heavy crop one year and little or no fruit the next, but with clean culture, pruning, fertilizing, water, and care to keep the sun coming into the bearing branches, most apples can be coaxed into annual bearing. The Indians treated their oaks in the same way. It would not be that surprising if they had had the same result.

For more than half a century, the Mono, the Chukchansi, and all the other surviving tribes have not been allowed to burn. Even after the white man came, for a time, it was still common to burn in the autumn. Cattle and sheep men, who summered their beasts in the high country and who often hired Indians to cowboy, burned the meadows and surrounding hills when they brought the animals down in the fall. That way, they were assured of new grass for the coming year. Then, it all stopped. Fire suppression became and remained the ruling creed.

The land began to change. In the Indian view, it began to die. Without the active relationship between people and plants, both suffered. The meadows—even big ones like Jackass and Beasore in the high country near where Bohna lives—have begun to fill in with lodgepole pines and with other pioneer trees and scrub. Hillside grasslands have turned to forest. Oak groves have been invaded by bull pine and other tall fast growers, forcing them to grow higher to compete and so making the acorns less reachable. Acorn weevil and acorn worm now take a large proportion of the acorn crop—since they are not controlled by burning—and the trees have returned to alternate bearing. The sourberry, the redbud, and the other stick makers no longer offer a fresh crop of sticks every year or two. They have become, said Bohna, a useless mess, full of deadwood, lateral branches, cankers, and gray and colorless wood. Without burning, the soap root—a bulb that had wiry hairs, and made a fine household brush—no longer gets hairy. "They are as bald as a cue ball," she sighed. The deer grass is moldy, and a whole plant yields only one or two useful stems. The tall stems of blue and black oaks are pockmarked with knots of parasitic mistletoe. It is not an invasive, not a new problem. It is becoming a serious issue now only because it is not controlled by fire.

We went for a walk on land that had belonged to Bohna's grandparents. She and her husband had just fenced it and were building a house and barn there. She took me out looking for a stick of redbud long enough for her to demonstrate how to split it. First we passed a sourberry, a lump of shrub in the landscape with small light green oak-lobed leaves. She had cut it several years ago with a chain saw to get sticks for a baby basket, but since then it had grown into a rat's nest of branching, intersecting stems, some living and some dead. She broke off a stem and held it toward my nose. "Smell that," she said. The other name for the plant is skunkbush, and it is a name well given. When you work with sourberry, the first thing you have to do is peel the bark off it. She uses a piece of obsidian or a sharp knife. You have to reach out and draw the tool toward you along the stick, again and again. If you go back and forth, you scar the stick.

"I saw a friend last week in Coarsegold," she said. "'Boy, have you been peeling sourberry!' I told her.

"'No I haven't!' she answered. She paused and reddened. 'Or maybe I have . . . but I took a bath after.'

"'Honey, you've still got some on you somewhere.'"

Bohna was not only rich in knowledge and experience. She was also a born tale teller. Every time we thought we had finished talking, she started up again. A village life materialized around us as we walked through a landscape now long disused. You could see how, absent conquest, it might have persisted. "It used to be so open here," she said. "My aunt Rosie said it was so open you couldn't find a place to pee without somebody seeing you."

She pointed to three tall dead digger pines among a thick grove of tall trees. "All those trees are dying," she said, "hundreds of thousands of them." Like so many pines in North America, they are dying from infestations of boring beetles. "What would your people have done about those beetles?" I asked.

"They never would have been there in the first place," she responded. "They don't belong." Fire would have kept them down. (It would likely also have prevented the recent outbreak of boring beetles that has killed millions of conifers in the West and in Canada.) "Those trees are over-growth," she continued, "like parasites on the land."

Bohna thinks that the uncontrolled growth of the pines is one cause of the droughts that trouble the foothills. "Fire and water go together," she said. "If you don't have fire, you don't have a lot of water." The roots of the big pines compete for water, drying the ground. In winter, the closed canopy catches falling snow, and a lot of it evaporates instead of reaching the dirt. When snow or rain does get to the bottom, it hangs up in a deep layer of duff. Again, a proportion evaporates before it gets into the ground. "Water's not going into the soil where it belongs," she said. The same thing happens in the big meadows higher in hills, so they no longer soak up the water like a sponge and trickle it downhill.

She showed me a dry creek near which a small patch of bracken fern grew. "This fern grows higher up in the hills," she remarked. "I think my aunties may have brought it and planted it here." Why? "The black threads in the acorn-sifting basket I showed you, that's bracken fern," she said. "But the roots are rust color when you dig them. You have to dye them black." She had a favorite method, she said. She put acorn shells and rusty nails in a pot and boiled them together. Then she sat the pot on the back of the stove for a week. "It gets blacker every day," she said with pleasure. "Dip the coils of bracken in, and they go jet black. Permanently. That's my white-man way to dye fern root." Many plants are endemic to California. Not bracken fern. It is one of the five most common plants in the world. The rhizomes can spread over an area larger than a football field. If it is regularly burned, a single clone can live for a thousand years.

When she was a child, Bohna ate acorn almost every week, but her mother had eaten it every day. Her mother's mother, Hazel Helen Harris, was born in a cedar bark house in 1910. For most of her adult life, she would spend a whole day pounding and sifting acorn to a fine powder, then another day leaching and cooking it. She cooked it in a basket that held about five gallons, enough to feed her family of six for a week. She put in the ground meal and added water. Then she put one hot rock in the basket at a time. "It's a volcanic explosion when the first rock goes in," said Bohna. "The acorn boils right in the basket." She might make *yumana*, a thin mush about the consistency of chocolate milk. More rocks and more boiling turned it into *ikiba*, a mush more like a pudding. With a little more cooking, the paste got thick enough to make water biscuits, *conowoy*. She used a small basket to dip out a dollop of mush at a time, then ladled on cold water and rolled the mass into ready-to-eat biscuits. "That way, you could clean the big basket right away," Bohna said. "It didn't stay nasty with acorn the whole week." When someone was sick or too old to make their own, Bohna's grandma would sometimes double up, making ten gallons instead of five.

Bohna showed me where soap root grew. "I can still get good soap root if I try," she said in passing. "Anybody who has any in their garden and uses a weed eater on it will do. For some reason, the cutting helps the hair grow on the bulbs." She showed me a patch of sedge, an important warp material in almost every basket. "If you don't cut it down every year," she explained, "you lose it." We walked by some thorny buckbrush, with pale green leaves the shape of mouse ears: it was good for the warp of baby baskets, if it was well burned.

We passed some poor-looking redbud and made for the new fence that marked the edge of the property. It had been built in the spring. She suddenly sped up and her boots clacked on the rocks. "Look at that!" she exclaimed. "This is beautiful! I mean, look at this thing! Fine and straight!" Where they had cut down redbud with a chain saw to make room for the fence, it had sprouted back with incredible vigor. There were wonderful rust red stems six or even seven feet long, with no branching or only one branch. "I've got to tell my friends about this," she breathed. "The thing about a baby basket is you can't splice in the middle of the basket. If you're doing an arrow design, you start in the middle, and you've gotta have a stick long enough to go clear out to the edge and wrap around!" These were just long enough. She was delighted.

Now, as the year wound to its end, was the time to cut redbud. It would hold its color if you did. If you waited until January to cut it, you might find the red bark sloughed right off. "Usually, I'd cut these and cover them up with a tarp and let them sit for a few days before I split them," she said. She cut off a six-foot piece and whittled the fat end flat with her knife. Then, to my complete surprise. she put the cut end in her mouth.

Kat Anderson had compared a basket maker to a concert pianist; Bohna was an orchestra conductor. She held her head up high—one-third of the stick's fat end between her four front teeth. Bringing her two hands to her mouth, she took two more thirds of the stick's butt, one between each forefinger and thumb. Then, precisely like the conductor calling the orchestra to attention, she slowly spread her hands in what looked like a gesture of welcome. As she did so, the stick split into three nearly equal pieces, their lengths extending as she pulled her hands apart. At one point, she tucked the end of one of the three split stems beneath one arm. The other dangled free. She brought her hands back to the center of the stick, just at the point where it was splitting, and pulled gently and evenly again, the third end still in her mouth.

As she was pulling one stick into three basket fibers, she kept telling me what she was doing. I had trouble keeping up, because she was speaking through clenched teeth. "You wan the budts on the outsie," she mumbled, "'cause you're gonna split dow through the muddle of thm." She closed her eyes. "The truck is ta pall evnly," she continued. "When you git dow hur, you gotta be reayiy caful. You want it exacly in holf."

As she neared the thin end of the stick, she said that she usually did this with her eyes closed, or while watching a movie. It was easier to concentrate if you didn't focus on the visuals. The idea was to make each strand of precisely the same width, no fat spots, no skinny spots. You never took a knife to it until you were ready to weave. Then you could cut off the buds. She reached the end, and the stick came apart into three nearly equal threads. "Once, you know how to do this," she went on, "you're better off not looking at it. 'Cause my thumb tells me. It'll tell me if I'm pulling too much." Once she was done, she had to go back and split each thread again the same way, until she had pieces of the thickness the basket needed. When they died, the women of California often had a notch in their front teeth, where they had held sticks to split them.

How much intelligent work went just into making the strands for a basket. And then she had to weave it, into different shapes and sizes, some flat, some cupped, some deep, some shallow, some waterproof, some sifters, some taller than a standing child, some with straps to carry, some hooded and cradled to hold a baby, some to catch a salmon, some to snare a rabbit, some to ladle water. If there was patterning on the basket—a repeating pattern of circles, or lightning bolts, or rattlesnakes, or people—she had to figure out ahead of time how many stitches went between each figure, so the pattern worked out right. "My grandmas were mathematicians," said Bohna. "Say they wanted a pattern of people around the bowl. They had to see how many stitches the widest part would take, then count the couple thousand stitches in the first whorl beneath where they were going to go. They divided one into the other, and so found out how many people would fit. I use a calculator. They did it in their heads."

But it must have been so much work. So must it have been to grind acorn with a stone that weighed twelve pounds. Their pounding stone was usually buried with them, and some of their baskets. The rest were ritually burned.

Was this a hard life that we should be glad to be done with? Fire needs something to work on. So does love. The baskets and the life they made could be ill done, haphazardly finished. The makers were doubtless often competitive, trying to do outdo one another, or sloughing off, doing perfunctory work. But here in the making and the working with one another were the opportunities for love. And the love made its own sign: a meal that might be quickly eaten but with lasting thanks, or a basket that lived as long as its maker.

And they worked less hard than we do. They worked fewer hours, and were not often worried about where the food or the rent would come from. They had time for festival, time to sit around the fire, time to tell stories, time to play games, time to give thanks. One remarkable thing about the Hearst Museum stacks is how many toys and games are among the artifacts. Maybe the California Indians were smarter than we are. Their regular burning avoided the destructive wildfires that plague the state today. Belatedly, in the twenty-first century, even the Forest Service has come round to the notion that a regular burn is good not only for preventing wildfires but also for creating the most diverse and healthy landscapes. The Karuk have begun to burn again, and they are teaching others. The increasing number of prescribed burns—not just in California but across North America—is homage to the way of fire coppice. Maybe these hundred-plus cultures were not backward, but beckoning.

THE PARADISE OF SPROUTS

The last time that I was at Big Basin Redwoods State Park, I was four years old. The redwood trees had been so tall, so many, and so thick that I had scarcely noticed them. I felt dwarfed just by my parents and their friends. Here was I, so little, so little I could use the kitchen table as a fort, and they so big they could get into the freezer without a stepstool. And they went on and on talking about the trees and about the other mysterious questions that parents address from their strato-spheric elevation. My job as a kid, I had felt, was to squeeze out of their shadow.

There was a tree that had a black cave at its base where the trunk had hollowed out. I snuck into the cave. Out its back door, I could see a running creek, and I ran to it. My father had often pulled strange and interesting creatures out of running water. Once it had been a huge biting larva, once a huge biting crayfish. It seemed that everything that came out of such water was big and it bit. This frightened but also excited me.

I was dabbling in the cold water, pulling up nothing but pebbles, when I heard a deep voice say something inarticulate behind me, and I was lifted up by my underarms. My father threw me up with a spin, so I was facing him when he caught me again. "There you are, young sprout," he said. "You shouldn't run off like that!" He was trying to look stern, but he was doing a bad job of it. I smiled at him.

Sixty years later, I was back at Big Basin. We had dropped my father's ashes a decade earlier from a tugboat in San Francisco Bay near Angel Island and my mother's much earlier than that—far too early—on the Pacific shore just outside the Golden Gate. Likely, both of them now had circumnavigated the Pacific Rim. And here I was, one of the big people, actually noticing the trees and wondering about their size and age and their habit—very odd for a conifer—of regrowing in immense fairy rings. My own children were now adults, and I think I am shrinking, so I am not exactly in the position my father was in. I am more a granddad, and an admirer of the persistence and the unruliness of sprouts.

It was about two weeks before Christmas, and thank god it was rainy, breaking California's drought. As I climbed up onto Skyline Drive, the old highway that reaches 3000-feet elevation on top of the Coast Range, I drove straight into the clouds. This is the way that redwoods like it: live in the cloud in winter and in the fog in summer. The rest of the time it can be as dry as it likes. This explains why 65 million years ago redwoods were common across the whole joined continents of North America and Eurasia, and survive now only in a thin band along the Pacific Coast and a valley enclave in China. This cloud life, once common in the warmer world of the past, is now rare. On a ridge, I passed a sign that read "Cloud's Rest." Yes. When you drive in this weather, you feel rather as though you were a tide-pool creature, with the roiling swirl of the waves above your head, sometimes a little higher, and sometimes a little lower, a sinuous roof of frosted glass.

I felt lonely, so I turned on talk radio. It had been so long since I lived here that I did not recognize the station or know the male/female duo who were bantering along. They were talking about cutting Christmas trees. The male had recently done it. He had managed the truck, while his wife had spoken to the tree farmers. "The wife got the Talk," he remarked. "'Leave a few whorls of branches at the bottom,' they said." The female host laughed. "What the heck for?" she asked. "I don't know," he replied. "Do they sprout from the top again?" He reflected a moment. "Weird!" he breathed into the microphone, and went on to the next topic.

Instinctively, I agreed with him, since conifers generally do not resprout from the base. But I had the sense he thought it would be weird for any tree to sprout. And it is indeed a practice among some Christmas tree growers to keep stumps with living whorls of branches. Although the stump will seldom sprout, the branches in the lowest whorls will turn upward toward the sky. Selecting the best of these, the grower can get another Christmas tree from the same roots. Some call them limb trees, and they take two or three years fewer to mature than would new seedlings. A few customers demand that their new Christmas tree come from the same roots as their old one. Not a bad wish. Here too was a way that the ancient conifers could persist, sprouting, as it were, without sprouting. The redwoods were an enormous exception.

The top of Skyline was meadow balds for a good way south from San Mateo. Then the trees closed in. You had to turn right down the hill on the ocean side to get to Big Basin. Just off the crests the redwoods began, thickening in the creek bottoms. Often they appeared one by one, but as I descended a pattern started to form. Three, six, eight, even twelve or fifteen trees appeared in groups. Sometimes, they formed the spokes of a wheel, with the rotting stub of an old stump at the hub. Sometimes, there was no hub, only a depression in the ground. Sometimes, the wheel was broken. Sometimes, there were all or parts of several concentric circles, the inner ones with much thicker trees than the outer ones.

I wondered what my radio host would think here. Really weird! I have seen fairy rings of trees all over the world, including the self-coppiced basswood near my home in upstate New York. As the parent dies or declines—and sometimes even before it shows any signs of stress—new young specimens sprout from the old trunk's edges, all around it. A lignotuber is the reason, the special organ that some trees have. From the moment the seedling is a brand-new thing, in the axils of the very first leaves, called the cotyledons, dormant buds begin to form. They proliferate as the tree grows, forming a solid, durable, and self-renewing ring of embryonic new trees around the base of the old one.

Redwoods sprout again from the base prolifically, dependably, repeatedly, millennially. A circle of them looks just like a fairy ring of mushrooms, only some of the sprouts are more than 200 feet tall and themselves hundreds of years old. In 1977, loggers found a redwood lignotuber that was forty-one feet in diameter and weighed more than 525 tons. What must have been the size of the tree at whose base it had been. Never mind the seven huge trees it now supported!

There was a narrow, barely paved road called the Big Basin Highway that led into the park. Erosion had pulled soil off some of the banks, exposing the roots of redwoods. There were times when I seemed to be driving into the world of the dirt. I have always wanted to see that hidden world, out of which all life comes. As beautiful and unique as may be the tops of the redwood trees—hiding, among other things, the nests of the diminutive marbled murrelet and strange leaves specifically adapted to face the sun—I have always been more interested in the mystery close at hand.

It started right in the parking lot. I did not feel too different than I had as a four-year-old. The tops and even the midsections of the trees were lost in the clouds. The average redwood around the parking area had a diameter and a height greater than the 139-foot tulip tree that I take care of in the Bronx, and that is the second tallest tree in New York City. Redwoods top out at more than 375 feet, almost three times what to me is the breathtaking elevation of our tulip tree.

The more remarkable thing about them, however, was not their size. It was the geometry they made on the forest floor. The redwoods were constantly squaring the circle. Not content to sprout once from the base, many of these continued sprouting, creating generations of the same kind of concentric rings I had seen as I entered the forest. Right by the parking lot was a marvelous example. It was a full ring of sixteen sprouts. The biggest three were each more than five feet in diameter, many were three to four feet in diameter, a few were only eighteen inches in diameter and there was a baby that was six inches in diameter, another one four inches. Elsewhere on the trails, I found examples where the largest was six or eight feet in girth and the smallest three inches. The biggest of these trees was certainly more than eight hundred years old, and the amazing thing was that they were sprouts from previous ancient trees. How far back did their line stretch unbroken?

Even the biggest oldest trees in the place were likely sprouts from vanished elders. One called Father of the Forest had its own plaque, bragging about its size. It was 16 feet 10 inches in diameter at breast height when they measured it for the sign, and stood 250 feet tall. If you looked at the base, however, you could see that the pattern of its roots on the ground suggested that they had once been part of the circumference of a circle of roots. In other words, it had been one among a fairy ring of redwoods that had surrounded a more ancient tree. If this tree were more than a thousand years old, what if it had grown from another that was a thousand years old? And so and so on back in time. Somewhere in the redwood forests perhaps there was an unbroken chain of filiation for 64 million years.

A fairy ring of resprouted redwood trees.

Not all the geometry was radial, however. Often, when a young stem fell to the ground, it sprouted where it fell, creating a linear grove of new progeny. In a wonderful story about the redwoods subtitled "Immortality Underground," the botanist Peter del Tredici included a picture of a twenty-inch-diameter trunk lying on the ground, with half a dozen eight- to 12-inch-diameter trunks emerging from it in a line as straight as a ray of sunshine. As I walked around Big Basin, I found two young trunks that had been broken by falling branches in recent storms. On the ground, these trunks had already responded by giving birth to two or three dozen sprouts each. A new sprout can grow six feet in a year. Many of these young'uns would likely die, but it was not impossible that were I to make it back here during my dotage (god willing) a couple of decades from now, I would find two straight lines of tall redwoods making their way toward the canopy top.

Redwoods don't sprout only from the bottom. Great bulbous masses form above wounds on the trunk and gradually drip until they

A straight line of redwood sprouts arising from a fallen trunk.

reach the soil, where they can root and return new trees. They look like boiling water frozen in midboil, as if the trunk were roiling with dormant sprouts. When I was a kid, people would harvest chunks from these burls and put the cut ends in water. They sprouted as reliably as avocado pits, and in fact in our house the two sat side by side on the windowsill, everyday miracles. You could buy chunks of burl in most of the roadside gift shops in redwood country. People now are much more careful with the trees, since there are far too many people and too few trees, but the burl is yet another way in which the redwood absolutely refuses to die.

While I got out of my car at Big Basin, the clouds settled lower, until I was inside them, as though the frosted glass had decided to include me, like a scene in a paperweight. I remembered arguments my father and I used to have while tide-pooling or hiking. "It's raining!" I would complain, flipping drops off the peak of my raincoat hood. "No," he would insist, "it's just heavy fog." Whatever it was, it was wet and misty. Reluctantly, I started to walk, but in less than a minute I had forgotten the discomfort.

There was a big full-color sign at the trailhead touting the "Amazing Ever Living Redwood Tree." The copy did not even mention the just as amazing thing standing right behind it. The entry had a canopy, like rainbows arching over the trail. It wasn't made by hands. Two canyon live oaks—plants that normally open into a bouquet of multistem tree—had here instead leaned out of the shade in which they had sprouted, making an archway directly over the trailhead. The average light penetration in the redwood forest is only 12 percent of what it is at the summit of the canopy, so resourcefulness is at a premium. Leaning out into the relatively bright space cleared for our passage, the two wooden rainbows had each released four stems from their top sides. These upright sprouts, using the parent branches as a launching pad, had grown up and out like eight new trees. It was an arboreal welcome portal to what turned out to be the paradise of sprouts.

In some ways, the redwoods were the least of it. They were the dominants, the big winners, easily five times taller than their nearest competitors. Nothing could grow in their fairy rings and few things directly under the shadow of their boughs. The creativity of the forest that indeed had grown up among them was as astonishing as the redwoods themselves. My four-year-old self felt a great affinity with these dwarves that had found a way to thrive among the giants, in just the way that I had, by getting out of their shadow.

Consider *Notholithocarpus*, the tan oak. I started walking off trail, and as soon as I did I found my boots tangled in an ivylike mass of leaves. I thought it *was* ivy, but what was it doing there? No, the leaves were large, oblong, slightly leathery, and had sharp little drip tips arranged around their edges. This ground cover was tan oak, putatively a tree that grows to heights of eighty feet or more, but here about six inches off the ground.

As I followed it, I learned what it was up to. It would stay close to the ground until it found a light gap. It might be the trail edge, or the border of a stream, or a spot where a taller tree like a redwood had fallen. There it would shoot up toward the light. Like as not, the promised light would turn out to be a chimera, or at least in a different direction than first surmised. The trunk would change direction to fine-tune its approach to the life-giving radiance. The tan oak could make living boughs as the live oak had, but some of these boughs were severely bent, like hog backs. Fresh stems jumped up from these. In other circumstances, it might realize that it had really gone wrong, or perhaps a new fall had blocked its source of sun. In such cases, the trunk might suddenly shift, growing out straight sideways at a slightly rising angle, rather as Joyce imagined Leopold Bloom, ascending into heaven "at an angle of 45 degrees . . . like a shot off a shovel." When it felt the radiance increase, it might release a bud straight up to reach it, the new bud taking almost all the tree's energy, and the old crown thinning and declining. It was very likely miming what the first broadleaf plants had done inside the conifer-dominated forests of the early Cretaceous.

Then there was the California huckleberry. It was a shrub, so it liked to spread from the base, not from the tips. You could draw a light map of the forest in the Waddell Creek drainage by mapping the course of spreading huckleberry across the ground, as it sent up one after another new shoots from the root crowns. Its cheerful little bright green leaves and its white flowers produce tasty black berries, even in the shade of redwoods, where it loves to grow. The groves of the huckleberry were never much more than six or eight feet tall at most, but they spread in winding paths over acres of ground. I am not sure if anyone has ever tried to see how many clones compose this dense understory or how old they are, but a huckleberry along the Juniata River near Harrisburg, Pennsylvania, stretches through the woods for a mile and is claimed by some to be more than thirteen thousand years old.

One of the most beautiful opportunists in the redwood forest was the native azalea, *Rhododendron occidentale*. It rose only twelve or fifteen feet tall and was daintier than its neighbors the tan oak and huckleberry, more likely to get elbowed out. Still, it was among the most common plants in the understory on my walk. Wherever it was wet on the ground and there was even a little extra light, its colonies of straight stems rose, topped in early winter by yellow whorls of leaves that fluttered to the ground as I watched them. In early spring, it had white or pink flowers borne before the leaves emerged, and it emitted a delicate fragrance. It is one of the parents of the hybrid Exbury azaleas, but long before it was an ornamental, it had everyday uses and medicinal uses for the Indians who lived in and near the redwoods.

The more I walked, the more I saw. It was a landscape of broad brush-strokes and skyrockets, the shrubs covering any even slightly sunny ground and the trees jumping up to fill any gap made by a trail, a stream, a tree fall, a road, a parking lot. It was the paradise for sprouting organisms. Where in my adopted eastern woodlands I find many sprouts that come from seedlings chewed down or knocked down by a branch fall or reduced by a pest, here it was hard to tell in what deep of time there may have been seedlings here. Everything, it seemed, came from a brother or sister, growing a bud on a stem or from the roots. How old and how long has the land existed? Did it stretch back to the Cretaceous? Were these the last strongholds of plants that once stretched from California to southern China? The fog settled down on all of us, and there we were, a scene in a paperweight: the paradise of sprouts.

The redwood forest is not pristine. It is rather the product of continual regeneration, unending succession. It gives a whole new meaning to the phrase "old growth." In the twentieth century, fire had been largely suppressed in the redwood forests, but prior to that, fire had been frequent, very frequent. Del Tredici related fire scars on older trunks to the successive rings of sprouts around them at Big Basin and determined that prior to European contact, fires likely occurred here every twenty-five years at least. In 1992, Mark Finney and Robert Martin found by counting fire scars on ancient stumps that from about the fourteenth to the middle of the nineteenth century, the trees there had suffered burning every six to twenty-three years. (Many sprouted again from the base or from a burl, but some simply resprouted prolifically up and down the stem, creating leafy fire columns.) A few showed fire scars every two years. While in ancient times the ability to sprout may have been a response to lightning fires, the ability was certainly honed by millennia of contact with humans. The peoples who occupied California at that time burned the land frequently (see page 213), to renew their food plants, to open the country for game, and to coppice small plants to get straight new stems. In fact, the redwood forests as we see them are as much the artifact of this millennial relationship as of random seasonal fires.

The Indians used the redwood forest. They ate the understory huckleberries, worked the huckleberry and azalea stems into arrows and baskets, and made a porridge of the tan oak acorns and a medicinal poultice of its bark. They split out redwood boards with elkhorn wedges to make houses and sometimes even lived in the great hollow bases of the trees. The Indians fired patches of forest to get fresh hazel stems, huckleberry, spruce roots, redwood sprouts, and bracken ferns. They also maintained what the whites called "prairies." These open spots might be on hillsides or on summits, and in each the forest stood back, making room for grass, ferns, sunflowers, and other herbaceous plants. The uninstructed might nearly die of starvation in the deep forests, unless they came upon one of these prairies, where edible plants and deer, elk, and bear were plentiful. The Indians knew the way from prairie to prairie as well as they knew their own names. Their idea of a healthy woodland was one in which they were active participants. They made their life out of what it gave them.

WHEN WOOD WON'T SPROUT

How do you make use of a tree that does not sprout? Most conifers don't sprout from cut limbs or from the base. When you have cut a branch or a bole, that is the end. The ancestral Puebloans of the American Southwest did not have much to choose from. They used a little wood from broadleaf trees—cottonwood and aspen—but mainly a suite of conifers: ponderosa pine, Douglas fir, juniper, pinyon pine, spruces, and firs. The evergreens were stronger and lasted much longer. The people needed firewood. They also needed wood for roof beams and for lintels, at least. The wood needed to be straight and as little knotty as possible: from four to twelve inches in diameter and from eight to twelve feet long.

How were they to get this wood from trees that would not sprout again once cut? A great deal of it they simply harvested by removing young trees at the appropriate diameter using the revolutionary sharp Neolithic stone axe, which could make a kerf in a log, not just bludgeon dents. Many stems were likely cut this way, and for firewood, they might harvest only deadwood. Because their conifers didn't sprout back except from seed, however, the people might more easily denude their landscape.

Late in the history of the Mesa Verde cliff dwellings, at least, by imagination and observation, they found a possible solution. All trees and shrubs, conifers or not, share a peculiarity. If you bend a stem over from the vertical toward the horizontal, you will release whatever dormant buds are alive near the surface of the stem, and any lateral branches that have already sprouted will change their minds. Instead of becoming laterals, each will try to become a new young tree, re-creating the pattern of the original tree. These newly released stems will grow straight and true, just as though they were saplings. This is the process of phoenix regeneration (see page 51).

Someone at Mesa Verde saw this happen, maybe in a Douglas fir that had been knocked over by a falling branch or fallen in a storm. They decided to try it intentionally. Scientists during the 1960s looking for the oldest Douglas firs in the Mesa Verde area in order to complete their dendrochronology came upon a series of very old specimens that had apparently been intentionally bent over almost flat—centuries before, when they had still been young trees. Intriguingly, each of these ancient trees had wounds on top of the bent stems that seemed to have been made by stone axes.

The people in the late phase of Mesa Verde building—only a few decades before the place was abandoned—apparently had turned lateral branches into straight new young trees. They were thus able to harvest straight poles for lintels or roofs without destroying the tree. When they harvested the dominant reiteration, the next strongest would become the dominant stem and would increase its rate of growth, eventually providing the next pole. Because they were dendrochronologists, of course, the scientists were expert at reading the width of annual tree rings. They noticed that there were periods when a stem suddenly increased dramatically in its ring widths, without any climate events that might have caused the change. The increase, they believed, was caused by the stem's becoming the new dominant on the flattened trunk.

Once cut, the stem had to be debarked to create a smooth pole. It was very hard to get the bark off Douglas fir, even in spring when the bark is at its loosest. The carpenters learned, however, that if you cut the wood when the bark beetles were in flight and left the wood around for a few weeks, the beetles would get into it and loosen the bark for you. Then, the bark was more easily removed. Some pole wood in the ancient Puebloan sites showed the characteristic larval galleries made by bark beetles.

Brilliant ideas indeed, or rather brilliant observations, but they were too little and/or too late. It is notable that at the end of the Mesa Verde occupation, house lintels would be made or repaired with stones, not wood. The three ancient trees that had been tricked into reiteration stood on a very steep and difficult-to-access talus slope. Although nobody knows exactly why the cliff dwelling was abandoned, it is very possible that a shortage of wood was among the reasons. The Puebloans had built and cooked themselves out of house and home. However, they did not simply disappear. Rather, they moved to mesa-top sites near more well-watered and wooded bottomland, where pinyon pine and juniper were thick and accessible.

All of the southwestern tribes—including the Navajos, the Puebloans' rivals for more than five hundred years in the same landscape—had a similar need to respect scarce wood and to use it sparingly. The term Anasazi, the word once usually used to name the ancient Puebloans, is now little spoken because it is a Navajo word that means "our enemies." The Navajo had a specific way to preserve the trees out of whose wood they made cradles. Thus, the tree served both physical and spiritual needs, since the tree's long life was wished upon the baby.

The father typically made the cradle. He would find a tall straight tree. Some say ponderosa pine was the preferred wood, though juniper and other woods were also used. The tree had to be broad enough to be able take a piece from it without harm to the whole. It had to be healthy and not have been struck by lightning. It had to be in an out-of-the-way place where the tree was unlikely to be harvested. The father would make two transverse cuts on the east side, the sunrise side, and split out a three-foot-long section of the trunk.

Sometimes, when he was done, he sang this song:

I have made a baby board for you, my son,
May you grow to a great old age.
Of the sun's rays I have made the back . . .
Of rainbow I have made the bow . . .
Of sundog I have made the footboard. . . .

Since the wood's making was the result of sun-driven, rain- and air-mediated photosynthesis, the statements were not inaccurate. The tree would close the wound again, continuing to grow as before. The making may indeed have expressed a wish to borrow the long life of trees and their resilience when damaged.

Interestingly, it was often the trees themselves whose lives were extended by respectful human treatment of them. When scientists discovered those ancient Douglas firs at Mesa Verde, they were not looking for human-influenced wood. They just wanted a tree old enough to complete their chronology, but they could not find one. They had the tree-ring patterns of the ancient wood from the buildings and they had the tree-ring patterns of still living trees. They looked and looked for specimens that would bridge the gap between the dead and living trees. Their archaeological chronology came up to AD 1275. The oldest they could find in a living tree was AD 1285. Close but no cigar. They were ten years shy of completing the chronology.

A year later, a park ranger found what he thought was a very old tree. He took a tree-ring core sample and sent it to Edmund Schulman, one of the dendrochronologists. Schulman was back on site in a flash and took twenty-six more cores from the same tree. It turns out this Douglas fir first sprouted in AD 1170. He had completed his chronology with more than a hundred years to spare.

Not until sixteen years later, in the course of preparing a museum exhibit, did students notice that this tree had had a section cut in prehistoric times with a stone axe. They then found the two nearby trees that had likewise been bent and subsequently had a reiterating stem removed. The eight-hundred-year-old tree that had completed the chronology was a tree that had been cultivated and cut by human beings. The human use of the tree had not shortened its life; it had lengthened it.

SAMI PINE

The great northern boreal forest.

There if anywhere the great untouched virgin forest is intact. Right?

For centuries—at least since the botanist Linnaeus, who traveled among the Lapps—visiting Europeans have wondered about the scars found about breast height on the north sides of scots pines in the forests where Sami people live or lived, in present-day Norway, Sweden, Finland, and Russia. Some decided that the elliptical openings were marks made by farmer settlers in the nineteenth century. But study of the growth rings of the folds of wood closing the wounds showed they were far too old for that. The Lapps, the Sami, had made them. Were they sacred signs? Were they trail markers? Were they records of reindeer migration? What were they doing there, and why were there so many of them?

After much questioning, some native informants shamefacedly admitted that when their ancestors had been starving, they might have harvested some of the tasty and nutritious phloem, or inner bark, the carrier of the food elaborated in the pine needles, to make a famine bread.

But, they contended, they had learned this practice from others, and now eschewed it. So ingrained was the notion that they were an inferior people, who had only lately benefited from God's gift of cereal grains, that they would not own a practice as old as their people.

I found a similar attitude in New York City in the 1990s, when I went to teach poetry in a bilingual class in a public school. I started the class in Spanish. *"¿Quién domina el español?"* I asked. "Who speaks Spanish here?" Not a single hand went up. I asked a few kids whom I thought must be native speakers. *"¿Ud. no habla español?"* I asked. *"¿Yo? Yo no,"* responded a nine-year-old boy. Whoops. I realized that I embarrassed him in front of all his friends.

I had better do something quick. I had been planning to transition into fun with tongue twisters in both Spanish and English. Instead, I said in English, "The great language for poetry in the twentieth century is not English. It is Spanish." I started in on the rich names of the poets: Federico García Lorca, Pablo Neruda, Gabriela Mistral, Rafael Alberti, Antonio Machado, Octavio Paz, César Vallejo. As I pronounced the names, I could tell from the ears pricking up who really spoke Spanish, but I could also see they were dreading a lesson.

"Who can pronounce the Spanish double *r*?" I asked.

The same young man who had not spoken Spanish, ventured "err-rre." It rolls and rattles your lips and the roof of your mouth. When you were a child, did you ever tie a playing card to the back of your bike frame, so it made a rattling motorcycle noise as the spokes struck it? That is the errrre.

"Yes!"

"Rrrrapidos rrrrapidos corrrren los carrros del ferrrocarrrril."

[How quickly how quickly run the cars of the railroad train.]

I asked everyone to say it. With hesitation, all did.

We said it again and again until the whole room was chanting it.

A girl volunteered, "El perrro de San Rrrroque no tiene rrrrabo. . . ."

[Saint Roque's dog has lost his tail. . . .]

I finished it with the proper rejoinder, "Porque Rrrramon Rrramirez se lo ha rrrrrobado."

[Because Ramon Ramirez stole it.]

We chanted that too.

Eventually, we found we had a lot of Spanish speakers, and those who were just beginners wanted to speak Spanish too. From there it is was not far to:

¡Oh, ciudad de los gitanos!
En las esquinas, banderas.
La luna y la calabaza
con las guindas en conserva.

Oh, city of the gypsies,
with flags on every corner.
The moon and the pumpkin
and the jars of cherry jam.

That is García Lorca, and it turns out you can chant that as well.

The Sami too are again finding pride in what their ancestors did, and in the deep knowledge through which they thrived in the north. Not only is pine phloem tasty and nutritious, but you can harvest it without destroying the trees, so your resource is perennial.

Scholars get angry when you tell them something has happened since time immemorial, but they are just going to have to get used to the fact that there was a time when measuring its passage was not so important. The truth is, no one knows when the Sami began to do this. They peeled back the bark and harvested strips of the long blond- to buff-colored inner bark. They did it in the spring, when the bark and the phloem peel easily. From the tree's point of view, it is also a good time, because a wound will most quickly begin to close. It is the season for making and growing cells. The Sami then wrapped the strips in bark and buried them, building a slow fire above to cook the stuff. (Recently, they have slowly cooked it on direct flame.) The prepared phloem was ground into a flour. Just like rye or wheat flour, it was mixed into everything—in the Samis' case, from cloudberries to reindeer blood.

And it turns out the Lapps were not the only ones to harvest and reharvest conifers. If you draw a circle with a compass around the northern cap of the world, almost everywhere it finds land and trees, it finds a people who lived by them: in the Adirondacks, in the Northwest Territories, in Siberia.

HARVEST OF MAST

American Indians are supposed to have had the luxury of virgin land. Raised in the lap of a verdant nature, they had the luck to be able to live off her. We admire—or, more precisely, envy—this supposed good fortune. There is some truth to this legend. Because American mountain ranges run north to south—whereas those of Europe run east to west—it was easier for plant species to repopulate North America after the Ice Age than it was for them to come back into Europe. (The seed and pollen of European species had to go over the mountains, while the American mountains and the prevailing winds guided the trees north.) There are more than eight hundred species of native tree in eastern North America, and only around eighty in Europe. But the idea that the Indians lived passively in the lap of the land is both condescending and false. They shaped and maintained their land as thoroughly as did the Nordic peoples or the Basques. Only they responded to what they themselves had been given, a different gift.

Fruits and nuts in many parts of North America were readily available. Acorn was elegant. You just popped off the cup, broke the husk, and out popped the nutritious kernel. Chestnut was just as easy to eat, though a little starchy. Hickory nuts were not so easy to get at. In fact, they were something like a Chinese puzzle. You first had to extract the nut from its four-beaked covering, then open the tough husk and try to remove the seed, which was held to the husk by veining. If you have ever tried to open a hickory nut with a walnut opener, you know it is no easy proposition. The Indians who ate hickory nuts—mainly shagbark and mockernut—whacked the nut with a rock or a wooden mallet. Then they threw the broken mass into boiling water and let the heat and agitation sort out the meat from the skin. Or they picked out what shell they could and worked the remains into an oily ball called *kanuchee*. When they later soaked the ball to dissolve it, the shell bits floated to the surface, where they could be removed. Black walnut and butternut (or white walnut) both had a slimy, squishy outer husk that had to be removed before you got to the nut from which to extract the meat, but at least once that was done, the nut came out cleanly.

As comparatively laborious as they were to get at, however, hickory and walnuts were much easier to eat than acorn. Acorns had to be leached to remove the astringent tannins. The hickories and walnuts could be popped in the mouth. Furthermore, they were oily. If you put a butternut in your mouth, for instance, you learned why it was so named. An explosion of oil filled your mouth, and for a moment you were not sure if it was delicious or disgusting. All of them, unlike acorn, could be boiled to extract an oil for use in cooking and in medicine.

From around 8000 years ago until about 200—in other words, for almost eight millennia—these principal nut trees, along with about two dozen other trees and shrubs, formed the staple diet of the Indians of the eastern woodlands. The Indians did not climb the trees but waited for the nuts to fall. Throughout the river-bottom villages of the forestlands, the chief archaeological finds in middens and house sites were pieces of charred nut shells. Through the use of these plants, the Indians learned how to process and preserve vegetable foods to carry them more reliably through what could otherwise be the starving times of late winter. Even at the end of this period, during the third quarter of the eighteenth century, the plant collector and writer William Bartram reported in his *Travels* a number of Creek and Cherokee villages that were surrounded by what he described as orchards of hickory and other nuts. He had not the least doubt that the Indians cultivated the trees. In one Creek household, he found stored away for winter about one hundred bushels of dried hickory nuts. At eight gallons to the bushel, that was about eight hundred gallons of nuts.

Without burning, however, these mast forests would not have lasted a century, never mind seven-plus millennia. All the nut species love sun. Without clearing, they are outcompeted by trees that tolerate shade: maples, hemlocks, beeches. (Thanks to Smokey the Bear and his fire suppression campaign, forests in some parts of the East, once dominated by oak and hickory, are now turning to red and sugar maple.) In most of the eastern woodland—except the far north and far south—the Indians burned parts of the woodland on a cycle of one to fifteen years. Studies of fire scars on ancient trees and studies of witness trees—those used to mark boundaries in deeds—show that the nut-bearing trees were very often close to Indian villages. The term Indian summer very likely referred to the red, hazy weather occasioned by regular autumn burning—not, as some have said, to Indian hunting season.

Burning the understory on a regular basis did not damage the large trees. At most, it may have caused them to release a few sprouts or suckers at the base. Dormant buds waited in broadleaf trees for a stimulus to release them. In the case of hickory, the appearance of basal sprouts was desirable, because the wood was in demand for bows and for tool handles of all kinds. (Hickory is still the preferred axe handle.) Burning removed diseased and infested nuts. It cleared away competitors and low ground covers that made gathering difficult. It brought more light to the understory. It killed the seedlings of the shade-tolerant trees that might otherwise have outcompeted the nut trees.

Clearing by fire also burned the tops, and sometimes the entire crowns, of the smaller plants that gave nuts and fruits to both animals and people. Redbud, serviceberry, hawthorn, *Aronia*, pawpaw, plum, hackberry, chokecherry, elberberry, sassafras, crab apple, black haw: all have edible fruit. The firing of the land acted as a kind of coppice, removing all or most of the plant to the base, from which it sprouted again. This brought low, straight, easily harvested stems for human users and readily available provender for deer and other animals upon which humans also fed.

The regular burning also gave rise to the first agriculture in eastern North America. The Indians of the eastern woodlands did not adopt corn agriculture until fourteen hundred years after the southwestern Indians. They had no need for it. The annual weeds along the flats by the river— marsh elder (a relative of ragweed), lamb's-quarters, pumpkins and other squash, knotweed, little barley, and maygrass—all yielded large quantities of edible seed. Lamb's-quarters gave back 50,000 seeds in exchange for 1, marsh elder 5,000 for 1.

What we call weeds, they called dinner. Opportunists that sprouted where the sun reached, these plants gave seeds to be ground for porridges and breads. In the fall, the women and children harvested the plants, saving seeds to plant again next spring. As they burned the nut-tree corners of the forest, they could plant the new crops in the sunny spaces. In this way, the Indians of the woodlands created a rich and enduring culture, driven not by scarcity and population pressure, but by orders-of-magnitude improvements in access to food.

NAGEREBA

My obsession with sprouting and with the antiquity and scope of people's life with trees had taken on the quality of a quest. Everywhere I went, someone sent me further. While I was talking to the Indians about fire coppice in California, someone told me about the culture of coppice oak forests in Japan. They said that classical Japanese culture had been based on coppice woods. It was shocking news to me. Off I went.

In ancient Japan, there were thought to be five elements, not four. Earth, air, water, and fire were four, just as in the West. The fifth element was wood. "Fire cannot sustain itself," reasoned a seventeenth-century shogun. "It requires wood. Hence, wood is central to a person's hearth and home. And wood comes from the mountains. Wood is fundamental to the hearth; the hearth is central to the person." It is hard to put it clearer than that.

Near the town of Tono in Iwate, a winter-cold northern prefecture on Japan's main island, stands a footbridge across the Kesen River. At first glance, it looks to have been made by an idiot. There are nice broad cedar planks for a walking platform, but they are not joined end to end. Instead they are in three sections, each butting against another section simply by placing the two ends beside each other, overlapping, on a support. So you walk a straight line, then sidestep, then walk another line, then sidestep back, and finally reach the other side, about two hundred

A *Nagereba* bridge, showing the deck planks, the crosspieces, and the coppice piers.

feet from the start. From the air, it would look like diagram of a dance step. The piers themselves stand in the water like the jointed legs of insects. Upside-down coppiced crowns of walnut and chestnut flex as though about to pounce in the river bottom, each piece on two or three legs, the former crown branches of the coppice. These spider legs run in rough pairs across the river. Joining each pair as a pier cap or headstock is a planed board that is mortised to receive the tenoned trunk of the trees. The walking platform is simply laid atop these and a bamboo rail is lashed along one side. The bridge has been there—well, sort of—since about the seventeenth century. It is called a *nagereba* bridge.

Nagereba is an inflected form of the Japanese verb *nageru*. Kenkyu-sha's *New Japanese English School Dictionary* gives the definitions as follows: "throw, hurl, fling, cast, pitch, toss, thrown down, or throw away." The inflection gives roughly the meaning "In case it should be thrown down, hurled, flung, cast, pitched, tossed. . . ."

When a big storm hits, if the water is high and rough enough, the *nagereba* bridge comes apart. Like the Scarecrow in *The Wizard of Oz*, its legs go one way, its headstocks another. The big planks of the bearing beams are tethered to the shore. They turn to mime the stream flow. The river rushes over them until the storm is over. Then out come the townspeople from both sides. They look for the piers and the headstocks. If they need to, they cut new ones. They reel in the beams. Working as a team, they put the bridge back together.

Nagereba mo. If it is thrown down, put it back.

About six hundred miles away in the city of Kyoto is the Philosopher's Path, a lovely creekside walk that leads tourists from one stately temple to another. In the great Zen temples, the gardeners rake parallel channels of sand around the islands of selected rocks; they match moss floors and canopies of pale green maple leaves. They have no compunction about treating those Japanese maples just as the country people do their trees to

make the *nagereba* bridge piers: Where they want new branching to ramify a crown, they make selected pollard cuts on the ends of branches. And
bang, back come three or four new branches, sprouting just behind the
cut. On the ground beneath, they rake away dirt and channel the moss,
so the root tops are exposed. Crown and root do not mirror but reflect
each other, showing their similar idea and different execution.

My wife, Nora, and I were walking that Kyoto path. We were completely exhausted from temple viewing. Each place was so grand and so
perfect, even in its smallest corners. I envied several of the pruners I
saw. They simply carried their homemade tripod ladders from one tree to
another for their whole careers, meticulously snipping and shaping their
one astonishing garden.

A small bridge across the stream had a sign pointing to a *jinja*, a
Shinto shrine. It was uphill all the way, we sighed, but why not? It might
prove a change of pace.

Shinto and Buddhism were formerly commingled in Japan, but in the
modernizing Meiji period, the Japanese decided to forcibly separate them.
Among the bad results was the strident deification of the emperor, who—
though in fact a puppet of the rising military oligarchs—was represented
as the god figurehead under whose banner the nation was to go to war. It
was also the Meiji sages who imported the word "religion" to Japan. (It first
appeared in a commercial treaty with the Germans in 1868.) Prior to this
time, there were Shinto gods in Zen temples and Buddhist deities in Shinto
shrines, but no one thought to sort it out or to call any of it "religion."

We struggled up the hill, with one or two rests. (At one house, I saw a
simple combination of two hydrangeas and one nandina, making a lovely
front garden, no larger than a love seat, out of modulating whites, reds, and
greens, with short, fat light green leaves mingled with sharp-spear-tip dark
green ones.) Finally, we came to the *torii* gates that led to the very edge of
town, where mountain meets houses. Each Shinto shrine is guarded by a

pair of spirits, one standing tall with its mouth open and the other seated with its mouth closed. These are meant to show the two ways of resisting evil: by attacking and defeating, or by enfolding and converting. The deities are often lions, dogs, or even foxes. Here, however, they were mice.

Nezumi-sama. Komanezumi. Honored mice. Guardian mice. In the beginning times, a prince fell in love with a beautiful maiden. Her jealous father told the young man to fetch an arrow that he had shot into the middle of a field of grass. As soon as the suitor set out, Dad set the field on fire. As the prince was about to be consumed, a mouse appeared and gave him entry to her hole. The fire passed harmlessly over. (This, by the way, is the best hope to survive a wildfire: Dig a shallow hole and lie down. It is still taught to woodland firefighters around the world.) As soon as the flames passed, the mouse handed the prince the arrow.

At this shrine, one of the mice stands with her mouth open and what is interpreted as a sutra scroll held in her forepaws. The other is bowing, closemouthed, over something that looks like a child's top but that is said to be a sake bowl. The latter augers a healthy baby, long life, and luck. Young lovers and expectant mothers often pray here. The same thing happens at a church in the South of France dedicated to Mary Magdalene. Young wives go there to scrawl upside-down *U*s on the dark, damp wall of the crypt where the relics of the saint are enshrined. Within it, they scratch vertical lines, one for each hoped-for child.

In the South of France, things became sacred by association with the holy ones of scripture. In Japan, there was in theory nothing without a soul. Rock, river, hill, cave, tree, fox, mouse, chicken, man, woman, smallpox, cancer, and the cure for cancer: all had been enspirited. Often in the larger shrines and sometimes even in the countryside, one comes upon ropes made of a white paper folded into streamlined quadrilaterals like cartoon lightning bolts. These may be wrapped around an immense Japanese cedar (a cryptomeria), a small boulder, a statue, a lamppost, or the street where a procession will pass. They are most often seen within the precincts of shrines, but sometimes also in the landscape. Each signals that in that place a *kami* is among us.

There is no shortage of different *kami*. One shrine in Tokyo is said to enshrine more than 2 million of them. They are not transcendent gods or abstract spiritual entities. It is in fact hard to say just what they are. They are a little like Heisenberg's uncertainty principle for quanta: you can't simultaneously fix their location and their path. They are perhaps the energy by which a thing acts among other things. "Energy is eternal delight," wrote Blake, always and only expressed through a particular thing, place, or person. *Kami* may be grand in their effect or almost trivial: A pair of these *kami* is said to have created Japan and all that is in it, for example; another *kami* is said to cure (and yet another to cause) toothache.

People then cannot act as a realm that is apart from nature. Everything has spirit, energy, and everything is enmeshed with everything else. The Japanese are therefore not shy about acting on the world around them. There is little thought of a pristine Nature, apart from human beings. Praying to mice is one aspect of this way of living. So is the deep pruning of a tree. The *nagereba* bridge is another: It is not superior or inferior to the natural world. It is part of it. The overwhelming energy of a big storm takes it apart; the enfolding energy of the townspeople puts it back together.

The shrine of the *nezumi-sama* sat on the very edge of Kyoto. The roads led down from it, but above was steep, untracked woodland. (There were in fact a number of makeshift plywood and metal barriers behind the shrine to keep the one from flowing down onto the other.) Almost every shrine, except for some at city centers, is so located: on the edge between steep and level ground. Such land is not hard to find in Japan. Seventy percent of the rural landscape consists of short, steep mountains with narrow valleys at their base. It is the signature landscape of the countryside, and from it a people was made.

No one knows when rice was first grown in paddies in Japan. The technique certainly came from China and from Korea. Perhaps it came not once, but a number of times. The first evidence of a rice paddy in Japan dates back 6000 years, during the Neolithic Jomon period, but not until about 2500 years ago did it become the normal and pervasive way to grow a staple food so important that the name for any meal is *gohan*, which literally means "rice." The phrase for "peace and prosperity" is *gokoku hoojyoo*, which means "a good rice harvest."

Though the farmers complain that people are now abandoning them for horrible things like croissants, spaghetti, and buttered bread, it was still remarkable to see the extent of rice paddies through the entire countryside. A broader valley had them by the dozen, a narrower one had all that would fit, and even the narrowest defile between canyon slopes had one or two. The lower part of a steep coastal slope might be terraced into a brocade of paddies descending the hill in stages. Even in the small towns, instead of a garden beside the house, four times out of five there was a paddy. The strangely modulated green of them—winking lighter and darker as the light on the water comes and goes—becomes a part of your eyescape. When the color and sheen of them is absent, you think that something has gone wrong.

For at least two millennia, the paddy field has been at the center of Japanese culture, but it did not stand there alone. The grasslands beside the paddies were regularly harvested for thatching, for bedding, and for fodder, and the trees on the woodland slopes fueled and warmed the villages. One poem in the ancient anthology *Manyōshū* calls Japan "the rice-abounding land of reed plains." Rain falling on the hillsides soaked into the ground through the trees and the grasslands, emerging near the bottoms in springs, the indispensable source of water to keep the paddies wet. The hills served as reservoirs of groundwater. The growing trees— mainly the two Japanese oaks, *konara* and *kunugi*—trickled the water off their leaves and trunks into the dirt. The water percolated into the ground instead of running off. The farmers took up the fallen oak leaves and the grasses, either composting them directly or feeding them to their draft animals. The manure and compost went into the paddies as a fertilizer, all that was needed to supplement the nitrogen supplied by the blue-green algae and the fish and frogs and other animals living in the water.

Before the people ate the rice, they cooked it over charcoal made chiefly from the *konara* and *kunugi* oaks. They coppiced a part of every hillside every fifteen to twenty years, cutting back a section of the trees to a few inches above ground. The woods were called the *booga mori*, the forests of sprouts, the sprout lands. As the trees grew back, different plants also sprouted among them, some brought in by birds or the wind, some from the dormant pool of seeds. It was not an impoverished landscape but as rich a land as the place has ever known. Where uncut woodlands have about 176 different species of plants living in them, the whole mosaic of the *booga mori* has 351. It is twice as diverse as an untouched forest.

The tree roots stayed in the soil to hold the water and feed the springs. The trees quickly sprouted back. The cut wood went for firewood or for charcoal. (In 1940, the woods still yielded 2.7 million tons of charcoal.) The brushy tops might be kept for fire starter, used to dry sea salt, or even thrown into the water to make habitat for fish or oysters. Some of the trunks were cut into logs, each inoculated with mushrooms. Year by year, people would cut another section, so there were always parts of the woodland in different states of growth. It was a way to make edges, and edges within edges, multiplying the conditions in the landscape, so creatures that loved different habitats all could thrive. In the new-cut lands, the giant purple butterfly (now the national butterfly) lived, along with stag beetles and longhorn beetles, both prized as pets by children. Dragonflies cruised the paddies and the grasslands, straying into the open young forest. Rice fish, frogs, and freshwater molluscs inhabited the paddies. Bumble bees and wildflowers coevolved, so that the order of flowering and the shape of the flowers corresponded to the time when different bees and different bee life-stages were present. The flowers were long and wide when only the bumblebee queen was gathering pollen and short and fat when the smaller workers were out and about.

As the trees grew in, overhanging the paddies and the rice fields, the gray-faced buzzard and the golden eagle perched atop them, waiting for frogs to reveal themselves, harvest mice to nest in the waving grasses, and rabbits to run across a new-mown field. As the grasses grew back and the rice matured, the birds moved into the woods to hunt. Eighty-five different butterfly and moth species fed or reproduced on the regrowing *konara* and *kunugi*. The two great songbirds of Japanese poetry—the springtime *uguisu* and the summer-visiting *hototogisu*—both live in the regrowing coppice and in the tall grass. When you walk on a paddy edge in June, the call of the *hototogisu* is sometimes almost constant, along with the last songs of the springtime *uguisu,* whose song is said to name the Lotus Sutra.

The youngest sprouts—growing in discrete mounds like a colony of tortoises—shared their sunny space with wildflowers and grasses. The people enshrined those they most valued. The sacred rope around them was made out of language. *The Haru no nanakusa* (Seven Spring Herbs) were gathered for a New Year festival, *Nanakusa no Sekku,* on January 7. These were the first herbaceous sprouts of the coming spring. People ritually laid out their cooking utensils, sang a song, and went to hunt the plants. They made the catch into a tart soup.

The first sections of the *Kokinshu* and the *Shinkokinshu,* two of the principal imperial poetry anthologies, each have more than a dozen poems about going to pick the wild spring herbs. Even today, there is a great deal more seasonal wild food available in Japan than in most other developed nations of the world. Tempura is often made with wild herbs of the paddy, the cut grassland, and the coppiced hill. *Yamaudo, taranome,* and *koshidowa* are three whose stems and leaves are battered and quick-fried. *Taranome* in particular is valued for its tart, almost astringent flavor. The bulb of *katakuri*, a trout lily that grows in the new-cut woods, is powdered to make a starch to coat and to thicken other foods. The little purple trumpet flowers carpet the ground in early spring under the regrowing coppice.

The *Aki no nanakusa* (seven autumn grasses) were likewise crucial for both cooking and culture. Among them, the *hagi* was used to flavor rice or made into a tea, and the *kuzu* root was ground and used to thicken foods. The glory of these plants, however, was their place in Japanese poetry. In all the great imperial anthologies, the defining classics—the *Manyōshū*, the *Kokinshu*, and the *Shinkokinshu*—the autumn flowers are keys to the season.

They are among the chief *kigo*, or season words, by which autumn is announced. *Hagi*, the bush clover, droops gracefully, but sprouts with wild abandon. It was admired for its feminine grace and its perennial fruitfulness. It flowers white even as its leaves are reddening, just as the deer call to their mates. It became a symbol of *mono no aware*, the evanescence of life and love. The plant appears in 137 autumn poems in the *Manyōshū*, and in many more in the later anthologies. *Ominaeshi*, the yellow, fragrant maiden flower, was celebrated for scenting the autumn air and for its waving blossoms. It reminded people of love in autumn and even apparently tempted Buddhist priests to ignore their vows of chastity and nonattachment. A great poetry contest of the Heian period was called the Tenjinoin Maiden Flower Contest.

Here and there in the anthologies, the coppiced oaks themselves appear. The coppice forests were called *hahaso*. In one poem the mountainside woods were called *Hahaki*, a pun, or *kakekotoba*, meaning both oak woods and mother woods.

This landscape of dynamic edges has recently been dubbed *satoyama*, marking the interface between *sato* (village) and *yama* (mountain). So central to the Japanese was this kind of place that when commoners were required to adopt surnames at the end of the nineteenth century—the better for the Meiji modernizers to be able to tax them—the majority chose names that located them in the *satoyama* landscape. Tanaka was from the middle field, Shibata from the firewood hill, Ikeda from the paddy pond, Kimura from oak wood village. Nishimura came from a village west of there, and Hasegawa lived along the river in the long valley. Yamaguchi lived where the road climbed into the mountains, Morita by the field at the woods' edge. Maeda lived by the first field out of town, Yamada by the field deepest in the mountains. Takata was from the highest field, Yamamoto from the hill bottom. Koyama lived by a little hill, Takayama by a tall one. The west river of Nishigawa fed the west field of Nishiyama. Oohira and Hirayama came from the broad reed plains. In a hard rain, Uchida got dirt that came down the channel from Ueda's field above. Wada came from a quiet field and Honda from the center one. Kawasaki lived near the river mouth, Nakagawa in the middle of it. Takagi lived by the tall tree. Kozawa's field was by the little swamp, and Hamada's field was on the seashore. A third of the one hundred most common Japanese surnames have either *yama* (hill or mountain) or *ta* (paddy, rice field) in the name.

In Japan, the field and forest together created a culture that endured for two and a half millennia. It was not without problems. Early, in the AD 600s, the rise of metallurgy and its need for abundant charcoal seem to have led to overcutting of the *booga mori*. Some woods were lost, and erosion ruined rice fields. The people put the forests back. A document in AD 821 commented, "The fundamental principle for securing water is found in the combination of forests and trees." People learned what they could and could not do. In the late Edo period, before Japan opened to the West, rising population led to overexploitation of the forests. The result was the same. The Meiji authorities reined in the excess, and the *satoyama* recovered.

The third time the coppice woods have been threatened is the present. After World War II, Japanese culture was itself in ruins. Petroleum came into the burned land like a miracle. You could heat the house with it and cook with it. You could even fertilize the rice fields with it. Who needed that laborious old *booga mori*? Who needed the *hahaso*? Indeed, who needed the *Manyōshū*, the *Kokinshu*, and the *Shinkokinshu*, silly elitist books? Let's get people off the land and into the factories! We will become instantly modern! We will have all kinds of stuff! Instead of destruction and starvation.

The *booga mori* declined rapidly. Annual charcoal production dropped 99 percent, from 2.7 million tons in 1940 to 28,000 tons at the turn of the century. During the 1960s and 1970s, around the big cities, *satoyama* landscape was turned into new towns and suburbs at a rate of 150,000 acres per year. The area of coppice woods around Yokohama, for example, declined by two-thirds between 1960 and 2005. The Japanese had always prided themselves on being self-sufficient in food. To this day, farmers as a group are protected, and designated farmland can only be bought and sold among farmers. During that same period, however, the ability of the Japanese to feed themselves dropped from 73 percent to 34 percent. And when the coppice woodlands were not urbanized, they were often converted into plantations. Huge tracts of land in rural northern and western Japan were converted from *konara* and *kunugi* to Japanese cedar and red pine, marketable timber.

Tama New Town was the archetype of postwar development. To prevent the chaotic suburbanization of Tokyo, as thousands of people moved there, the metropolitan government in 1965 began a meticulously planned project to convert the Tama Hills, twenty miles from the center of the capital, into a network of connected suburbs. Heretofore, it had been almost entirely *satoyama* landscape. To make the apartment buildings, malls, stations, and parking lots, they cut the tops off mountains and dropped the dirt in the valleys, making flat heights for building and flat bottoms for parking. In 2017, Tama New Town was eight miles long and two miles wide. A quarter of a million people lived there.

Tama Center is its commercial hub. The train from Shinjuku station takes you there, and from there you can fan out on suburban buses and rail lines. Don't try to walk, however. You cannot cross the street from the station to the mall with its high-rise hotel unless you go up and down half a dozen flights of stairs. Barriers prevent pedestrians from simply walking across the street. This was not an accident of development, but a thoughtful scheme on the part of the developers. For safety's sake, they decided to keep the human and vehicle traffic separate, but the vehicles did not have to struggle up and down stairs. We people did.

My wife and I made the crossing one Friday in June. Once across, we stood in the remains of a *satoyama*. It was now called Parthenon Avenue. A wide masonry pedestrian mall bordered by two raised beds with about fifty trees, it was flanked by hotels, department stores, and shops. It sloped up, just as it did when it was *hahaso*, but at the top, instead of a mountaintop, was a parody of a parody: a three-bay set of concrete uprights topped with concrete plinths. It was hard to tell if it looked more like Stonehenge, an exposed building foundation, a Greek temple entry, or a shrine gate. Mussolini would have been proud of it. Tama Center is known as the City of Hello Kitty. The chief crossing avenue leads to the Sanrio Puro, a Hello Kitty–themed amusement park. On this summer evening, the sunset was obscured by the imitation rainbow arch that invites you there. Schoolgirls in their white shirts and black skirts trooped in and out.

There were once more than 350 plant species in Tama's woodland. Now, in Tama Center, there were maybe 10 or 12, all disciplined to fit inside the long planter beds that flank that paved avenue. On the other hand, there were thousands of different products for sale. The Mitsukoshi department store alone had an entire floor of restaurants. They had traded one diversity for another: given up the dynamic and living diversity that depended upon intelligent human interaction to maintain and preserve it, in exchange for a vast selection of goods. Where you might have had many different roles in a *satoyama*—forester, farmer, basket maker, bamboo shoot collector, mushroom farmer, *mochi* maker, potter, blacksmith, collier, homemaker—there were only three on the Tama Center mall: buyer, seller, or support staff. It was a terrific department store, but somehow it didn't seem like a fair trade.

Many Japanese agreed. There were protests in the streets. Two great *anime* movies arose to defend the *satoyama*. One of them, known in its English release as *Pom Poko*, though in Japanese its title means *The Heisei Raccoon Dog Wars,* was actually a saga about the building of Tama New Town. The *tanuki,* or raccoon dog, is a small mammal that in Japanese legend is adept at transforming itself into other creatures. The film recounts the efforts of the *tanuki* to prevent the destruction of their habitat by the rapacious humans. This is the best place to see what Tama looked like as a *satoyama*: there are *anime* scenes that clearly show the coppice woods and the rice fields together. In one scene, all the *tanuki* together exert their shape-shifting powers to transform the brand new high-rise suburb back into *satoyama*. The people looking out their apartment windows are delighted and surprised. One recognizes her mother on a village path. But the effect is temporary.

The second movie is the most popular film ever made in Japan. *My Neighbor Totoro* tells how two young girls and their father move to a small farm house in a *satoyama* village not far from Tokyo in the Sayama Hills, to be near the mother, who is recovering in a sanatorium. There, the girls—first four-year-old Mei and then her eleven-year-old sister, Satsuki—meet a gigantic purple egglike creature whom Mei dubs Totoro. (There are also smaller Totoros running everywhere, as well as living herds of charcoal dust.) The girls first meet Totoro together on a rainy evening when he appears beside them at a bus stop. The girls lend him an umbrella. He loves the way the rain sounds when it patters and pelts on the canvas. He appears to think they have given him a musical instrument. Their father says that the girls are lucky. They have met the spirit of the forest. When Totoro helps them, they go to the largest tree in their woods to thank him. *My Neighbor Totoro* is exactly about the spirits infused in the living world. The Totoro are *kami*. In the antidevelopment protests, it was often a Totoro banner that led the way, and one rallying cry was "If you destroy the *satoyama*, we will no longer be Japanese."

Who were they kidding? Or perhaps it was not such an exaggeration after all. If you took away the rice fields, with their calling frogs, their rice fish, their *sansai* for seasonal gathering, their hunting buzzards and eagles, their planting, growth, and fruiting; if you took away the coppice woods, with their woodcutters, their singing *uguisu*, with the seven spring herbs and the seven autumn grasses, with the red autumn leaves of the *hahaso*; if you took away the grasslands with their annual cutting or burning, their *hototogisu* singing, the harvest mice swaying on the stems, then what remains to connect a people to their own story?

In the early tenth century, the poet and compiler Ki no Tsurayuki wrote the preface to the *Kokinshu*. "The seeds of Japanese poetry," he said, "lie in the human heart, and they sprout the countless leaves of words." To describe what people see and hear around them, he asserted, was the way in which poets could sing the feelings of human beings in the round of the four seasons. People were not the only singers. "When we hear the call of the *uguisu* in the cherry blossoms or the voice of the frog in the water, we know every living being has its song," he continued. If the voices of the creatures were stilled and the words of the poets faded into the barely remembered pastel once-upon-a-time, then where were the Japanese? What would become of the words that could "move heaven and earth, arouse the *kami* and the spirits, calm the relations between men and women, and pacify the hearts of fierce warriors," when the things that they referred to were no more? Are the contents of a Mitsukoshi department store, lovely as they are, enough to make up that loss?

Many Japanese have thought not. From protest, they went into action. They had the model of the *Nagereba* bridge: *"Nagereba mo,"* "If it is swept away, put it back." The volunteer movement began in the very shadow of Tama New Town, at Sakuragaoka Park. A concession to the citizenry, the park opened in 1984. It was all hill and valley, all former coppice woods and rice paddies. If you walked into the woodland today, you would see hundreds of *kunugi* and *konara* that have not been cut for more than half a century. Each of their multiple sprouting trunks are now as big around as a barrel. If you were to cut the trees again, they might not answer well. They have been let go for too long. The forest they have created is now dark.

In the sun on the edge of one such wood, however, were three long garden beds. Each was planted with the perennials and shrubs that once grew in the *satoyama* here. The plantings were separated into the three seasons of flowering: spring, summer, and autumn. It was a study garden. Members of the Sakuragaoka Park Volunteers, a group founded in 1990 and now numbering about eighty-five members, learn their plants here, so when they go to restore the woodland, they know what not to cut.

That Saturday morning, when I went to meet them, their room in the park office was a forest of human sounds: scraping of chairs, sharpening of tools, footfalls, giggling, passing woodland gossip, greeting the visiting *gaijin* (foreigner), comparing bamboo baskets, getting their assignments, filling their water bottles. Kishimoto Koichi, a retired software engineer who knew not a single plant when he first volunteered a decade ago, was their leader. In certain seasons, they cut trees. In others, they found and marked out rare or important plants. At almost all times, they cut back the persistent *sasa*, a small but very vigorous and fast-spreading bamboo, along with other weeds. *Zasso* is the name for weeds in Japanese. It is wonderfully onomatopoeic.

The others had gone out to work before we were ready to follow. We walked on an asphalt-paved park path. Suddenly, Kishimoto made a left turn between two newly planted sweet potato plots. "We planted these," he said in passing. He was walking straight into a wall of bamboo overhung by large old once-coppiced oaks. He pushed his way into the thicket. "Come on," he told me. Just inside, there was a clean dirt trail, completely invisible from the path. There was a small sign saying that this area—about 4 of the park's 40 acres—was reserved for the volunteers. He smiled as I came up behind. "Our secret garden," he said.

Their restoration went up and down hill, in sun and in shadow. They aim to bring back both *konara* and *kunugi* coppice, with all the plants of the *booga mori*. When they started in the 1990s, they simply tried to cut back all the bamboo and coppice all the oaks. It was a disaster. The *sasa* came back faster than the trees, and they were unprepared to keep after it. They made several false starts before they learned how to manage a regenerating coppice wood. (It heartened me to hear it. They were just like we were at the Met, with no manuals and no information online.) Now, they used a carefully plotted set of thirty-seven field boundaries. Some are designated for active work, others to make a buffer between managed and unmanaged woods. It was an oak and bamboo ballet, measured in a tempo of years. Each year, they cut one of fifteen areas, bringing back its trees. In a decade and a half, they return to the same area. Meantime, the volunteers visit all the actively managed areas at least once per year, keeping back the bamboo and the other invasives.

There were strange tiny flexible arcs in blue or white plastic that marked off certain patches of ground. These protected where the volunteers had found rare or coppice wood species. More than sixty differ-

A selection of resprouting *konara* and *kunugi* oaks, at Sakuragaoka Park near Tama New Town, Japan.

ent species had returned since they began, almost all from the dormant seed pool in the overgrown woods. (Animals had also returned. A newt thought to be extinct in Metropolitan Tokyo was recently found in a stream here.) Kishimoto showed me a tall multistem shrub that they have brought back and nurtured. It was a honeysuckle called *Uguisu kagura* that flowers dark pink in early spring, just when the bird called the *uguisu* begins to sing, and develops bright red ovoid fruit in summer. The bird loves to sit on its stems and swing while it sings, so the com-

mon name for the plant means, "where the *uguisu* does its sacred dance."
As if responding to a cue, a bird started piping in the trees around us,
dodleeeedo, dodeleeedoo. Do deedoo deedoo. The call would follow us for
the next half hour, sometimes making it hard to understand one another.
It was the *uguisu,* just at the end of its season of song.

The volunteers were in a shady hollow, armed with shears, small
saws, hedge trimmers, and a lot of bottled water. It was a muggy morning. Their talk was much quieter here. The work was not glamorous.
Mainly, it was weeding what was invasive and precisely not weeding what
was meant to remain. But it was work done together, and they obviously
enjoyed the company of their fellow weeders. When they looked to the
edge of the area, where a buffer section was, they saw how much difference their work made. Even in the buffer, the bamboo was as thick
as the stuffing in a pillow. For two hours in the morning and another
three in the afternoon, they would keep it up. The oaks here had been
cut five years ago, and they were now back to twelve feet tall, each stem
as big around as a person's arm. A rectangle of white arcs surrounded a
stand of a low plant that looked like Solomon's seal and was clearly in
the same genus. *"Miyama narukoyuri,"* Kishimoto said. "A lily that has
come back."

The Sakuragaoka Park Volunteers have restored no great area here.
Most of the park was beyond their reach, both logistically and contrac-
tually, but they have restored the connection of hundreds of people to
their own land and their own past. Every year, they have festivals. One
in July celebrates the huge golden spider lily that has returned to sunnier
spots of the coppice woods. The volunteers give guided tours to find it. In
autumn, they hold an acorn festival, at which they plant new *kunugi* and
konara. In February, there is a rice festival, at which they make *mochi*
cakes. They compost rice bran, *nuka,* to fertilize their sweet potato fields,
and they learn to make *nukazuke,* pickles in fermented rice bran. "We

used to get more volunteers than we do now," said Kishimoto, ruefully, but that is not because the idea is dying out. It is because there are now more than two thousand such groups in the Tokyo area alone.

Not far away, on the border between Metropolitan Tokyo and Saitama prefecture, are two of Tokyo's principal reservoirs: Tama and Sayama. Urban sprawl rapidly overran the Sayama Hills here, just as it had in Tama. An aerial photograph shows a wave of silver, gray, and white, the buildings and roads, their light colors washing up against little fingers of green forests that hug the shore of the reservoir and the courses of streams. This was the place where the director Hayao Miyazaki had set *My Neighbor Totoro*. Here in 2017 Totoro was not leading protests, but preserving *satoyama*.

The Totoro no Furusato Foundation (Totoro's Hometown Foundation) was founded on the model of the United Kingdom's National Trust. Funded in part by Miyazaki himself, it aims to prevent development of what remains of the rice fields and the *booga mori* in the Sayama Hills and to restore degraded ones. In response to the protests over vast projects like Tama New Town, the Japanese government made it much more difficult for large developers to acquire and develop whole swathes of countryside. On the other hand, they put no restrictions at all on small developers. The result was a piecemeal destruction of the remaining *satoyama* niches. In particular, developers from elsewhere in the Tokyo region bought small parcels as dumps for contaminated soils and construction debris. Especially valuable were hill-bottom wetland areas, where the dumping was easy.

The Totoro Foundation started to outbid them, and when the developers could not be outbid, the owners have often been persuaded to sell the land for preservation rather than to have it buried in garbage. Sometimes, the foundation bought degraded land, as well, and restored it. As of 2017, there were forty-one *Totoro no Mori* (Totoro Forests) in the

Sayama Hills. They amount to only about twenty acres in total, but those parcels have cost the foundation more than $5 million. In some places, they simply preserved coppice woods, without putting them back into cycle. In others, they begin the cutting anew, and plant new oak when needed. Some remove the fill from ruined paddies and restore them as working rice fields. We walked with Tsushima Ryoichi and Andoh Naoko of the foundation beside a restored paddy about to be planted. There were houses on one side, palm trees escaping from their gardens and chestnut groves on the other, but the frogs were setting up a terrific din. "The frogs are thanking us!" said Andoh. "They said, 'Don't invade here! Give us back our paddy pond.' And we did." The goshawks on the overhanging branches must also thank them, for providing abundant frogs, as must the fireflies that have returned and the *tanuki*. Here at least was one refuge for the displaced raccoon dogs.

Volunteers were important to the success of these efforts. So were local governments. While we were looking at one forest, Tsushima, the foundation's executive director, met a random visitor and signed him up to help. To restore a paddy, it was necessary not only to remove fill soil but also to turn the original soil and pull the aggressive weeds—not once, but three times per year, until the paddy ecosystem is reestablished. "It takes a lot of biomass energy to restore a field," joked Tsushima, watching his young recruit walk off. The foundation was not allowed to buy farmland, so sometimes the city or prefecture bought the land and gave it to Totoro to manage. Local governments also bought up forests adjacent to Totoro Forests, extending the preserved areas. Private citizens' groups also helped. One owner of a small golf driving range organized his neighbors to resist development and begin preservation. "He is the reason there are Totoro Forests in this place," said Tsushima.

A test came when Waseda University decided to build a satellite campus in the Sayama Hills. The original plans cut hilltops and filled paddy lowlands to make the campus. Totoro objected. So did the local governments. So did the local citizens. Instead of fighting, the university joined them. They resited the buildings and preserved the wetlands. Waseda became responsible for the annual management plan to maintain the restored paddies, reed lands, and grasslands, and the university contributes money each year to the maintenance. At first, the foundation thought it would make paddies, then leave them fallow for a decade to save money, but where sixty or more species had come back from the buried seed bank when they established the paddies, most of them went away again when cultivation stopped. The diversity depends upon the activity of the people.

Beside one field of six-foot-tall *susu* grass, the university faced a new laboratory building away from the wetland and screened all the windows on that side. The idea was to keep night lights from disturbing the rhythms of the creatures who live there. "Now the researchers complain it is too dark," said Tsushima. He smiled just a little, then caught himself. There were persistent birdcalls and answers as we bushwacked through the *susu*, the grass that once was used for thatching and for fodder. It was the first of the *hototogisu* and the last of *uguisu* together. The former was a kind of cuckoo who, like western cuckoos, had a penchant for laying eggs in other birds' nests. In this case, the *uguisu* was most often the recipient of the *hototogisu*'s eggs. Both birds were common in the woods and grasslands.

Recently, their work has also brought back the *kayanezumi*, the harvest mouse. It is a tiny native mouse. The scientists who named it wanted us to be sure about that: *Micromys minutus* is its Latin name, which, loosely interpreted, means "Tiny mouse. I mean really really tiny." It is small enough that it actually nests on the grass stalks themselves. These mice build the small ball of their nests out of the grass itself, high on the stems. The nest starts out green and turns brown.

At the shrine in Kyoto were the protector mice. In the Totoro Forest, the mice were protected. There was not just human largesse here, but a kind or reciprocity. The iconography of the Shinto prayer card—you bought it at the shrine and hung it there with your prayers—was almost exactly the same as a natural history drawing of *Micromys minutus*. In both, one mouse stood tall, the other stooped, enfolding. Coincidence? I think not. Rather I think that in some places there has remained a common understanding that all creatures share these two modes of being, in science, in song, and in prayer. One challenges the enemy directly, the other surrounds evil and causes it to surrender.

Near the big cities, it is a struggle just to keep back the buildings and the dumps. In the countryside, most coppice oak woods have been cleared and replaced with plantations of Japanese cedar (*Cryptomeria japonica*), pine, and hiba cedar (called *ate*). Where they have not been cleared, they have simply been abandoned. But on the Noto Peninsula, on the western coast of Honshu, there is a move not only to restore but also to reuse the *hahaso*.

Ohno Choichiro inherited a charcoal business started by his father in woodland near the town of Suzu on Japan's far western Noto Peninsula. The area did not escape the postwar mania for profitable plantation forestry. A lot of it was indeed planted with the then fashionable red pine. But the soils were too good. The pine didn't like them. When a major pest appeared, the pines went down, and the oaks came back.

Ohno called his business Hahaso. It was modest: He had three employees, three trucks, a splitter, chain saws, a mowing machine, and two charcoal kilns. These last stood in a wood-framed hut with corrugated plastic walls and a corrugated iron roof. When you walked in, you seemed to have entered an amateur exhibit about Eskimos. There were twin igloos fashioned out of concrete. Ohno invited me to go inside one of them. "In you go," he chuckled. "Just like the wood!" It was a tight fit. Inside, three or four hundred upright sticks of finished charcoal, each about three feet tall, leaned against the back wall. They were cooling. It took about a week to cook the charcoal, and another week for the batch to cool.

Some of the charcoal went to city barbecues, where it was in demand. Sacks full of cooled and cut charcoal—made from twenty- to thirty-year-old coppice—stood in ranks in the shed, almost ready for sale. Ohno made the best money on charcoal for the tea ceremony. For this purpose, he used only *kunugi*, which burned hotter, and he cut it young, when the stems were only about ten years old. He chose the straightest stems. When they were cooked, cooled, and cut into six-inch lengths, each was a thing of beauty: obsidian black all over, inside and out, but look from the end of the stem and you saw a perfect pattern of growth rings punctuated by the sunburst pattern of rays cells, each of which runs from the pith out to the bark. Every year, Ohno cut about four square kilometers of woodland and made about twenty thousand tons of charcoal.

We went to see fresh-cut coppice beside a dirt road. The other side of the road was lined with rice paddies. Until recently, the wood had belonged to a ninety-year-old man who cut it in cycle to get firewood and logs for growing shiitake mushrooms. When he died, his children had had no use for either, so they asked Ohno, their neighbor, to manage the woodland. This was its first coppice since the old man had died. There was nothing picturesque about it, from a distance. It looked like a clear-cut bit of hill. with leftover stumps, some brushwood scattered here and there, and a tremendous amount of grass and weeds.

Only when you came close did the beauty begin to emerge. Nine-tenths of the stumps were sprouting back. There were fresh herbaceous greens tinged with the red of new leaves and purply twigs just beginning to turn woody. Here were *konara* and a little cherry, both coppiced alike. Ohno pointed out *taranome* and *katakuri* growing up in the opened land. One will make tempura, the other its batter. He looked over his work. "This now will wait twenty years," he said. "Then I will cut it again. If I am lucky, I may get to cut it twice in my lifetime."

In a nearby woodland of fifteen-year-old trees, I had the feeling I was swimming in a seaweed forest, just as in the pollard grove in Golden Gate Park. Five or six wrist-thick trunks rose from each stump, like bull kelp from its holdfast. Uphill and down, the clumps of stems rose and waved. The canopy was closed here, but it still felt open. Sun reflected in off the light-colored leaves. The *sasayuri*, an endangered lily, and rhododendrons have now occupied the understory. This was Ohno's family's land. His father had first cut it forty-five years ago. Three decades later, he had trained his son there. "He sent me into the hardest places," recalled Ohno with a laugh.

To manage a *booga mori* requires successive generations. Ohno was not sure who would follow him, but he has not slowed down. He enlisted the internet, which may provide him with a new generation. He recently bought land on another slope nearby. There, he has already begun to plant *kunugi*, hoping to expand his tea ceremony business. The new land had been in mulberry and chestnut, but it had gone wild for at least a decade. He used volunteers to help clear it and prepare the soil. "It was really hard work!" lamented a young forester, Ifumi Yuho, who had been among them. For the new section, therefore, Ohno decided to hire professionals to prepare the soil. In two weeks, he raised $18,000 on a crowdfunding website. The work was about to begin.

It was such a small enterprise, compared to the vast conifer plantations that now occupy much of the land that was once in *hahaso*, but it was a beginning. Above the twin kilns in his corrugated shack was a *kamidana*, a Shinto home altar. It presided over the space with a rope that marked the presence of the *kami*. Standing on the altar were tiny facsimiles of two trees, *konara* and *kunugi*. "Here he works with fire," said Ifumi. "It is dangerous and sacred, so he calls on the *kami* to bless the work."

INTO THE WOODS

To restore and preserve *satoyama* landscapes is still possible in much of Japan, particularly on the edge of urban areas. Not twenty-five miles from the center of Tokyo, beside another new town, there are 4006 little forests of *konara* and *kunugi*, each about three acres in size. They are now cut in rotation, on a cycle of twenty years, a proportion each year. With this woodland, they can make an estimated thirty thousand tons of wood per year, enough to heat, cool, and light almost ten thousand homes in the area.

But in the countryside, the former coppice woodlands often have been completely extirpated. In the postwar era, as wood became less important for heating and cooking, the authorities decided it might instead become a great modern industry. Not only in Japan but in Scandinavia and in other densely wooded lands, they ripped out mile after mile of coppice woodland, replacing them with vast plantations of fast-growing, board-producing conifers. In Japan, the main species were Japanese cedar and red pine. The idea was to both supply the whole domestic market for wood and to create an export market. When one drives through western Sweden today, one thinks that the whole country is by nature an unbroken forest of spruce; similarly, in northern Japan it seemed that every hillside was clothed from top to bottom in Japanese cedar, or *sugi*. In neither case were they spontaneous natural forests. They were both installed.

Like so many marketing ideas, this one did not work out as planned. In the 1960s, the Japanese got 80 percent of their building wood from their own plantations. At the beginning of the twenty-first century, they got less than a quarter of it. Because they insisted upon living wages for the people who grew and harvested the wood, it became far cheaper to import the boards from Southeast Asia and from Canada. Just like the Swedes, in fact, the Japanese were left with acre after acre of conifers, wondering exactly what to do with them.

Nagereba mo. If it is thrown down, put it back. In 2018, there were 25 million acres of plantation forest in Japan. Rather than despair at the enormity, some people, both in Japan and Scandinavia, began to ask the question What did the *booga mori*, the coppice woods, the sprout lands, give us as a culture, and can we somehow use these plantation forests for the same ends? You cannot coppice or pollard a Japanese cedar or a spruce, but perhaps you can use and treat their woodlands in a way that yields the same physical and cultural rewards as the coppice woods.

What were those benefits? The trees provided local needs—for heat, craft, building, fodder—from the local area. They involved ordinary individuals in providing their own livelihood. They created an intimate—if often laborious—connection between people and the place they lived. They preserved the cultural language—the poetry, the saga, the dance—that had been created and sustained by the life of the woodlands.

Near the city of Morioka in Iwate prefecture in northern Honshu is Shiwa New Town. Local forestry, local agriculture, and local benefits are its watchwords. It is in every way the opposite of Tama New Town. When

I visited in 2017, Shiwa consisted of fifty-seven houses, a city hall, a library and community center, a hotel, and a restaurant. Ground was being broken for a hospital and a town swimming pool. The wood for the buildings all came from surrounding plantations; the laminated posts and beams were all made inside the prefecture.

The energy station was the town's hub. It was a red corrugated steel shack about the size of an average American garage. Inside was a clean, smooth-sided green and aluminum-silver cube about as big as a walk-in closet in a high-class house. Just outside the door was an immense, half-buried bin full of wood chips. It had a red corrugated cover that could slide over the top of it when it rained. Four days a week, a dump truck refilled the bin. In winter, the truck might visit four or five times a day. In summer, it came at most but twice. The chips were burned in the walk-in closet. The fire there heated and cooled all of the houses and all of the public buildings, 365 days per year. When I visited, the staff had just cleaned out a month's worth of ash. It lay in clear plastic bags—two dozen of them—in a low pile. Later that day, it was to be given to a farmer to fertilize his fields.

Thus far, it might have been a technocrat's dream of efficiency: a little bit of waste wood heated and cooled a whole town. Wunderbar! This alone was remarkable, but what made Shiwa really different was how they got the wood. Nearby was the plant that made the wood chips to stoke the boiler. Called the Shiwa Town Noorinkyoosha, or Agroforestry Company, it was a public-private partnership.

Most of the place consisted of long stacks of raw logs. Some were red pine that thanks to climate change had died of a disease that had now at last reached Iwate. (Before, it had been too cold for the vector insect to live.) Some were thinned Japanese cedar from woods as close as the nearest hill and as far as northern Iwate. Some were half-burned wood from a recent forest fire. Some were even from the woods knocked down by the tidal wave at Fukushima. It aged on site—the infected pine was smoked to kill the beetles—and then into the chipper it went. The machine was Austrian and shiny, and it took up a whole building. Most of the resulting chips went to the new town's boiler. Some went to wood chip and pellet stoves that heated other local buildings.

How did they harvest the wood? Foresters brought some of it, but almost half was brought to the chipper by the citizens of Shiwa, Morioka, and surrounding towns. They got the equivalent of 500 yen per 100 kilos of wood that they brought to the site, and the town organized conveyance parties, when foresters left thinned wood by the sides of roads for people to collect and bring to town. Professor Harashina Koji, who helped design this system based on Scandinavian models, had gone on several collecting trips himself. He comfortably brought enough wood in a day to earn 5000 yen. But the pay was not in yen. It was in a currency that Harashina dubbed the ecobee coupon.

The coupon was good at most of the stores in Shiwa. The town itself was a postwar entity, created out of nine different villages, each of which had had its own farmers market. All of these markets were still in business, plus a tenth market that specialized in local wines. The stores were broad, light, and beautiful. There were fresh and dried vegetables, fresh and dried fish, meat, cereal, pickles, vinegars, soy, wine, candy. There was a great deal of *mochi*, the sticky rice paste for which Shiwa is famous. (The town is the number one producer of *mochi* in the nation.) Traditionally eaten on New Year's, *mochi* is also the base of many Japanese desserts and may be accompanied by everything from strawberries to mugwort. Recently, *mochi* rice had been used as a feed for cattle, and Shiwa was a leading producer of the succulent *mochimochi* beef. (The word is another *kakekotoba*, a poetic pun: one "*mochi*" for rice paste, and the other a form of the verb *motsu*, which means "containing.")

The point was to draw a larger circle in time—one that embraced the idea of the *hahaso* with its repeated local harvest—and a smaller circle in space, which like the *satoyama* landscape kept the goods and the benefits circulating inside the town. The coupons kept the money local. At the Shiwa Central Station, where the railroad stopped to take people to Morioka and more distant places, there was a wood chip stove and a solar roof. The fuel for the stove came from the Noorinkyoosha, and the solar panel roof was a product of local investors. The solar industry in Shiwa was funded entirely by local people, who benefited from the profits that the panels generated.

It was a way to rebuild a community. Some people grew and harvested the food and made it into finished products; others collected the wood and bought the food or invested in solar. Harashina recently did a survey and found that only 6 percent of people in the most rural parts of Iwate still heated and cooked with collected wood, but here in Shiwa they could still have a direct and intimate connection to the woods and fields.

An hour and a half by a winding road higher and deeper into the northern mountains stood Sumita, a town that since World War II had lived by plantation forestry. Tada Kinichi had been mayor there for sixteen years. The changes he spearheaded could be seen in the contrast between the old town hall and the new one: the former was a bunker of crumbling concrete and glass. It squatted like a toad only a couple hundred yards from the new hall, which was all wood and glass. The new building needs no columns, because its roof and walls are suspended on open-cambered trusses. Each of the trusses was made of larch imported from Hokkaido. At the lumber mill down the street the wood was made into bonded wood—strengthened by cutting, layering, and gluing—and formed into trusses. The walls were made of Japanese cedar from the surrounding hills. The interior was breathtakingly open, the trusses spreading like a forest canopy overhead. The light came into it as though into a well-thinned woodland.

The wood from the lumberyard supported the whole building in another way. The industrial planer generated sawdust, which was blown into a tank that fed a humming and rattling Rube Goldberg contraption. In went sawdust, out came wood pellets by the kilo. Three boilers beside the new town hall converted the pellets into all the energy needed for heat and for cooling the building. It was meant to provide a model for the surrounding area, and indeed the pellets—bagged and palletized—have found a wide market all over Iwate prefecture. Azuma Atsuki, the leading expert on the gray-faced buzzard in *satoyama* landscapes, checked the price of these pellets and ordered a pallet for his house in Morioka. The mill was the means by which the citizens could support their own town and their own efforts.

The town intended to put the ash residue from the boilers back into the rice paddies, but they could not. Sumita is less than one hundred miles from the Fukushima Daiichi nuclear power plant, the one that had melted down in the 2011 tsunami. When the wood was burned, the ash concentrated traces of radioactive cesium that had settled out of the air onto the forest. It was too radioactive to put back into the ground. The lesson was not lost on the people of Sumita: use what you are given, in and for your place, rather than depend upon miracle solutions.

In Shiwa and Sumita, the citizens benefit from the woodland and are involved in its maintenance, but only tangentially. Near the town of Tohno in Iwate, a small nonprofit called Tohno Econet has begun to make it possible for ordinary people to care for plantation forests. Its founder and head, Chiba Nagomi, got the funds to take over a disused lumber mill and turn it into a headquarters for his group of fifty volunteers. They thinned forests on private land, removing sick trees and opening up the forest to air and light. Doing so increased the plant and animal diversity, in just the same way that the *hahaso* did. Chiba built a charcoal oven and created a classroom. Some of the volunteers came to make charcoal. They learned to watch the smoke, how it turned from white, to yellow-white, to blue, to clear. Clear meant it was done. They made charcoal of the pine they have thinned, and also of willow. They have even made charcoal out of old beehives, out of carrots, and out of Japanese radishes. They drew with willow sticks, hanging their drawings in the room. They made furniture out of the thinned wood. They used wisteria and walnut bark to make baskets. An old woman showed them how to make boxes out of grass to store the charcoal. One group made firewood and took it home.

The central work was the thinning itself. There was a dramatic difference between the light of the thinned forest and the deep shadows of an unthinned one. More different plants grew in the thinned woods. More animals lived or hunted or bred there. The air and light helped reduce the incidence of disease among the forest trees.

They did not hire professionals to do the thinning, although the trees they removed were fifty feet or more in height, growing in tightly planted forests among other trees of equal and greater stature. An eighty-year-old forester came regularly from Morioka to teach a class in the proper use of the chain saw and proper felling techniques. The tools were not only substantial Stihl saws, but also felling levers, peaveys, a portable winch, and a Logosol, a portable lumber mill. Almost half the students were women. "Young ladies, old ladies," mused Chiba. "They all love to learn to thin. When they start the day, the forest is dark and deep. When they finish, it is light and open."

To demonstrate, he set the four of us up in a section of *sugi* wood that they were actively working. With Harashina and Azuma, we selected which of the trees we wanted to remove. The one we chose was about fourteen inches in diameter and about fifty feet tall. It had the white streaking on the bark that indicated a fungal disease. At first, however, it was hard to see how it could be brought down in the dense forest. Where was an open path for it to fall? We had to walk 360 degrees around it before we found the one alley along which it might come cleanly down. Then the dance began.

By happenstance, Azuma had recently taken a felling course with the same instructor. He agreed to do the work. Chiba told him to name the five principles. Azuma paused. He could not remember them. Together, they worked it out.

1: Look UP. There should be no crossing branches and no obstacles aloft to the fall. There should be no heavy cross wind moving the branches.

2: Look DOWN. There should be no grass or other obstacles to prevent a clean cut.

3: Look AROUND. The tree was 20 meters tall. He needed to look 40 meters all around it to make sure it was safe to fell.

4: Look for ESCAPE. There had to be a clear escape route for the cutter if something went wrong.

5: Look at the DIRECTION OF FALL. It should be clear of obstacles.

Azuma donned a hard hat and put a whistle on a lanyard around his neck. With Chiba's help, he fired up a chain saw, with its twenty-four-inch bar. Now the work began in earnest. Chiba asked the key word of each principle as a question. Azuma responded "Yoshi!" meaning he had taken it into account:

Joohoo? Yoshi!

Ashimoto? Yoshi!

Chuuin? Yoshi!

Taihibasho? Yoshi!

Bajutohooko? Yoshi!

Azuma blew his whistle to warn everyone to stand away. Then he started to make a pie cut on the trunk. This open-mouth cut would determine the direction of the fall. When he was done, he moved to the opposite side of the tree. With the saw resting on his hip joint, so any kickback would go around his body and not into it, he began the back cut. The hinge closed and the tree fell, but it hung up in another tree.

Unfazed, Chiba cinched up the tag line he had attached to the trunk just in case and instructed Azuma to roll the base of the tree with the felling lever, keeping in mind the *taihibasho* should the trunk jump when it sprung free. After a few dozen grunts, the two worked the crown loose, and the tree fell with a satisfying crunching thud. Then we cut it into eight-foot lengths, dragged them to the mill with the portable winch, and began to saw them into boards. A Japanese cedar board is a beautiful thing. It is pale cream in the sapwood and rust red in the heartwood. The bark is charcoal gray. Each board looks like a magnificent slice of bacon.

When we were done, we lunched. Casually, Chiba said that he had to practice for the Hayachine shrine festival that afternoon. Would we like to come watch? He knew I was eager to see woodlands, not dances. "All the people there," he cajoled, "are foresters and farmers. You can ask them lots of questions."

"Okay," I said. I had no idea what we were getting into.

Mt. Hayachine is the tallest thing around. It stands up out of the lowlands like a rumpled fedora. It is a *kami*, and it is full of *kami*. Some version of the shrine has been there since the eighth century, at the latest, and since at least that time people have danced the *kagura*. We walked through the great gate of weathered green-brown wood into a precinct of huge trees and the stumps of huge trees, all of them ancient Japanese cedars. Around both trees and stumps were the white lightning sacred braids that mark the place where a *kami* lives. Off on the west side lay the *kaguraden*, the small building where the dancers practice and where they store their costumes and equipment. There was one main room. We sat on the floor, and someone brought us soft drinks. Off went Chiba with a wave. He disappeared behind what looked like a stage curtain, a deep purple and dark gray cloth adorned with a pair of emblematic cranes facing each other.

Kagura is sacred dance. It almost ceased at the end of World War II. Most of the practitioners had died. In some places, only a single dancer survived, and he revived the dance there. (One man succeeded by offering a free meal to whoever would attend the practices.) I did not know then but have later learned that Hayachine Kagura is one of the two leading schools of the art in Japan. Like most such things, it ends up getting some odd acronymic designation from the government and from things like UNESCO, calling it an Intangible Cultural Heritage of Humanity. The dancers happily perform for tourists and for visitors, and they sometimes go on the road, but the vocation of all *kagura* dancers—there are now more than four thousand groups of them in Japan—is to enshrine, invite, delight, and embody the *kami*. The very first *kagura* was danced by the goddess Ame-no-Uzume to attract the sun goddess, Amaterasu, out of the cave where she had hidden herself. The wild and ribald dance was so impassioned that thousands of *kami* all laughed at once. Wondering what the commotion was about, the sun goddess peeked out and was tricked and cajoled into reappearing, saving the world from eternal darkness. Once, *kagura* had been a tradition handed down among lineages of professionals; since the war, it has been managed and sustained by foresters, farmers, and shopkeepers. What had once been an aristocratic tradition was now a democratic vocation. Indeed, some young *kagura* dancers now begin to learn their craft in high school clubs.

Three men entered from a side door. One was old, his face drawn and thin as though he had been dried over a fire. The other two were middle-aged, one the shrine's head caretaker and the other a local forester. The first man was carrying a pair of small cymbals, the second a two-headed drum, and the third a little undecorated cloth bag. From the bag, he drew two flutes and handed them to us. They were clearly made by him, rather roughly, out of single joints of bamboo. It is said that someone once came from Iwate University to write down the music of the *kagura*, but that he couldn't. Each flute was made by the person who played it, and the tones and intervals of each one were unique to it. We handed them back, and he joined his fellow musicians.

We drank the fizzy pop. The three men milled around and finally settled in a line beside the curtain. With a bang on the drum, it began. The three played a stately music—if you have heard No or Kabuki music, you know what it is like—all alone. We stopped drinking and faced the stage. The drum set the deep tempo. The flute danced impossibly high over the top of it, and the cymbals punctuated the phrases.

Parting the curtain, two figures appeared. It was impossible to tell whether either was Chiba. Both were costumed in long full white robes, and they wore what amount to helmets with side flaps as big as elephant's ears. On top of each helmet was the outline of a seated chicken, white with a red comb. I was about to chuckle when they started to move. They danced in a position that was almost squatting, their backs erect, their heads looking out six meters into the distance, their thighs held low, a fan held high in one hand and in the other a sprig of bamboo. They stamped and shuffled, shuffled and stamped, in steps in sets of three as they circled in different directions to mark out the sacred space for the dance. For the next twenty minutes the two followed each other, joined in a common circle, then followed again. When the dance ended, it seemed that they have indeed finished something, but I had no idea what. It could have gone on for another hour, and I would not have tired of it.

Ten minutes later, Chiba and his wife emerged. They had just performed the dance of Izanagi and Izanami—the inviting man and the inviting woman—through whom the world was created. (Eight of their children were the eight islands of Japan.) They had not just played them, but embodied them and invited them to attend. We knew none of this then. My wife asked Chiba what it was all about. "Male and female," he said in slow, careful English. "Plus and minus. Gratitude."

It occurred to me that there was no very great distance between the morning Chiba invoking the five questions to ask before felling a tree and the afternoon Chiba who had just been Izanagi. In both, there was a movement toward a world that is kinetically enspirited, in which engagement brings thanksgiving. Here was a way in which a forest initiative, modeled on the spirit of *satoyama*, had not only a material but a bracing cultural effect.

Nagereba mo. If it is washed away, put it back again.

EVER MORE

A shoot shall come out from the stump of Jesse
and a branch shall come out of his roots.

Isaiah 11:1

When you are pruning trees as severely as you must when you coppice or pollard, it is reassuring to think, as Neville Fay asserts, that "trees have a tendency towards immortality." The Hebrew prophet Isaiah wrote clearly about this idea, using the language of sprouts. Establishing the unbroken line that must lead to the birth of the Abrahamic Messiah, Isaiah wrote, "A green shoot will sprout from Jesse's stump, from his roots a budding branch." He did not seem to be sure whether the Messiah was to be a stump sprout or a root sprout, but whichever it might be, he was going to be a sprout of the same tree. It was phoenix regeneration, just what Job had longed for (see page 25). A tree doesn't necessarily die. It can improvise a new life from the old one.

Trees are functionally immortal. Even the dumbest conifer can find a way to begin anew, however hard its life. A sawara cypress on Long

Island started life as a single-stem beauty in a robber baron's garden, but as it grew old and as the garden was neglected, its lowest branches hung down until the tips hit the ground. There each tip set roots, and a whole ring of new *Chamaecyparis* arose on the circumference of its mother. Again, the branches hung down and rooted, and another ring arose. And once again. A tree that was once 75 feet tall with a crown 70 feet in diameter is now, about a century later, 60 feet tall and 360 feet in diameter. It embraces four generations of itself. Is it an individual or a colony?

Creosote now covers much of the open plains of the American Southwest and northern Mexico, where it is an invasive pest (although a native) in range and pasture. Its spreading stems arch over, touch the ground, and root there. In this way, one plant can eventually cover acres of ground. The botanist Frank Vasek radiocarbon-dated the oldest dead stems at the center of a very large ring of creosote. He then measured the radius of the ring and calculated an average rate of growth. Finding an even larger circle so wide and old that the center plants were no longer even there, he used his average growth rate to calculate roughly the age of this immense clone. The figure was 9400 years.

Disease knocked down the American chestnut beginning in 1904, but that did not destroy it. From the roots of the dead giants sprung sprouts that grew up again. Before they reached fruiting age, the disease killed the new stems, but not before they had themselves made basal sprouts, which in their turn sprang up again. A century later, all over its former range, you can still find chestnuts, but the onetime giant has metamorphosed into a serial shrub. In theory, it could remain so forever.

Clonal groves that spread by root sprouts are likely the champions of tree longevity, although no one has yet found a way to reliably estimate their age. They send up new sprouts again and again from the same

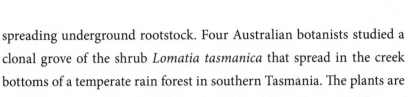

spreading underground rootstock. Four Australian botanists studied a clonal grove of the shrub *Lomatia tasmanica* that spread in the creek bottoms of a temperate rain forest in southern Tasmania. The plants are triploid, and so sterile. They flower but do not fruit. Genetic analysis of plants taken from three separate patches there showed no genetic diversity at all. They were identical not only with their current peers but with fossil plants known to be more than 40 millennia old. The living plants are clones of the fossils: the plant is at least 43,600 years old.

There are even grander claims for Pando—which means "I spread"—in southern Utah. It is a clonal grove of quaking aspen that covers almost one hundred acres on a mountainside in Fishlake National Forest. There are 47,000 stems in the grove. Most, though not all, come from the same root. Estimates of the age of this tremendous organism range from 10,000 to 1 million years. The age is not so important, unless you take the Guinness Book of World Records point of view about life: biggest, oldest, fastest, best. (Botanists gloat that Pando is now clearly the heaviest organism on Earth.) The point is rather the one raised by Darwin. After he observed a colony of sea pens—colonial organisms each of whose rising fingers had its own mouth, body, and tentacles, but all of which moved as one and reproduced as one—he wrote, "Well may one be allowed to ask, 'What is an individual?'"

The facts of sprouting wonderfully complicate the thought. Surely each clone is an individual, but also each one is part of a community. It is a little like the quantum in the superposition experiment: you shoot the thing at a gate, and rather than choose one or the other path, the same thing goes both ways at once. Life in this sense is a kind of shimmering, where you see the uniqueness of an organism at one moment and its ramified countlessness on the other. In the starlight of this thought, you begin to glimpse another view of ever more.

Immortality and individuality don't mix. The Christian or for that matter the Buddhist assertion about eternal life become less credible the more you think that immortality is a property of individuals. In the old days, Roman Catholicism opposed cremation, since the idea was that you had to keep the body intact waiting for resurrection. No one who thought this must ever have explored the facts of decomposition or the fauna of the grave, or for that matter the fact that part of what digests our bodies when we die is what helped us digest others when we lived.

Even while we live, we are hardly isolate individuals. Ninety percent of our cells are not the human genome, but others, chiefly bacteria. More than one hundred species of these organisms inhabit our guts, and they help us to parse the countless creatures from the world out there whom we eat and whose cells go to sustain us. Our immune systems are built through our intimate relationships to others—sometimes parasitic, sometimes symbiotic, sometimes just commensal—within the supposed castles of our bodies. We are continually pumping out of these bodies what from one point of view is refuse, but from another is life to the world around us. Our own genome is a composite of others.

The Christians' Gospel of John is clear on this point. A person is only really alive, wrote John, if he or she is a branch attached to the growing vine. God may prune the branch to make it bear more fruit, but as long as it is attached to the parent vine, it will prosper. If it is severed, it withers and is thrown into the fire. Like the reiterating growth on a tree's trunk and branches, the vine branch is both an individual and a member of community.

A green shoot shall spring from the shoot of Jesse, wrote Isaiah. "Abide in me," wrote John, conveying the assertion of Jesus that he was the vine through whom the branches lived. The tree and the vine both teach about the shimmering: it is not true that there are no individuals,

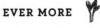

and it is not true that there are. When a branch is pruned, it sprouts back. Even when a tree appears dead, it may arise again from the roots. And it can apparently do so for ever more. It is the same and not the same. It is the shimmering. This is what the sprouts teach: immortality is not a matter of holding on, but of letting go.

VOLUNTEERS

The word "recruit" in French literally means the sprout that comes back after pollarding or coppicing. When trees and their sprouts appear in a place, unbidden and persistent, I think of them not as recruits, but as volunteers. They insist upon occupying the land, and little by little they transform it. Even where we forget or neglect the woods—particularly in urban areas—they do not abandon us. My most and least favorite woodlands in New York are places where the power of sprouting reaches out to scratch you.

The first is at Gerritsen Beach. I feel that if I stayed the night, I might wake up covered in creeping twigs. I try not to go there on weekends, since then I am liable to be run down by a speeding dirt biker on one of the sand paths. And if I go near sundown, I try to make sure I get through while the light lasts. I always go to the fire circle, where I have found everyone from groups of teenagers to the apparently homeless gathered around on benches made of logs and of discarded guardrails from old roads. I hunt up the outcrops of concrete and count the carcasses of burned-out cars. I check to see what new is growing in the open meadows, what seeds are most plentiful in autumn and winter and how their fruits can be broken open, and who is winning the battle where phragmites, sumac, and mugwort meet.

One hundred years ago, this place wasn't a woodland. In fact, it wasn't there. The forest here grows on made land. Until 1934, most New York City garbage—the solid waste from trash cans, the building and road debris, the sand dredged to open or deepen channels—was barged out to sea and dumped in the New York Bight.

Then, the city's wise men had a bright idea. Population pressure was growing. That meant lots more garbage and not enough lebensraum. Why waste all that trash in the open ocean? Why not use it to make land? "The city's lowlands . . . form an almost unlimited supply of dumping ground," wrote the predecessors to New York's Sanitation Department, and they made the smart connection: "The possibilities of land reclamation are almost boundless."

The edges of New York are thick with fill. Once, Coney Island was indeed an island. The water in between was filled. La Guardia and Kennedy Airports were built on landfill. So was the World's Fair site in Flushing, Queens. (It had been an early dump dedicated largely to coal ash. In Fitzgerald's novel *The Great Gatsby,* the hero calls the landscape "the Valley of Ashes.") Battery Park is dredge fill. Borings find old ships' timber and wharf pilings at thirty-foot depth. And all of the land in Brooklyn south of Avenue U from Sheepshead Bay to Kennedy Airport is made out of about 1 trillion yards of fill: 23,000 acres, or 36 square miles, of the stuff. Soil scientists have named a soil class to describe these places, the Big Apple Series, which is officially described as "anthrotransported"— in other words, brought there by us. In the early days, before landfill engineering, the stuff was not sealed or capped, just dumped.

The land at this, my favorite woods has been woven mainly out of three kinds of trash. One is the sand dredge, spewed up to clear passageways for ships and at the same time to make new land. A layer of solid waste—household trash and municipal leavings—enough to cover the whole area to eight feet deep, is the second thread. The third is the debris from excavation, construction, and demolition.

Some city fathers apparently decided that they had not done enough to make real soil for the real estate developments they planned. In a few spots, they thoroughly mixed sand and sewage sludge, topping it with alfalfa plowed into the new soil annually for three years. They left off when they realized how expensive the work was, and when they saw that plants were coming up all over anyway. They had no idea of the slow, relentless, healing power of woodlands, or that they heal not by means of wealth but through poverty and time.

When Hurricane Sandy struck in 2012, only about seventy-eight years after the dumping had begun, it rolled right over the woods, across the avenue and into the flatland, fill-based neighborhood beyond. Cars floated up and down the street, coming to rest in flocks, nose to nose, like herds of deer at salt licks. The power was out. Every house and business in the neighborhood was damaged. The London plane street trees were defoliated, their bark changed to the color of rusty pipes, and the white pine needles had turned a brittle dead bronze. But on the other side of the street, the wild forest shrugged off the storm. A few trees were down. That was it.

East of the avenue and east of the rough ballfields—their lawns so corrugated that any ground ball stands fair to be a base hit—the motley forest waves, a strip of greens and yellows and purples and more brownish yellows and bronzes and waxy pale blues between the neighborhood and what is left of a tidal creek. It is a mutt woods. Groves of ailanthus and black locust stand beside outcrops of concrete blocks, the understory thick with waving mugwort. Along the shore, the waves expose the shore dirt and the evil plans of phragmites, whose matrix of tangled rhizomes can grow thirty feet in a season through the black nutrient-rich soil and whose stolons run over the surface almost as fast as flowing rivulets, expanding the front of the giant reeds. Among the groves stand meadows on pure sand, dotted with emerging black cherry and sumacs, and edged with banks of balsam-smelling bayberry. Switchgrass, little and big blue-stem, and Pennsylvania sedge rise from the billows of sand. Crustose and foliose lichens splotch bare patches.

Without the aid of tilling, of alfalfa, of any care at all, Great Nature is bringing forth a triple soil on the three kinds of spoil she is given. You could call these leavings "waste," but as the compost man Clark Gregory once put it, "It isn't waste until it's wasted." Great Nature will not waste it.

The dirt based on rubble and excavation debris is well drained, but full of concrete and mortar, which contain high-pH calcium oxides. The plants this stuff attracts—ailanthus, black locust, hackberry, mugwort—like just such limy dirt. Where the soil is black with decaying solid waste—very high in organic matter—the nitrogen-loving phragmites sprawl over everything, driving out most other plants. Where the buff tan soils are little more than pure sand dredged out of the water, the dirt is very low in pH, very low in organic matter. It is downright poverty stricken. On this poor soil, the native coastal plants are directly emerg-ing: the switchgrass, the black cherry, the sumacs, the bluestems, the lichens, the bayberry. In some places, you will even see black tupelo.

Because the dirts are woven together one with another—according to what barge dumped which spoil where—you can find a lens of one soil woven into the matrix of another. In a field of switchgrass and sumac—whose leaves flash white beneath when the wind overturns them, like a field of oblong mirrors—grows an emerging grove of ailanthus. If you search at the base of the ailanthus, you will find chunks of rubble and other construction debris.

One path leads to a rough rectangle of pavement whose origin and use are unknown. At first glance, it seems that the center and the south edge of this opening are fringed with twin sumac groves. Their typical staghorn multistem look—caused since their flowers occupy the ends of stems, forcing new growth to emerge like branching horns beneath the tips—gives them away. But as you come closer, you see that one is indeed a grove of sumac, with its rust red obelisks of terminal fruit, but the other is a clonal grove of multistem ailanthus. One is on sand, the other on broken concrete, and both are spreading in the same ground-covering plural-trunked way.

That this landscape is less diverse than the salt marsh that preceded it is unquestionable. But so much was happening here! A bird's nest in a black cherry was armored with a white plastic frame, apparently from a six-pack of beer. A dense colony of night herons, their droppings festooning an ailanthus grove, screamed at me as I passed, making a sound like snow shovels skip-skidding over pavement.

Here, the poorest substrate gave the strongest results. We think from our vegetable gardens that a good soil is full of nutrients, but at Gerritsen Beach that "good soil" bred only the bullying phragmites. The dredge sand blossomed, slowly it is true, with lichens, grasses, shrubs, and trees, although it started with almost nothing. The dirt made of concrete was likewise a slow starter, but it could only accept those species that would tolerate the very high pH.

Perhaps not in a human lifetime, but over time, the calcium compounds will leach through the dirt and be gone. The concrete will melt and disappear. The organic garbage will break down, part going to the air and part flowing into the groundwater and away. With patience, the life-giving poverty of this sandy seashore landscape will return, the sandy soil slowly enriched by the life and death of its native flora.

It is amazing to me that this will be accomplished not only by our earnest efforts at restoration, but by neglect. Nobody except walkers,

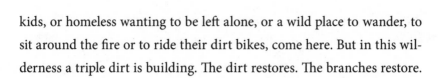

kids, or homeless wanting to be left alone, or a wild place to wander, to sit around the fire or to ride their dirt bikes, come here. But in this wilderness a triple dirt is building. The dirt restores. The branches restore. We only help or hinder.

———

About twenty miles from this woodland is another. It cannot be called beautiful for how it looks, but only for what it does. Fresh Kills is the largest manmade structure on Earth. Until it closed in 2001, it had been New York City's principal dump. Every kind of leavings that an industrial society can make had landed up there. Hills and mountains rose where there had been wetlands. Methane vented through cracks in the dirt. It was the opposite of the mutual respect that people and trees showed for each other in a coppice woodland. It was a place in which to hide the unspeakable, so the bright, shining city could continue to polish its windows, to attend its operas and symphony concerts, and to dine out in peace.

We had been asked to assess about two thousand trees in a small section of the place. In a late winter blow with heavy snow, a lot of trees had come down. It was not surprising, since they had been planted atop big gray riprap gravel, red clay, piles of varicolored bottles, and plastic shards. This was a modern landfill—not just fill, but a place that had been sealed beneath and capped above to keep the detritus and its leachate from escaping. There was hardly any dirt to speak of, but the trees had come up anyway. There were ailanthus, black cherry, royal paulownia, mulberry, black locust, red maple, box elder . . . weed trees every one, and none taller than about thirty-five or forty feet. Many were completely wrapped in choking vines: oriental bittersweet, poison ivy, grapes, and porcelain berry. One fallen black cherry had turned up a root plate about six feet in diameter. Roots had wound in and out of the rough surface, like the filigree in some Tiffany brooch, trying to get a hold in the strange dirt. Packed among the exposed rootlets were green, clear, and brown bottles of a dozen sizes, half a child's red plastic dump truck, fragments of plates, cups, and dishes, red and yellow labels that for some reason were slow to decay. Stretched taut in one corner was a beige nylon stocking, one end of which adhered to the top of the root plate while the other end clung stubbornly to the ground.

It was neither a healthy nor a pretty place, except perhaps when the paulownia was flowering. In fact, it was the ugliest woodland I had ever walked. Many trees were dead or dying. The vines had covered some trees and taken them down. The branches and the vines together made impenetrable thickets of fallen wood, like the chaotic scribblings of an enormous, troubled child. There were many fungi: Ganoderma shelves at the base of many trees, the reflexed, bone-colored tongues of Dryad's Saddle in cracks on the stems, turkey tails all up and down the dying trunks. Even the fungi seemed unhappy, many stained a yellow-green by something saprophytic.

The just fallen trees looked like Mathew Brady's pictures of the Civil War dead, sodden and crumpled, but those that had collapsed in previous years had not been slow to rise again. One big three-stem black cherry—it had certainly come from the stump of a previous specimen there—had split at the base, each trunk falling to the ground. One was dead, but a second had turned one of its lateral branches into a rising tree, and the third had three branches that were in the process of becoming trees. None would likely ever make its own roots, so all would eventually perish. Nearby, another cherry had been luckier. Its branch had rested on a smaller stem that did not arch but reached the ground. The trunk had already decayed, but the former branch was putting down its own roots. By hook or by crook, the woodland said, I will grow over and into this place.

It was a cold day, and I was tired. There were many more trees in the area than our client had at first told us. My supposedly waterproof boots were stained dirty brown where I had been standing in the slush. It seemed an endless and a thankless task. On a slope in Section 9, I came upon a tangle of greenbrier that covered the ground like barbed wire. There were indeed trees among them, so I had to go in. The prickly miasma covered at least an acre of ground.

I tried to follow what looked like paths, but they led nowhere. When I finally had to step into the briars, they caught at my boots, my shoelaces, my pant legs. Turn one way to escape one tendril, and the act caused another, opposite-facing spiral to wind me up into its coils. In one place—I think it was near Tree 9889—I couldn't get away. I wound tight in one direction, then spun in the other. I could go neither forward nor back. I felt like a corkscrew, and I wondered as I whirligigged back and forth whether I would eventually disappear underground. It took a quarter of an hour to escape from there.

When I did, I felt grateful to be walking on nothing more noxious than broken bottles and old shoe soles. The thick, capping gravel appeared again. I slid down a slope on the riprap and almost into a creek full of dead green filaments of slime. What the #$@%)%8*, I remarked. When I turned, I slipped. I unintentionally went down on my knees. I was looking out over the floor of the forest, littered with unsightly piles of dead trunks, fallen branches, and collapsed serpentine vines. Right in front of me rose the ripped-out roots at the base of a fallen black locust. On the top of one root—five feet high in the air—a new black locust had sprouted.

My god, I breathed. And despite the fear that my knees might get infected, I did not want to get right up. It was suddenly, momentarily beautiful. From a coyote's eye view, you could see what the trees were up to. Decay, repose, and the drip of acid water through the gravel were mixing a dirt out of the detritus. This hideous forest, I suddenly realized, was there to repair the damage done, and not at our bidding. Its intent was not to look good. Its intent was to stay alive, year by year, century by century, until at last it had cleaned and renewed even the nylon stocking. Stems failed. They decayed. Branches fell. They decayed. Vines covered whole groves in a mass of thick stems until all of them together collapsed. They decayed. Organic acids came from the rotting mass. The rain and snow did their work. The dump was slowly changing.

On posts in the industrial harbor of Pasaia near San Sebastián in Spain, the administration has put up a wonderful sign to discourage people from dumping into the water. It tells how long it takes most kinds of leavings to return to the earth. Organic material goes quickly: cardboard in three months, wood in one to three years, a pair of wool socks in one to five years, an apple core in two. From there, the time mounts up. A cigarette butt may take a decade, a plastic shopping bag ten to twenty years, a plastic cup fifty. All of these are at least within the range of a human lifetime. Not so the major industrial materials. An aluminum can is with us for two hundred years, a glass bottle for five hundred, a plastic bottle for seven hundred, and a Styrofoam container for a millennium. The sign is written in Basque and Spanish. Its legend reads *"Ez daukagu B Planetarik," "No hay planeta B."* ("There is no Planet B.")

The forest does not think this. It just acts as though it were so. Because it is so good at sprouting, resprouting, repeating, reseeding, it can keep up the living and dying for as long as it takes, even if that is a thousand years. It would require the whole time that Bradfield Wood has operated in Sussex to break down one Styrofoam tray, but as both Bradfield and Fresh Kills show, the trees, the vines, and the fungi are up to it. The trees are not conscious. They are something better. They are present.

My colleague Laura found the genie of Fresh Kills landfill lying in the dirt. It was not the only pale plastic doll's head that we had seen among the trash, but this one was different. The gray fettuccine of its plastic hair had become the matrix for a puke green crew cut of living moss. Well beyond the imagination of its makers, the doll was coming to life.

WHAT WHITE'S WILLOW SAID

It was time to cut the young London planes in front of the Metropolitan Museum again. Predictably, I woke around three a.m. with the anxious fear that this time I had done something really wrong. It was too late or the weather was too cold or too warm, or something exceptional and bad was going to happen. I was going to cut too much or too little. I was a mess, but the trees are faithful. It was when I touched them and looked up through the whorl of their growing branches that my anxiety subsided.

I had found many wonderful advisers in my journey to figure out how to prune them, but above all, the trees themselves have been my teachers. The woods brought us from the Neolithic to the edge of the modern world. They showed us how to work with them and with one another in a way that was good for all. I had started out looking for a book of instruction, and instead found a way of life that had brought us from the mesolithic to the modern. It involved not just trees, not just people, but each bringing help to the other.

The more I learned from the generosity of the trees themselves and of the people who still work among them, the less I felt the need for a set of rules. I had expected to have to shape my London planes and to nurse them along, but it is they who have been carrying me. They are smarter, stronger, older, longer living, and more generous than I am. They respond to my tentative efforts with dozens of beautiful stems. If one is not where I wanted it and I rub it out, they accept the gesture and shift their pattern of making. They appear unfazed that I want to keep them unnaturally young, always demanding new first-year stems of them. Even where a stem is weakened by the shade, the tree sends out another suggestion for my consideration. When I do my winter quadrille among them—winding in and out and twirling all the way around each, in order to see them clearly and assess the health of trunk and branch—I feel I am beginning to know each both as a responsive individual and as part of a young colony.

The London plane trees are teaching us the art of growing in place. It isn't natural to a human being, and we are not yet very good at it, but it is an art. We can make the cuts properly and each branch will live, but how beautiful will they be as they grow up? Will they make the rose window of shadow in winter? Will they be a pagoda of big maple-shaped leaves in the summer? An arborist is taught that trees arrange and dispose their branches so as best to let each leaf catch sun. We are faced with the need to help to make it so. In a naturally growing tree, it looks so effortless, and the results are often lovely. Working with each plane, we see how intricate are the chances and the choices.

Even today, they show me how they can serve a city. Our four little groves of London planes are not only strange and beautiful. They are also as right in their place as my favorite tall invading English elms are in the edge of the Central Park forest nearby. By staying small on the paved plaza, the planes do not grow big heavy branches, which they might drop in a storm on an unfortunate passerby. With the annual pruning, their roots too remain small. They do not buckle the pavement, lift the sidewalk, or create lips of concrete upon which a person might trip. They cast a shade that is cooling but not too deep and wide. Other plants can grow among and beside them. You can sit beneath them happily, without feeling dwarfed. In winter, they are beginning to cast an intricate web of shadow. You can even plant them under things like utility lines, without having to disfigure their branches to keep them out of the wires. They have a place beside us still, although today the cut sprouts serve only to make a playful wattle fence.

Trees return. Cut them. Chop them. Burn them. Bend them flat. And back they come again. There is no greater force on Earth than is shown in the power and persistence of branching. And certainly none more cheerful. Henry David Thoreau fire-coppiced a hundred acres of woodland early one spring in Concord. By autumn, the space was "clad in a fresher and more luxuriant green" than anything around it. The sprouts put heart in him. "Surely this earth is fit to be inhabited, and many enterprises may be undertaken with hope," he wrote, "where so many young plants are pushing up."

Tell me about it! The planes sprouted beautifully, despite my fears, but one hectic afternoon on the edge of June, I just didn't care. Here I was diligently learning to practice a rightly dying art, while I live in an age in which knowledge is communicated at the speed of light. Who cares about those old slow ways? The yard door stuck when I tried to open it. I had to kick it. It sprang open, framing the E. B. White willow. The fish-skin bark of the young trunks was shining with vigor. Each pollard cut we had made in March had sprouted a dozen new stems, every pencil-thick wand at least three feet long and covered in yellow-green leaves. This tree had probably been talking to me for all of the five years it spent there, but only now did I hear it.

I remembered the old willow in the Manhattan garden. As big and strong as the trunk had looked, it had been the plant's weakest point: hollow, fragile, buckling under its own weight, scarcely connected to a few decaying roots. Though once it had sustained a tall and lovely tree, nothing we could do would save it. It was too sick to fruit and set seed. QED. End of tree. We only learned the truth by accident, when we stuck a few of its young sticks in the ground: The trunk was dying, but the willow was not. The twigs sprouted roots, stems, and leaves, the only three organs that a tree needs. Since then, we have started hundreds of new trees from the first-year sprouts of our blooming young willow.

What if new life does not come only from the centers of power, wealth, resource gathering, and exchange? What if it comes too from the margins, the extremities, the growing tips, the sprout lands? Maybe new ways will come to us from places distant in time or space or both, where a living connection to the world renews. Maybe they will come from Grinde Farm, Osawa, Bradfield Wood, Leitza, Tohno, Beasore Meadow, the Somerset Levels, Hiyachine Shrine, Pasaia, Jolster, Kilimi, Etxarri Aranatz, Shiwa, Sumita, Star Carr, Federsee, Diss Mere, Sirok Nyírjes, Misterfals, Kussalid, Sakuragaoka. . . . Places we never heard of, times beyond our lives.

BIBLIOGRAPHY

Abrams, Marc D. 1992. "Fire and the Development of Oak Forests." *BioScience* 42 (5): 346–53.

Abrams, Marc D., and Nowacki, G. J. 2008. "Native Americans as Passive and Active Promoters of Mast and Fruit Trees in the Eastern USA." *The Holocene* 18 (7): 1123–37.

Acreman. M. C., R. J. Harding, C. Lloyd, N. P. McNamara, J. O. Mountford, D. J. Mould, B. V. Purse, M. S. Heard, C. J. Stratford, and S. Dury. 2011. "Trade-off in Ecosystem Services of the Somerset Levels and Moors Wetlands." *Hydrological Sciences Journal* 56 (8): 1543–65.

Alberry, Alan. 2011. "Woodland Management in Hampshire, 900–1815." *Rural History* 22 (2): 159–81.

Albion, Robert Greenhalgh. 1926. *Forests and Sea Powers: The Timber Problem of the Royal Navy, 1652–1882.* Annapolis, MD: Naval Institute Press.

Allison, P. A. 1962. "Historical Inferences to Be Drawn from the Effect of Human Settlement on the Vegetation of Africa." *The Journal of African History* 3 (2): 241–49.

Anderson, M. Kat. 2005. *Tending the Wild: Native American Knowledge and Management of California's Natural Resources.* Berkeley: University of California Press.

"Aprobación definitiva de modificación de ordenanza de comunales. Leitza." 2015. *Boletín oficial de Navarra* 113 (June 12, 2015).

Aragón Ruano, Álvaro. 2009. "Una longeva técnica forestal: Los trasmochos o desmochos guiados en Guipúzcoa durante la Edad Moderna." *Revistas Espacio, Tiempo y Forma. Series I-VIIÑ Espacio, Tiempo y Forma, Serie IV, Historia Moderna.* Madrid: Facultad de Geografía e Historia/UNED.

Arber, Agnes. 1937. "The Interpretation of the Flower: A Study of Some Aspects of Morphological Thought." Onlinelibrary.wiley.com/doi/10.1111/j.1469-185X.1937.tb01227.x/pdf.

Astatt, Peter R. 1988. "Are Vascular Plants 'Inside-Out' Lichens?" *Ecology* 69 (1): 17–23.

Austad, I. 1988. "Tree Pollarding in Western Norway." In *The Cultural Landscape, Past, Present and Future*, edited by H. H. Birks, H. J. Birks, P. E. Kaland, and D. Moe, 13–29. Cambridge: Cambridge University Press.

———. 1993. "Wooded Pastures in Western Norway: History, Ecology, Dynamics and Management." In *Soil Biota, Nutrient Cycling, and Farming Systems*, edited by M. G. Paloetti, W. Foissner, and D. Coleman, 193–205. Boca Raton: Lewis Publishers.

Austad, I., L. N. Hamre, K. Rydgren, and A. Norderhaug. 2003. "Production in Wooded Hay Meadows." In *Ecosystems and Sustainable Development*, edited by E. Tiezzi, C. A. Brebbia, and J. L. Uso, vol. 2, 1091–1101. Ashurst, New Forest, U.K.: Wit Press.

Austad, Ingvild, and Leif Hauge. 2008. "The 'Fjordscape' of Inner Sogn, Western Norway." In *Nordic Landscapes: Region and Belonging on the Northern Edge of Europe*, edited by Michael Jones and Kenneth R. Olwig. Minneapolis: University of Minnesota Press.

———. 2014. "Pollarding in Western Norway." *Agroforestry News* 22 (3): 16.

Austad, I., L. Hauge, and T. Helle. 1993. "Maintenance and Conservation of the Cultural Landscape in Sogn og Fjordane, Norway." Final report. 1–60. Sogn og Fjordane: Department of Landscape Ecology, Sogn og Fjordane University College.

Austad, I., and M. H. Losvik. 1998. "Changes in Species Composition Following Field and Tree Layer Restoration and Management in a Wooded Hay Meadow." *Nordic Journal of Botany* 18: 641–62.

Austad, I., A. Nordehaug, L. N. Hamre, and K. M. Norderhaug. 2003. "Vegetation and Production Mosaics of Wooded Hay Meadows." *Gjengroing av kulturmark, Bergen Museums Skrifter* 15: 51–60.

Austad, I., A. Norderhaug, L. Hauge, and A. Moen. 2004. "An Overview of Norwegian Summer Farming." In R. G. H. Bunce et al, *Transhumance and Biodiversity in the European Mountains*, 7–18. Wageningen, Neth.: Alterra.

Austad, Ingvild, and Arnfinn Skogen. 1990. "Restoration of a Deciduous Woodland in Western Norway Formerly Used for Fodder Production: Effects on Tree Canopy and Field Layer." *Vegetatio* 88 (1): 1–20.

Austad, I., A. Skogen, L. Hauge, and A. Timberlid. 1991. "Human-Influenced Vegetation Types and Landscape Elements in the Cultural Landscapes of Inner Sogn, Western Norway." *Norsk Geografisk Tidsskrift* 45: 35–58.

Barrow, Edmund. 1988. "Trees and Pastoralists: The Case of the Pokot and the Turkana." *ODI Social Forestry Network*, Paper 6B: 1–24.

Barthelemy, Daniel, and Yves Caraglio. 2007. "Plant Architecture: A Dynamic, Multilevel and Comprehensive Approach to Plant Form, Structure and Ontogeny." *Annals of Botany* 99: 375–407.

Bases técnicas para el plan de gestión de la Zona Especial de Conservación (ZEC) ES2200018 "Belate" Diagnosis. Natura 2000: 2014.

Batchelor, C. R., N. P. Branch, E. A. Allison, P. A. Austin, B. Bishop, A. D. Brown, S. A. Elias, C. P. Green, and D. Young D. 2014. "The Timing and Causes of the Neolithic Elm Decline: New Evidence from the Lower Thames Valley (London, UK)." *Environmental Archaeology: The Journal of Human Palaeoecology* 19 (3): 263–90.

Bean, Lowell J., and Thomas C. Blackburn. 1976. *Native Californians: A Theoretical Retrospective.* Ramona, CA: Ballena Press.

Bechmann, Roland. 1990. *Trees and Man: The Forest in the Middle Ages.* New York: Paragon House.

Beerling. David J., and Andrew J. Fleming. 2007. "Zimmermann's Telome Theory of Megaphyll Leaf Evolution: A Molecular and Cellular Critique." *Current Opinion in Plant Biology* 10: 4–12.

Billamboz, Andre. 2003. "Tree Rings and Wetland Occupation in Southwest Germany Between 2000 and 500 BC: Dendrochronology Beyond Dating, in Tribute to F. H. Schweingruber." *Tree-Ring Research* 59 (1): 37–49.

———. 2014. "Regional Patterns of Settlement and Woodland Developments: Dendroarchaeology in the Neolithic Pile Dwellings on Lake Constance (Germany)." *The Holocene* 24 (10): 1278–87.

Birks, Hilary H., et al., eds. *The Cultural Landscape: Past, Present, and Future.* Cambridge: Cambridge University Press, 1988.

Black, B. A., and M. D. Abrams. 2001. "Influences of Native Americans and Surveyor Biases on Metes and Bounds Witness Tree Distribution." *Ecology* 82: 2574–86.

Blackburn, Thomas C., and Kat Anderson. 1993. *Before the Wilderness: Environmental Management by Native Californians.* Menlo Park, CA: Ballena Press.

Blaustein, Richard J. 2008. "The Green Revolution Arrives in Africa." *BioScience* 58 (1): 8–14.

Bogdanova, Sandra. "Bark Food: The Continuity and Change of Scots Pine Inner Bark Use for Food by Sámi People in Northern Fennoscandia." MA thesis, Arctic University of Norway, 2016.

Bond, William J., and J. J. Midgley. 2003. "The Evolutionary Ecology of Sprouting in Woody Plants." *International Journal of Plant Sciences* 164 (S3): S103–14.

Bromfield, Louis. 1997. *Pleasant Valley.* Wooster, OH: The Wooster Book Company.

Brooks, A. 1937. "Castanea Dentata." *Castanea* 2 (5): 61–67.

Brundrett, Mark C. 2002. "Tansley Review No. 134. Coevolution of Roots and Mycorrhizas of Land Plants." *The New Phytologist* 154 (2): 275–304.

Buckley, G. P., ed. 1992. *Ecology and Management of Coppice Woodlands.* London: Chapman and Hall.

Carey, Frances, I. A. C. Dejardin, and M. Stevens. 2016. *Painting Norway: Nikolai Astrup, 1880–1928.* London: Scala Arts and Heritage Publishers.

"Chestnut Flour. (Castanea sativa, Mill.) 1890." *Bulletin of Miscellaneous Information* (Royal Botanic Gardens, Kew) 44: 173–74.

Claben-Bockhoff, Regine. 2001. "Plant Morphology: The Historic Concepts of Wilhelm Troll, Walter Zimmermann, and Agnes Arber." *Annals of Botany* 88: 1153–72.

Clare, John. 1984. *The Oxford Authors: John Clare.* Oxford: Oxford University Press.

Clark, J. G. D. 1954. *Excavations at Starr Carr.* Cambridge: Cambridge University Press.

Clément, Vincent. 2008. "Spanish Wood Pasture: Origin and Durability of an Historical Wooded Landscape in Mediterranean Europe." *Environment and History* 14 (1): 67–87.

Coles, Bryony, and R. Brunning. 2009. "Following the Sweet Track. Relics of Old

Decency." In *Archaeological Studies in Later Prehistory: Festschrift for Barry Raf-ferty*, edited by Gabriel Cooney et al. Dublin: Wordwell, 25–37.

Coles, J. M., and A. J. Lawson. 1987. *European Wetlands in Prehistory*. Oxford: Clarendon Press.

Coles, J. M., and B. E. Orme. 1976. "A Neolithic Hurdle from the Somerset Levels." *Antiquity* 50 (197): 57–61.

———. 1977. "Neolithic Hurdles from Walton Heath, Somerset." *Somerset Levels Papers* 3: 6–29.

———. 1983. "*Homo sapiens* or *Castor fiber*?" *Antiquity* 57: 95–102.

Conedera, Marco, P. Krebs, W. Tinner, M. Pradella, and D. Torriani. 2004. "The Cultivation of *Castanea sativa* (Mill.) in Europe, from Its Origin to Its Diffusion on a Continental Scale." *Vegetation History and Archaeobotany* 13 (3): 161–79.

Cronon, William. 1983. *Changes in the Land: Indians, Colonists and the Ecology of New England*. New York: Hill and Wang.

Curry, Andrew. 2014. "The Neolithic Toolkit." *Archaeology* 67 (6): 38–41.

De Jaime Lorén, Chabier, and F. Herrero Loma. 2016. *El chopo cabecero en el sur de Aragón: La identidad de un paisaje*. Calamocha, Sp.: Centro de Estudios Jiloca.

Delcourt, Paul A., H. R. Delcourt, C. R. Ison, W. E. Sharp, and K. J. Gremillion. 1998. "Prehistoric Human Use of Fire, the Eastern Agricultural Complex, and Appalachian Oak-Chestnut Forests: Paleoecology of Cliff Palace Pond, Kentucky." *American Antiquity* 63 (2): 263–78.

Delhon, Claire, S. Thiebault, and J.-F. Berger. 2009. "Environment and Landscape Management During the Middle Neolithic in Southern France: Evidence for Agro-sylvo-pastoral Systems in the Middle Rhone Valley." *Quaternary International* 200: 50–65.

Delpuech, Catherine. 2014. "La journee classique de *kagura* de Hyachine." *Cipango* 21 (2014). Posted online September 8, 2016, accessed April 21, 2018, http://journals .openedition.org/cipango/2205; doi: 10.4000/cipango.2205.

Del Tredici, Peter. 1999. "Redwood Burls: Immortality Underground." *Arnoldia* 59 (3): 14–22.

———. 2000. "Aging and Rejuvenation in Trees." *Arnoldia* 59 (4): 10–16.

———. 2001. "Sprouting in Temperate Trees: A Morphological and Ecological Review." *The Botanical Review* 67: 121–40.

De Witte, L. C., and J. Stöcklin. 2010. "Longevity of Clonal Plants: Why It Matters and How to Measure It. *Annals of Botany* 106 (6): 859–70. http://doi.org/10.1093/ aob/mcq191.

DeWoody, Jennifer, C. A. Rowe, V. D. Hipkins, and K. E. Mock. 2008. "'Pando' Lives: Molecular Genetic Evidence of a Giant Aspen Clone in Central Utah." *Western North American Naturalist* 68 (4): 493–97.

Dey, Daniel C., M. C. Stambaugh, S. L. Clark, and C. J. Schweitzer. 2012. *Proceedings of the Fourth Fire in Eastern Oak Forests Conference*. Newtown Square, PA: U.S. Forest Service.

Dods, Roberta Robin. 2002. "The Death of Smokey Bear: The Ecodisaster Myth and Forest Management Practices in Prehistoric North America." *World Archaeology* 33 (3): 475–87.

Etienne, David, P. Ruffaldi, J. L. Dupouey, M. Georges-Leroy, F. Ritz, and E. Dambrine. 2013. "Searching for Ancient Forests: A 2000 Year History of Land Use in Northeastern French Forests Deduced from the Pollen Compositions of Closed Depression." *The Holocene* 23 (5): 678–91.

Ewers, F. W., and M. H. Zimmermann. 1984. "The Hydraulic Architecture of Eastern Hemlock (*Tsuga canadensis*)." *Canadian Journal of Botany* 62: 940–46.

Favre, Pascal, and Jacomet, Stefanie. 1988. "Branch Wood from the Lake Shore Settlements of Horgen Scheller, Switzerland: Evidence for Economic Specialization in the Late Neolithic period." *Vegetation History and Archaeobotany* 7 (3): 167–78.

Fay, Neville. 2002. "Environmental Arboriculture, Tree Ecology and Veteran Tree Management." *Arboricultural Journal* 26: 213–38.

Fenley, John M. 1950. "Pollarding: Age-Old Practice Permits Grazing in Pays Basque Forests." *Journal of Range Management* 3 (4): 316–18.

Finney, Mark A., and Robert E. Martin. 1992. "Short Fire Intervals Recorded by Redwoods at Annadel State Park, California." *Madroño* 39 (4): 251–62.

Fisher, Jack B., and David E. Hibbs. 1982. "Plasticity of Tree Architecture: Specific and Ecological Variations Found in Aubreville's Model." *American Journal of Botany* 69 (5): 690–702.

"Forests: Regeneration by Coppice." 1907. In *Cyclopedia of American Agriculture: Crops,* edited by Liberty Hyde Bailey, 325ff. New York: Macmillan Company.

Fredengren, Christina. 2016. "Unexpected Encounters with Deep Time: Enchantment. Bog Bodies, Crannogs and 'Otherworldly' Sites. The Materializing Powers of Disjunctures in Time." *World Archaeology.* doi: 10.1080/00438243.2016.1220327.

Gardner, A. R. 2002. "Neolithic to Copper Age Woodland Impacts in Northeast Hungary? Evidence from the Pollen and Sediment Chemistry Records." *The Holocene* 12 (5): 541–53.

Genin, D., C. Crochot, S. MSou, et al. 2016. "Meadow up a Tree: Feeding Flocks with a Native Ash Tree in the Moroccan Mountains." *Pastoralism* 6: 11.

Girardclos, Olivier, A. Billamboz, and P. Gassmann. 2011. "Abandoned Oak Coppice on Both Sides of the Jura Mountains: Dendroecological Growth Models Highlighting Woodland Development and Management in the Past." *TRACE: Tree Rings in Archaeology, Climatology and Ecology,* vol. 10 of *Proceedings of the Dendrosymposium 2011,* May 11–14, 2011, in Orleans, France. Reprinted in *Deutsches GeoForschungsZentrum GFZ* 10: 71–78.

Goethe, Johann Wolfgang von. *The Metamorphosis of Plants.* 2009. Cambridge, MA: MIT Press, 2009.

Green, E. E. 2006. "Fungi, Trees and Pollards." In *1er colloque européen sur les trognes,* 1–4. Vendome.

Greenleigh, Jason M., and Langenheim, Jean H. 1990. "Historic Fire Regimes and Their Relation to Vegetation Patterns in the Monterey Bay Area of California." *The American Midland Naturalist* 124 (2): 239–53.

Grenier, Robert, M.-A. Bernier, and W. Stevens. 2007. *The Underwater Archaeology of Red Bay: Basque Shipbuilding and Whaling in the 16th Century.* 5 vols. Ottawa: Parks Canada.

Gross, Briana L., and Zhihun Zhao. 2014. "Archaeological and Genetic Insights into the Origins of Domesticated Rice." *Proceedings of the National Academy of Sciences* 111 (17): 6190–97.

Hæggström, Carl-Adam. 2012. "Hazel (*Corylus avellane*) Pollards." *Memoranda Societatis pro Fauna et Flora Fennica* 88: 27–36.

Hallé, Francis, R. A. A. Oldeman, and P. B. Tomlinson. 1978. *Tropical Trees and Forests: An Architectural Analsysis.* Berlin: Springer-Verlag.

Hammett, Julia E. 1992. "Ethnohistory of Aboriginal Landscapes in the Southeastern United States." *Southern Indian Studies* 41: 1–51.

Harding, P. 2014. "Working with Flint Tools: Personal Experience Making a Neolithic Axe Haft." *Lithics: The Journal of the Lithic Studies Society* 35: 40–53.

Hardy, Thomas. 1981. *The Woodlanders.* Oxford: Clarendon Press.

Hauge, Leif. 1998. "Restoration and Management of a Birch Grove in Inner Sogn Formerly Used for Fodder Production." *Norsk Geografisk Tidsskrift* 52: 65–78.

Hayashida, Frances M. 2005. "Archaeology, Ecological History, and Conservation." *Annual Review of Anthropology* 34 (1): 43–65.

Hibbs, David E. 1981. "Leader Growth and the Architecture of Three North American Hemlocks." *Canadian Journal of Botany* 59: 476–80.

Hofmann, Daniela, R. Ebersbach, T. Doppler, and A. Whittle. 2016. "The Life and Times of the House: Multi-Scalar Perspectives on Settlement from the Neolithic of the Northern Alpine Foreland." *European Journal of Archaeology* 19 (4): 596–630.

Holling, C. S., and G. K. Meffe. 1996. *Conservation Biology* 10 (2): 328–37.

Hu, Shiu Ying. 1979. "Ailanthus." *Arnoldia* 39: 29–50.

Huntley, J. C. 1990. "*Robinia pseudoacacia* L. Black Locust." In *Hardwoods. Agriculture Handbook, No. 654,* edited by R. M. Burns and B. H. Honkala, 755–61. Vol. 2 of *Silvics of North America.* Washington, D.C.: USDA Forest Service.

Iñaki Iriarte, Goñi. *Bienes comunales y capitalismo agrario en Navarra, 1855–1935.* 1996. Madrid: Ministerio de Agricultura, Pesca y Alimentación.

Innes, James B., J. J. Blackford, and P. A. Rowley-Conwy. 2013. "Late Mesolithic and Early Neolithic Forest Disturbance: A High Resolution Palaeoecological Test of Human Impact Hypotheses." *Quaternary Science Reviews* 77: 80–100.

James, Susanne. 1984. "Lignotubers and Burls—Their Structure, Function and Ecological Significance in Mediterranean Ecosystems." *The Botanical Review* 50: 225–66.

Jeník, Jan. 1994. "Clonal Growth in Woody Plants: A Review." *Folia Geobotanica* 29: 291–306.

Jett, Stephen C. 2005. "Navajo-Modified Living Trees and Cradleboard Manufacture." *Material Culture* 37 (1): 131–42.

Jurgelski, W. M. 2008. "Burning Season, Burning Bans: Fire in the Southern Appalachian Mountains, 1750–2000." *Appalachian Journal* 35: 170–217.

Kaplan, Lawrence, M. B. Smith, and L. Sneddon. 1990. "The Boylston Street Fishweir: Revisited." *Economic Botany* 44 (4): 516–28.

Kobori, Hiromi, and Richard B. Primack. 2003. "Participatory Conservation Approaches for Satoyama, the Traditional Forest and Agricultural Landscape of Japan." *Ambio* 32 (4): 307–11.

———. 2004. "Conservation for Satoyama, the Traditional Landscape of Japan." *Arnoldia* 62 (4): 2–10.

Lamikis, Xabier. "Basques in the Atlantic World: 1450–1824." *Oxford Research Encyclopedia of Latin American History.* Posted online October 2017. doi: 10.1093/acrefore/9780199366439.013.4.

Lancashire, Terence. 2010. "A Discussion of Nagasawa Sōhei's *Hayachine take kagura: Mai no shōchō to shakaiteki jissen.*" *Asian Ethnology* 69 (1): 159–69.

Leach, Melissa, and James Fairhead. 2000. "Challenging Neo-Malthusian Deforestation Analyses in West Africa's Dynamic Forest Landscapes." *Population and Development Review* 26 (1): 17–43.

Lightfoot, Kent G., and Otis Parrish. 2009. *California Indians and Their Environment: An Introduction.* Berkeley: University of California Press.

López Sáez, José Antonio, Pilar López García, Lourdes López-Merino, Enrique Cerrillo Cuenca, Antonio González Cordero, and Gallardo Prada. 2007. "Origen prehistórico de la dehesa en Extremadura: Una perspectiva paleoambiental." *Revista de estudios extremeños* 63 (1): 493–510.

Lynch, A. J. J., R. W. Barnes, J. Cambecedes, and R. E. Vaillancourt. 1998. "Genetic Evidence That *Lomatia tasmanica* (Proteaceae) Is an Ancient Clone." *Australian Journal of Botany* 46 (1): 25–33.

Maclean, Murray. 2006. *Hedges and Hedgelaying.* Ramsbury, U.K.: Crowood Press.

The Manyōshū: The Nippon Gakujutsu Shinkōkai Translation of One Thousand Poems. 1965. New York: Columbia University Press.

Marinova, Elena, and S. Thiebault. 2008. "Anthracological Analysis from Kovacevo, Southwest Bulgaria: Woodland Vegetation and Itsuse During the Earliest Stages of the European Neolithic." *Vegetation History and Archaeobotany* 17 (2): 223–31.

Martin, Roy W. (1998.) 2001. *Resource Inventory: Plant Life. Big Basin Redwoods State Park.* http://www.parks.ca.gov/pages/21299/files/bbplant.pdf.

Mason, S. L. R. 2000. "Fire and Mesolithic Subsistence—Managing Oaks for Acorns in Northwest Europe?" *Palaeogeography, Palaeoclimatology, Palaeoecology* 164: 139–50.

Meier, Andrew R., M. R. Saunders, and C. H. Michler. 2012. "Epicormic Buds in Trees: A Review of Bud Establishment, Development and Dormancy Release." *Tree Physiology* 32 (5): 565–84.

Mellars, Paul, and Petra Dark. 1998. *Star Carr in Context: New Archaeological and Palaeological Investigations at the Early Mesolithic Site.* Oxford: Oxbow Books.

Menotti, Francesco, and Aidan O'Sullivan, eds. 2012. *The Oxford Handbook of Wetland Archaeology.* Oxford: Oxford University Press.

Michener, D. C. 1988. "The Introduction of Black Locust *(Robinia pseudoacacia* L.) to Massachusetts." *Arnoldia* 48 (4): 52–57.

Minnis, Paul E., ed. 2003. *People and Plants in Eastern North America.* Washington, D.C.: Smithsonian Books.

———. 2004. *People and Plants in Western North America.* Washington, D.C.: Smithsonian Books.

Mitton, J. B., and M. C. Grant. 1980. "Observations on the Ecology and Evolution of Quaking Aspen, *Populus tremuloides,* in the Colorado Front Range." *American Journal of Botany* 67: 202–9.

———. 1996. "Genetic Variation and the Natural History of Quaking Aspen." *BioScience* 46 (1): 25–31.

Miyazawa, Kenji. 1973. *Spring and Asura*. Translated by Hiroaki Sato. Chicago: Chicago Review Press.

——. *Selections*. 2007. Translated by Hiroaki Sato. Berkeley: University of California Press.

Moe, Dagfinn, and Oliver Rackham. 1992. "Pollarding and a Possible Explanation of the Neolithic Elmfall." *Vegetation History and Archaeobotany* 1 (2): 63–68.

Molloy, Karen, and Michael O'Connell. 1988. "Neolithic Agriculture: Fresh Evidence from Cleggan, Connemara." *Archaeology Ireland* 2 (2): 67–70.

Moore, Christopher R., and Victoria G. Dekle. 2010. "Hickory Nuts, Bulk Processing and the Advent of Early Horticultural Economies in Eastern North America." *World Archaeology* 42 (4): 595–608.

Morgan, Ruth A. 1982. "Current Tree Ring Research in the Somerset Levels." In. *Archaeological Aspects of Woodland Ecology*, edited by Martin Bell and Susan Limbrey, 79–84. Cambridge: B.A.R. Publishing.

Morimoto, Yukihiro. 2011. "What Is Satoyama? Points for Discussion on Its Future Direction." *Landscape and Ecological Engineering* 7: 163–71.

Munson, Patrick J. 1986. "Hickory Silviculture: A Subsistence Revolution in the Prehistory of Eastern North America." Paper presented at Conference on Emergent Horticultural Economies of the Eastern Woodlands, Center for Archaeological Investigations, Southern Illinois University, Carbondale, IL.

My Neighbor Totoro. 2006. Directed by Hayao Miyazaki. Burbank, CA: Walt Disney Home Entertainment. (Original, 1988. Tokyo: Toho.)

Nichols, Robert F., and D. G. Smith. 1965. "Evidence of Prehistoric Cultivation of Douglas-Fir Trees at Mesa Verde." *Memoirs of the Society for American Archaeology* 19: 57–64.

Nicholson, Rob. 2011. "Little Big Plant: Box Elderberry (*Gaylussacia brachycera*)." *Arnoldia* 68 (3): 11–18.

Nordbakken, J. F., and I. Austad. 2010. "Epiphytic Biophytes on Pollarded Trees of *Ulmus glabra* in Sogn og Fjordane, W. Norway." *Blythia* 68 (4): 245–55.

Notes on Pollards: Best Practices' Guide for Pollarding. N.d. Donostia: Diputación Foral de Gipuzkoa.

Nyerges, A. E. 1987a. "Development in the Guinea Savanna." *Science* 238: 1637–38.

——. 1987b. "The Development Potential of the Guinea Savanna: Social and Ecological Constraints in the West African 'Middle Belt.'" In *Lands at Risk in the Third World: Local-Level Perspectives*, edited by P. D. Little, M. N. Horowitz, and A. E. Nyerges, 316–36. Boulder: Westview.

——. 1989. "Coppice Swidden Fallows in Tropical Deciduous Forest: Biological, Technological, and Sociocultural Determinants of Secondary Forest Successions." *Human Ecology* 17: 379–400.

——. 1992. "The Ecology of Wealth-in-People: Agriculture, Settlement, and Society on the Perpetual Frontier." *American Anthropologist* 94: 860–81.

——. 1994. "Deforestation History and the Ecology of Swidden Fallows in Sierra Leone." *Culture and Agriculture* 14: 6–12.

——. 1996. "Ethnography in the Reconstruction of African Land Use Histories: A Sierra Leone Example." *Africa* 66: 122–44.

———. 1997. "The Social Life of Swiddens: Juniors, Elders and the Ecology of Susu Upland Rice Farms." In *The Ecology of Practice: Studies of Food Crop Production in Sub-Saharan West Africa*, edited by A. E. Nyerges, 169–200. London: Routledge.

———. 2001. "Is There a Political Ecology of the Sierra Leone Landscape?" *American Anthropologist* 103: 828–33.

Nyerges, A. E., and G. M. Green. 2000. "The Ethnography of Landscape: GIS and Remote Sensing in the Study of Forest Change in West African Guinea Savanna." *American Anthropologist* 102: 271–89.

Oosthuizen, Susan. 2011. "Archaeology, Common Rights and the Origin of Anglo-Saxon Identity." *Early Medieval Europe* 19 (2): 153–81.

Parvulescu, Adrian. 1987. " 'Coppice' and 'Coppicing' in Old Forestry. A Note on the Etymology of Grk. drios 'Coppice' and Skt. Vana 'Forest.' " *The American Journal of Philology* 108 (3): 491–94.

Peglar, Sylvia M., and H. J. B. Birks. 1993. "The Mid-Holocene Ulmus Fall at Diss Mere, South-East England—Disease and Human Impact?" *Vegetation History and Archaeobotany* 2 (2): 61–68.

Peñuelas, J., and S. Munné-Bosch. 2010. "Potentially Immortal?" *New Phytologist* 187: 564–67.

Peterken, George F. 1996. *Natural Woodland: Ecology and Conservation in Northern Temperate Regions.* Cambridge: Cambridge University Press.

Pollard, E. 1973. "Hedges: VII. Woodland Relic Hedges in Huntingdon and Peterborough." *Journal of Ecology* 61 (2): 343–52.

Pollard, E., M. D. Hooper, and N. W. Moore. 1974. *Hedges.* London: William Collins.

Pom Poko (The Heisei-Era Racoon Dog Wars). 2005. Directed by Isao Takahata. Burbank, CA: Walt Disney Home Entertainment. (Original, 1994. Tokyo: Toho.)

Posey, Darrell A. 1997. "Indigenous Knowledge, Biodiversity, and International Rights: Learning about Forests from the Kayapó Indians of the Brazilian Amazon." *The Commonwealth Forestry Review* 76 (1): 53–60.

Rackham, Oliver. 1976. *Trees and Woodland in the British Landscape.* London: J. M. Dent.

———. 1977. "Neolithic Woodland Management in the Somerset Levels: Garvin's, Walton Heath, and Rowland's Track." *Somerset Levels Papers* 3: 65–71.

———. 1989. *The Last Forest: The Story of Hatfield Forest.* London: J. M. Dent.

———. 1991. "Landscape and the Conservation of Meaning." *RSA Journal* 139 (5414): 903–15.

———. 2008. "Ancient Woodlands: Modern Threats." *The New Phytologist* 180 (3): 571–58.

Raimbault, P., F. De Jonghe, R. Truan, and M. Tanguy. 1995. "La gestion des arbres d'ornement, 2e partie: Gestion de la partie aérienne: Les principes de la taille longue moderne des arbres d'ornement." *Revue Forestière Française* 47 (1): 7–38.

Raimbault, P., and M. Tanguy. 1993. "La gestion des arbres d'ornement. 1re partie: Une méthode d'analyse et de diagnostic de la partie aérienne." *Revue Forestière Française* 45 (2): 97–117.

Rasmussen, Peter. 1993. "Analysis of Goat/Sheep Faeces from Elgozwil 3, Switzerland: Evidence for Branch and Twig Foddering of Livestock in the Neolithic." *Journal of Archaeological Science* 20: 479–502.

Read, Helen. 2006. "A Brief Review of Pollards and Pollarding in Europe." In *1er colloque européen sur les trognes*. 1–6.

Read, Helen J., J. Dagley, J. M. Elosegui, A. Sicilia, and C. P. Wheater. 2013. "Restoration of Lapsed Beech Pollards: Evaluation of Techniques and Guidance for Future Work." *Arboricultural Journal: The International Journal of Urban Forestry*. doi: 10.1080/03071375.2013.747720.

Reid, Robin S., and James E. Ellis. 1995. "Impacts of Pastoralists on Woodlands in South Turkana, Kenya: Livestock-Mediated Tree Recruitment." *Ecological Applications* 5 (4): 978–99.

Richards, Paul. 2005a. "To Fight or to Farm? Agrarian Dimensions of the Mano River Conflicts (Liberia and Sierra Leone)." *African Affairs* 104 (417): 571–90.

———. 2005b. "West-African Warscapes: War as Smoke and Mirrors: Sierra Leone 1991–2, 1994–5, 1995–6." *Anthropological Quarterly* 78 (2): 377–402.

———. 2006a. "An Accidental Sect: How War Made Belief in Sierra Leone." *Review of African Political Economy* 33 (110): 651–63.

———. 2006b. "The History and Future of African Rice: Food Security and Survival in a West African War Zone." *Africa Spectrum* 41 (1): 77–93.

Richens, R. H. 1983. *Elm*. Cambridge: Cambridge University Press.

Rodd, Laurel Rasplica, trans. 2015. *Shinkōkinshū: New Collection of Poems Ancient and Modern*. 2 vols. Leiden: Brill.

Rodd, Laurel Rasplica, and Mary Catherine Henkenius, trans. 1984. *Kokinshū: A Collection of Poems Ancient and Modern*. Princeton, NJ: Princeton University Press.

Saqalli, Mehdi, A. Salavert, S. Bréhard, R. Bendrey, J.-D. Vigne, et al. 2014. "Revisiting and Modelling the Woodland Farming System of the Early Neolithic Linear Pottery Culture (LBK), 5600–4900 B.C." *Vegetation History and Archaeobotany* 23 (supp. 1): 37–50.

Sayers, William. 2004. "Marie de France's 'Chievrefoil,' Hazel Rods, and the Ogam Letters 'Coll' and 'Uillenn.'" *Arthuriana* 14 (2): 3–16.

Scott, Gilbert F., J. Sapp, and A. I. Tauber. 2012. "A Symbiotic View of Life: We Have Never Been Individuals." *The Quarterly Review of Biology* 87 (4): 325–41.

Simpson, Jamie, and Luke Barley. 2012. "Ensuring Ancient Trees for the Future Guidelines for Oak Pollard Creation." *Quarterly Journal of Forestry* 106: 277–86.

Slomian, Sabina, M. E. Gulvik, G. Madej, and I. Austad. 2005. "Gamasina and Microgyniina (Acari, Gamasida) from Soil and Tree Hollows at Two Traditional Farms in Sogn og Fjordane, Norway." *Norwegian Journal of Entomology* 52: 39–48.

Slotte, Hakan. 2001. "Harvesting of Leaf Hay Shaped the Swedish Landscape." *Landscape Ecology* 16: 691–702.

Smith, Bruce D. 2011a. "The Cultural Context of Plant Domestication in Eastern North America." *Current Anthropology* 52 (S4): S471–84.

———. 2011b. "General Patterns of Niche Construction and the Management of 'Wild' Plant and Animal Resources by Small-Scale Pre-Industrial Societies." *Philosophical Transactions of the Royal Society B Biological Sciences* 366 (1566): 836–48.

Smith, Elise L. 2007. "'The Aged Pollard's Shade': Gainsborough's *Landscape with Woodcutter and Milkmaid*." *Eighteenth Century Studies* 41 (1): 17–39.

Smith, H., and D. Smith. 1971. "The Box Huckleberry, *Gaylussacia brachycera*." *Castanea* 36: 81–89.

Smith, J. Russell. 1953. *Tree Crops: A Permanent Agriculture*. New York: Devin-Adair.

Somerset Levels Papers. Number 3. Somerset Levels Project, 1977.

Steigerwald, Joan. 2002. "Goethe's Morphology: *Urphänomene* and Aesthetic Appraisal." *Journal of the History of Biology* 35: 291–328.

Stein, William E., and James S. Boyer. 2006. "Evolution of Land Plant Architecture: Beyond the Telome Theory." *Paleobiology* 32 (3): 450–82.

Stidd, B. M., 1987. "Telomes, Theory Change, and the Evolution of Vascular Plants." *Review of Palaeobotany and Palynology* 50: 115, 126.

Szabó, Peter. 2010. "Ancient Woodland Boundaries in Europe." *Journal of Historical Geography* 36 (2): 205–14.

Takeuchi, Kazuhiko. 2010. "Rebuilding the Relationship Between People and Nature: The Satoyama Initiative." *Ecological Research* 25: 891–97.

Takeuchi, K., R. D. Brown, I. Washitani, A. Tsunekawa, and M. Yokohari, eds. 2003. *Satoyama: The Traditional Rural Landscape of Japan*. Tokyo: Springer Japan.

Takeuchi, Kazuhiko, K. Ichikawa, and T. Elmqvist. 2016. "Satoyama Landscape as Social-Ecological System: Historical Changes and Future Perspective." *Current Opinion in Environmental Sustainability* 19: 30–39.

Tallantire, P. A. 2002. "The Early-Holocene Spread of Hazel (*Corylus avellana* L.) in Europe North and West of the Alps: An Ecological Hypothesis." *The Holocene* 12 (1): 81–96.

Terada, Toru, M. Yokohari, J. Bolthouse, and N. Tanaka. 2010. "'Refueling' *Satoyama* Woodland Restoration in Japan: Enhancing Restoration Practice and Experiences Through Woodfuel Utilization." *Nature and Culture* 5 (3): 251–76.

Thoreau, Henry David. 1962. *The Journal of Henry D. Thoreau*. Edited by Bradford Torrey and Frances H. Allen. New York: Dover.

Tomlinson, P. B. 1983. "Tree Architecture." *American Scientist* 71: 141–49.

———. 1987. "Architecture of Tropical Plants." *Annual Review of Ecology and Systematics* 18: 1–21.

Tomlinson, P. B., and M. H. Zimmermann, eds. 1978. *Tropical Trees as Living Systems*. Cambridge: Cambridge University Press.

Totman, Conrad. 1989. *The Green Archipelago: Forestry in Preindustrial Japan*. Berkeley: University of California Press.

Tusser, Thomas, and William Fordyce Mavor. (1812.) 2012. *Five Hundred Points of Good Husbandry*. Memphis: General Books.

Unsain, José María. 2014. *Balleneros vascos: Imágenes y vesitgios de una historia singular*. Donostia–San Sebastián, Sp.: Museo Naval.

Vandekerkhove, Kris, H. Baeté, B. Van Der Aa, L. De Keersmaeker, A. Thomaes, A. Leyman, and K. Verheyen. 2016. "500 Years of Coppice-with-Standards Management in Meerdaal Forest (Central Belgium)." *iForest—Biogeosciences and Forestry* 9 (4): 509–17.

Varien, Mark, S. G. Ortman, T. Kohler, D. M. Glowacki, and D. Johnson. 2007. "Historical Ecology in the Mesa Verde Region: Results from the Village Ecodynamics Project." *American Antiquity* 72 (2): 273–99.

Vasek, Frank C. 1980. "Creosote Bush: Long-Lived Clones in the Mojave Desert." *American Journal of Botany*. 67 (2): 246–55.

Warren, G., S. Davis, M. McClatchie, and R. Sands. 2014. "The Potential Role of Humans in Structuring the Wooded Landscapes of Mesolithic Ireland: A Review of Data and Discussion of Approaches." *Vegetation History and Archaeobotany* 23 (5): 629–46.

White, E. B. (1949). 1976. *Here Is New York*. New York: The Little Book Room.

Wilson, Carl L. 1942. "The Telome Theory and the Origin of the Stamen." *American Journal of Botany* 29 (9): 759–64.

———. 2005. "The Telome Theory." *Botanical Review* 71 (5): 485–505.

Windes, Thomas C., and P. J. McKenna. 2001. "Going Against the Grain: Wood Production in Chacoan Society." *American Antiquity* 66 (1): 119–40.

ILLUSTRATION CREDITS

Page 43: Illustration courtesy of Francis Hallé.

Pages 11, 36, 58, 76, 98, 252, 268: Illustrations courtesy of Nora H. Logan.

Pages 52, 69, 70, 100, 124, 126, 150, 202: Photographs by William Bryant Logan.

Page 199: Nikolai Astrup illustration, reprinted by permission of Leif Hauge, from his photograph in Austad, Ingvild, and Hauge, Leif. *Taer og Tradisjon*. Bergen, Norway: Fagbokforlager, 2014.

Page 160: *Ancient Trees, Lullingstone Park*, Samuel Palmer, 1828. Graphite; Sheet: 10½ × 14⅝ inches (26.7 × 37.1 cm). Yale Center for British Art, Paul Mellon Collection, B1977.14.308.

Page 211: Mrs. Mary Jacobs (Karuk) with baskets, by B. F. White, courtesy of the Phoebe A. Hearst Museum of Anthropology and Regents of the University of California (Catalog No. 15-9018).

Pages 231, 232: Courtesy of Peter Del Tredici, from "Redwood Burls: Immortality Underground," *Arnoldia*, vol. 59, no. 3 (1999), pp. 14–22.

INDEX